JEANNE VIALL
WILMOT JAMES
JAKES GERWEL

Grape

Stories of the Vineyards in South Africa

Tafelberg

Acknowledgements

We would like to thank Vernon de Vries of Distell and Russell Ally of the Ford Foundation for their support and encouragement. The idea of the book also came from Wilmot's discussions with colleagues at The Grape Company, especially David Powter, Hanno Scholtz and JT le Roux. Thanks to the people who were willing to be interviewed; they are mentioned at the end.

Thanks to those who went out of their way to help arrange interviews; thanks to friends and family for encouragement, in particular to Dorian Haarhof; Clé Latouf who accompanied Jeanne to the Northern Cape over hot and dusty roads, sharing her history notes; and Bernard Brom, for constant support.

Tafelberg
An imprint of NB Publishers
40 Heerengracht, Cape Town, 8000
www.tafelberg.com

Set in Janson Text
Cover design by Russel Stark
Book design by Nazli Jacobs
Edited by Linde Dietrich
Maps by John Hall
Photographs by Clé Latouf
Index by Mary Lennox

Printed and bound by Interpak Books
First edition, first printing 2011

ISBN: 978-0-624-04938-8

Timeline

500 Khoikhoi pastoralists move into the Southwestern Cape, inhabited by the hunter-gatherer San
1655 The first *Vitis vinifera* cuttings are brought to South Africa by commander of the new settlement at the Cape, Jan van Riebeeck
1657 Van Riebeeck releases nine Dutch East India Company servants to become full-time farmers
1658 The first significant number of slaves arrive: 228 from the coast of Guinea and 174 from Angola. More than half of the settlement now consists of slaves
1659 The first wine from the Cape is produced
1659 Khoikhoi mount a series of rapid and successful raids on free burghers' herds
1679 Simon Van Der Stel arrives as new governor; the following year he plants vines at Constantia
1679 The first free burgher settles in Stellenbosch
1687 More land is allocated to settlers in Drakenstein
1688 The French Huguenots arrive and settle in what is now Franschhoek
1694 Sheik Abidin Tadia Yussuf, an imam exiled from Indonesia, settles near Strand and soon has a following
1695 The slave woman Ansela van de Caab is freed, and marries a German freeburgher Lourens Campher
1700 The Land van Waveren (Tulbagh) is opened to farmers to graze their livestock on the loan-farm system; the cattle trade with the Khoikhoi is opened to the colonists
1705 Only two kraals of Khoikhoi are left between the Berg River and present-day Klawer
1710 Wagenmakersvallei (Wellington), the Swartland and the Land van Waveren are settled
1713 A smallpox epidemic greatly reduces the numbers of Khoikhoi
1754 The Slave Code is instituted, prescribing how owners may treat slaves
1759-78 A slave is sole cellar master at Constantia
1770 A plakkaat (statute) is issued that Christian slaves cannot be sold, discouraging farmers from baptising them
1798 There are 25 754 privately owned slaves in the Cape; up from 350 in 1690
1806 The British take over at the Cape
1809 The "Hottentot Proclamation" is passed, restricting the movement of Khoikhoi, a death knell to a way of life of a pastoral people
1813 Britain reduces import duties on South African wine by a third
1813 First amelioration measures passed to regulate the punishment of slaves

1816 Slave Registers are officially kept
1821 Wine exports amount to close to 63% of all exports
1822 A census identifies a Muslim community living at Strand
1825 The British suspend preferential duties on Cape wine and the industry collapses
1834 Slavery is abolished, but slaves must first serve a four-year apprenticeship period
1838 Slaves are now free people
1841 The Masters and Servants Ordinance passed to regulate labour
1843 Pniel established as a mission station by the Apostolic Union
1847 The Cape Parliament declares the Orange River the northern border of the Cape Colony; the region south of it is called Bushmanland
1861 Britain lowers tariffs on French wine imports, a blow to the South African wine industry. Exports drop and overproduction becomes a problem.
1863 Railway line from the Cape reaches Wellington
1866 Abraham Pieter Nel settles near Augrabies and buys the land in 1893
1865-1875 Brandy sales to the mines more than double
1878 The Cape government levies an excise tax on brandy to pay for the last Xhosa War of 1877-78 and the war with the Basotho
1879 The Afrikaner Bond, a new political party, is formed
1882 Abraham September is granted a farm just outside Upington, one of 81 people, mainly Basters, to receive land
1883 The earliest grapes are planted in the Northern Cape by a Canadian, Robert Frier
1886 *Phylloxera vastatrix* devastates the Cape vineyards
1886 Wine exports collapse
1892 The first table grapes are successfully exported
1898 The Dutch Reformed Church establishes a labour colony at Kakamas for "poor whites" destitute after the drought and an outbreak of rinderpest among cattle
1899 The South African War
1905 A commission investigates the depressed wine and liquor industry
1906 The first wine co-operative is formed but overproduction still a problem
1910 The Barlinka grape is imported by Dr Izak Perold
1918 KWV is formed
1925 Perold develops South Africa's own grape, Pinotage
1949 Mixed Marriages Act
1950 Population Registration Act
1950s Gibberellic Acid, which revolutionises table grape production, is discovered
1955 The viticultural and oenological research institute at Nietvoorbij is established
1968 Pniel is declared a "Rural Coloured Area" in terms of the Group Areas Act
1969 Strawberry Lane residents are removed under the Group Areas Act
1970s Automation and mechanisation of winemaking begin
1971 First wine route is established
1972 The Gariep Dam is opened, making it possible for thousands of hectares of agricultural land to be converted to productive irrigated land. In 1977 the Vanderkloof Dam opens
1973 The Wines of Origin certification system is introduced
1974 The Masters and Servants Ordinance repealed
1980s Table grapes begin to be a viable export

1990-1996 UK imports of wine increase from 1 million cases to 11million cases
1992 KWV's quota system abolished
1994 South Africa becomes a full democracy
1995 The first Pniel erf-holders are given title deeds to their land
1996 South Africa's first large-scale FAS study in Wellington
1997 The Basic Conditions of Employment Act is expanded to include agriculture
1997 The Extension of the Security of Tenure Act (ESTA) is passed, promising security of tenure to workers.
2002 The SA Wine and Brandy Co formed to implement Vision 2020 aimed at economic transformation of wine and grape industry
2003 Wine Industry Plan published
2009 Exports grow from 50 million litres in the 1990s to 395,6 million litres in 2009, with 49% of wine produced exported

Note on terminology

Although one may speak of many coloured communities, it is questionable whether one can speak of the coloured people at all. In this essentially residual category are to be found people of the most diverse descent, including slaves from the Indonesian archipelago and the descendents of the area's most truly indigenous groupings: the pastoral Khoikhoi ("Hottentots") and the hunter-gatherer San ("Bushmen"). To be "coloured" in South Africa today is merely to say that one can trace some ancestry from Africa or Asia, or both, and speaks either English or Afrikaans as a home language. That the very notion of a "coloured people" exists is due to the complex sociology of three centuries of European domination and more recently the classificatory madness of the apartheid regime. (For the genetics of being "coloured", see the chapter "Skin Colour" in Wilmot James, *Nature's Gifts: Why we are the way we are*, Wits University Press, 2010.) For stylistic convenience, the term coloured is used without quotation marks in this book.

Contents

Foreword

When we set out to write the social history of the grape, we searched for the stories of the people who had worked in South Africa's vineyards for more than 350 years.

We wanted to write about all the people of the vine, those who had been involved in the life and times of the grape in South Africa, in the wine, table grape and raisin industries.

We started with the people living here before the first vineyards were planted at the Cape, those who settled here and those who were brought here as slaves. We also wanted to tell the story of the people who have researched grapes, developed viticulture and taken risks to create a viable export market for wine and table grapes.

It was a tall order, of course. That's a lot of history, a lot of stories.

The three of us set out to write the book together, Jeanne doing the research and writing and Jakes and Wilmot reviewing, guiding and giving advice in an ongoing exchange of ideas. Wilmot was born and raised in wine country, in Paarl, and this project was close to his heart. He and Jakes had long been involved in discussions about how to research and write about the people who have come to be known as "coloured" people, without being ethnic or sectarian, and without casting their history as a perpetual state of pathology or victimhood.

We have striven, therefore, to craft stories about normal people struggling with normal things in life, and we hope that we have succeeded in this.

Very early on we became aware of how few stories there were about farm workers; fewer still were photographs and personal accounts. Perhaps, we thought, that will improve as we move past the era of slavery, where most accounts come from court records and reflect only a small part of lived reality. Search as we did, we found very, very little about the people who worked in the vineyards. Histories of estates documented the mostly white owners in detail; buildings, and their additions and restorations, were all there, with pictures. But there were few clues as to the lives of the workers.

Questions around land and housing, labour shortages, and the economic vagaries of the wine industry were common threads. That shadow of the vine, the *dop* system, was ubiquitous as we explored social issues and the marginalisation of farm workers.

There have been many changes in the world of grapes in the recent past, but much has also stayed the same. Even today conditions are horrible for many farm workers, good for some. There are good farmers and bad farmers; productive workers and unproductive workers. And everything in between. There are innovative empowerment projects; there are stories of tokenism. There are terrible housing conditions, abject poverty, hopelessness. There is also training and aspiration and a belief in a better future.

Change is not confined to the social and economic realm: today the effects of climate change and the power of the consumer are being felt, and some producers are adapting to them.

This is not a comprehensive social history of the grape; it cannot be. The grape's story is complex and cannot be oversimplified; the stories we found hopefully reflect this.

There are so many conversations still to have, so many other paths we could still explore.

The heart of *Grape* is people telling their stories. As outsiders – to the world of wine, grapes and farm work, to the lives and the struggles of farmers and workers – we have been closely watched, carefully questioned and challenged. But we have never been shut out. It has been a fascinating journey, as people eagerly share what they see as their untold stories.

The history of the olive is the social history of the people of the southern Mediterranean and north Africa; the history of the potato that of the nineteenth-century Irish famine and emigration to America; and the history of cod that of the city of Boston. We join the genre in retelling the story of the grape, which is the story of South Africa, mostly that of the Gariep/Orange River area and the Western Cape.

It is the story of the many people who produce the table grapes found in European supermarkets, New World wines of quality, and our high-quality raisins and sultanas.

JEANNE VIALL
WILMOT JAMES
JAKES GERWEL

INTRODUCTION

The invisible people – a history unrecorded

South Africa's wine industry, and later the country's table grape industry, was grown on the labour of the many people, free and unfree, who worked on farms through the past 350 years of viticulture at the Cape. But you will seldom find them mentioned in the histories of wine farms and the wine industry.

Slaves, Khoikhoi, and later the freed people who worked on the farms are surprisingly invisible, their stories largely untold. The story of our wine industry is not only that of gracious wine estates and landed gentry, nor is it just the story of European settlers and fine winemaking. It is also the story of the workers who toiled in the vineyards.

The story begins with the land where Khoikhoi societies (referred to as Khoekhoe by some authors) grazed their herds of cattle and sheep, and groups of San people lived by hunting and gathering.

It was here, at the southern tip of Africa, that the Dutch East India Company (the *Vereenigde Oostindische Compagnie*, or VOC) chose to establish a refreshment station in 1652. The indigenous people were gradually forced to move off their land to make way for poor Company servants who were granted farms by the VOC. Few of these had been farmers in their homelands, and they struggled to produce fresh goods for their masters. As the small settlement grew and labour needs increased, a decision was made to import slaves. The Khoikhoi only worked for farmers later, when they had been dispossessed of their land and their social structures had crumbled, and then reluctantly.

Over the years slaves from many parts of the world, Khoikhoi labourers and the servants of the Company established the vineyards that produced wine and brandy, albeit not always of good quality. The first attempts at winemaking yielded dreadful wine; it was only when Simon van der Stel arrived as commander of the settlement in 1679 that winemaking at the Cape began to improve. He was promoted to governor in 1691.

The Cape was at first a way station to the East, a place where passing ships could replenish their stocks of fresh vegetables and meat. Wine itself did not travel well, unless fortified, but soldiers and sailors would frequent the taverns and drink the locally produced wine.

The wine industry prospered in times of war, when more ships passed Table Bay. Some suggest that it was the different wars that kept the wine industry afloat, first under the Dutch and then under British rule. The industry, however, struggled under the VOC's monopoly and corrupt officials. When the British government imposed and then lifted tariffs on French wine in its strife with France, the industry experienced further ups and downs. Disease, especially an outbreak of phylloxera that largely destroyed the Cape's vines in the late nineteenth century, added to the difficult conditions which made wine production a tricky and unreliable business.

The South African wine industry is more than 350 years old. In that time it has seen many boom and bust periods; it has always been difficult for the majority of farmers to make their farms viable, let alone prosper. The question is, why then, after three and a half centuries of struggle, do viticulture and the wine industry that grew around it continue? Why were grapes first grown at the Cape, and why are they still grown? Overproduction of wine worldwide, fierce competition from other developing producers such as Chile and Australia (for high-end wines), a fluctuating exchange rate and paper-thin margins: these are some of the challenges facing producers today.

Mohammed Karaan, Dean of the Faculty of AgriSciences at Stellenbosch University, questions the intrinsic value of the wine industry. He describes it as "the most idiosyncratic of all industries, the most peculiar. I think it's an embedded thing. There is a sadness to this industry, more than wheat . . . "

What value, he asks, do wine and the viticulture that feeds the industry add to a world where food security is becoming a pressing concern and there is a surplus of wine? "The early farmers planted grapes – why not farm with sheep, goats and greens? What were their motivations for getting involved in wine? And why, 300 years later, are we still growing wine? People with too much money go into it for the image. It is an ego-based industry where the rich come and play. The tragedy of the industry is the workers – it destroys human capital."

Karaan's is bound not to be a popular viewpoint in the Winelands, but it is a question to ask of history and the present: why wine? Wine farming is lucrative for only a few; for most it is a battle for survival. It is like that now, and it has been that way since the first vines were grown. For new entrants, it is virtually impossible to do without other funding.

But wine farming is not likely to go away. Wine has been made and drunk for thousands of years, and has been used as a sacrament in many religions from ancient times. It is still a popular drink, from cheap wine in casks to bottled fine wines costing hundreds of rands. In South Africa, wine has been drunk since early times; among a certain sector of society, it is a mark of refinement and social standing. It is an export product and also consumed locally. Wine is a large contributor to the Western Cape's economy, and is here to stay.

In South Africa beer far surpasses wine in popularity, with only about 15% of people drinking wine in comparison to 65,5% drinking beer.[1] But wine and table grapes are still a big industry: in 2009 around 1,37 million tons of grapes were produced, with a total of 1 089 million litres of wine products used for wine (the bulk), brandy, distilling wine, grape juice and grape juice concentrate.[2]

Grapes are not grown only for wine in South Africa, and in the past 30 or so years table grapes have become a lucrative export business. In 2009, 125 002 hectares were under vines: 101 259 for wine grapes, 14 236 for table grapes (sultanas, rootstocks and currants made up the total).[3]

The story of grapes grown in the arid Northern Cape along the Gariep/Orange River, where land reform is still a pressing issue, is a fascinating one. Raisins and brandy have been around for longer there – about 100 years. How a grape such as Thompson Seedless, a small grape traditionally used for raisins, was transformed into a large juicy table grape, sought after in international supermarkets, is a riveting tale.

Some common threads run through the stories told in this book. "Who will work in the vineyards?" has been the cry of the farmer for three and a half centuries. This question informed the decision to import slaves in the late seventeenth century; it led to repressive laws to coerce the Khoikhoi to work on farms in conditions close to slavery; it was the question asked at emancipation, when slaves were free to leave their former masters – and did – much to the farmers' consternation. Incentives to keep former slaves on farms, such as providing housing, were partially successful, leading to the perpetuation of the paternalism begun in slavery. Alcohol was another incentive. The *dop* system (tot system) that evolved on farms in the Western Cape is infamous; with its legacy of poor health, alcohol abuse and the marginalisation of farm workers, it is the first thing that comes to mind for many people when you talk of the Winelands.

This feudal system, where labourers lived on the farm and the farmer was lord of the manor, determining working conditions and punishment as well as the provision of housing and education, has largely disappeared.

Or has it?

"Across the political spectrum there's large-scale agreement that the lives of farm women are not the kind of lives we would like people in South Africa to live," says Fatima Shabodien, the executive director of the Women on Farms Project, which is based in Stellenbosch.

Women farm workers are the project's focus: this group is still largely invisible, the most marginalised group in the country. "With the casualisation and feminisation of farm work, there are more women in agriculture than ever before," she says. "We operate in the context that farm workers have a specific history, rooted in colonialism, and the majority of farm workers are descendants of the original slaves. When it comes to power relations, legislation has changed, but the social dynamics which exist haven't – it is very evident that the roots of agriculture manifest in a particular way."

While the old paternalism of absolute authority may still exist in small pockets, it has largely made way for a new, more benign paternalism (but still paternalism), and in a few cases for a more corporate system of clear-cut labour relations.

The history of workers on grape farms is a sad one; indeed, the history of farm workers in South Africa in general, and also elsewhere in the world, is often one of hardship. But the *dop* system, and its ongoing effects over many generations, adds another dimension to disempowered and marginalised grape farm communities.

Farming today faces big challenges. After South Africa's transition to democracy in 1994, global markets opened up and local producers now face the same pressures as those in other countries in the South, without the subsidies enjoyed by their counterparts in the North. Supermarket chains have huge power, controlling prices and adversely affecting what farmers get paid for their produce. Climate change is making itself felt, while ethical trade initiatives have made trading on world markets a more complex – and costly – exercise.

There are some sterling examples of social development on farms; there are also some areas, for example the farming community over the Du Toit's Kloof Mountains, known in certain circles as the Badlands (for their labour practices), where little has changed for some farm workers. Transformation and black economic empowerment (BEE) are buzzwords that are bandied about, but how much change has really taken place?

Accurate figures for farm workers are difficult to come by. One estimate is that there are between 30 000 to 50 000 permanent farm workers employed in viticulture, and many thousands more seasonal and migrant workers.[4] There are many more employed in the cellars and support industries.

According to Shabodien, about one million people in South Africa are farm workers, with around 20% of those in the Western Cape. But in the past few years many permanent farm workers have lost their jobs. "There's a one-to-seven dependency on a farm worker – that's generations up and down. Where it's up, pensions help support the family; but where it's down, that wage supports children and grandchildren," she says. The minimum wage in 2010 is R1 231 a month.

Numbers have dwindled for many reasons – deregulation has meant that farmers operate in a more competitive market, and productivity has had to increase. Jobs have been lost. Labour laws and a minimum wage have put in place legal protection for farm workers. Security of tenure is still a vexed issue, however, and many people have moved or been evicted from farms.

Permanent workers on farms, who are often provided with housing, are in a far better position than the growing pool of seasonal labour, which has less legal protection. Migrant and refugee labour, from both within and outside of South Africa, has swelled the population numbers of small rural towns. Competition for jobs, or perceptions of foreign workers being willing to earn less than the locals, seems to have been behind the violent clashes that took place in the Western Cape town of De Doorns, a grape-producing area, in late 2009.

Many farmers complain that it is difficult to get labour in season; those who traditionally worked on farms no longer want to do so. With increased educational levels, young people prefer to find jobs off the farms, for better pay. There is also among the traditional labour force in many cases a resistance to working for a farmer.

The sustainability of farming systems, which are responsible for huge amounts of greenhouse gas emissions, is being called into question, and biological and organic farming, along with biodiversity, are now being seriously discussed. Add to the mix the pressure for the radical transformation of a traditionally very conservative sector, agriculture, and the wine and table grape industries become interesting places to investigate.

Who has worked on farms through the centuries? Why do farmers continue to grow grapes in spite of the wine industry being less than lucrative? The former question is easier to answer, although there are gaps in our knowledge; the latter remains a matter for speculation.

Mohammed Karaan – "where the clever ones go"

Mohammed Karaan was born in Stellenbosch, yet it was his grandfather's stories of farming in the Transkei that captured his imagination. "I had green fingers and kept animals," he says. "I always wanted to be a farmer."

But although he owns a farm today, he is only a weekend farmer. Karaan is Dean of AgriSciences at Stellenbosch University, the cradle of Afrikaner ideology in this town at the heart of the Winelands. His faculty is the only one in Africa to offer degrees in viticulture and oenology.

It is a measure of transformation at the formerly conservative university that the son of an imam, who grew up in the "coloured" area of Strand during apartheid, should today head a faculty that has promoted and defended the interests of wine farmers through its history of more than 100 years.

Karaan recalls: "I would accompany my grandfather (Abdul Rahim Adam) hawking cool drinks down Merriman Street, and he'd tell me, 'Those white buildings, that's where the clever people are. That's where you will go'." Not only did he attend Stellenbosch University, he made his way to the top of his faculty.

Quietly spoken and thoughtful, Karaan calls to mind the American writer John Steinbeck's novel *The Grapes of Wrath* as we speak of the social history of wine, agriculture and the evolution of the industry in South Africa.

Although he grew up in Strand, close to Somerset West, Karaan had never visited the nearby Vergelegen, one of the earliest wine farms, until a few years ago.

He knew of the area's history. As a young boy he would browse through the library, coming across the stories of settlements of "Hottentots" (as the Khoikhoi were known) and Malays in the area; he knew from oral history about Sheik Abidin Tadia Yussuf, an imam exiled from Indonesia in 1694, who was sent to live on the farm Sandvlei, today Macassar, near Strand. Runaway slaves came to live and learn with him.

In 1822 a census found a Muslim community in Strand, which has been researched recently by former school principal Ebrahim Rhoda. "My ancestors were these people," Karaan says, "their history unrecorded." In the 1960s, under the Group Areas Act, the community was moved to make way for white families. "History doesn't want to be reminded of this."

Knowing he was to attend a function at Vergelegen, Karaan chose to visit it the week before, mindful that it would not be easy for him.

"The Rajah of Tambora was a political prisoner at Vergelegen and was married to the daughter of Sheik Yussuf. I cannot verify the direct bloodline to him but consider him a forefather in the context of my Cape Malay ancestry. My direct ancestry can be traced back to great-grandfather Moosa Karaan who came from Java in Indonesia.

"There was a bronze plaque at Vergelegen, with the names and year the slaves arrived, and their ages. They were 11, 12, 15. They came from Sri Lanka, Indonesia and India, and in bondage. My ancestors were on Vergelegen. It's the saddest thing I've done. I cried. What does a Dutchman do with a young woman slave?"

Karaan was sent to school in Johannesburg when he was 12. "I missed the Cape every day, and we would travel back by train for holidays. The Karoo was beautiful in the morning, De Aar at sunset. As we came through the Hex River Valley, lush and pregnant, it had the sense of the celebration of nature – and the tragedy of people. It was so obvious to see the overworked people, and they were drunk. I couldn't figure it out: in the arid areas the people were big, they were Africans and well fed; in the lush areas, the people were small . . . "

Karaan heads a faculty that needs to grapple with questions of transformation in the industry and look beyond wine to the bigger challenges facing agriculture in the twenty-first century. These include climate change and food security. He is no stranger to difficult situations, change and being "other". As he explains, "In matric I applied to Stellenbosch University. I could speak Afrikaans, and I was the only black student in the faculty. I had many interviews with the rector, to make sure that I was 'okay'. I was asked questions such as 'What should we do with Mandela?' (Nelson Mandela was still imprisoned at the time).

"It wasn't easy, but it was good for me. I learned how to deal with racism and cultural issues in a non-threatening way. I would do it all again . . ."

After graduating Karaan worked at the Development Bank and the Rural Foundation, and then returned to academia. "I wanted to do my PhD, and I became junior lecturer. I was an agricultural economist for 12 years. When the dean's position became vacant, my boss nominated me." Outside university he had done policy work for the ANC, was chair of the wine marketing council and adviser to former agriculture and land affairs minister Derek Hanekom. "That all strengthened my application for dean."

The pace of change is slow, he says. "But genuine. There's no crisis to drive change. At faculty level only 17% of students are black; that needs to be doubled. The faculty is very Afrikaans, very embedded, and Afrikaans people feel more threatened, there's still a laager mentality. I'm fortunate I can speak the language well, and I'm non-confrontational. There's a sense that 'we've groomed him, he's the houseboy'."

Karaan believes South African farmers are agriculturalists *par excellence*. "They, and the Israelis, can really farm. The best livestock farmers are the Xhosa in the Eastern Cape."

While he followed an academic path, Karaan never let go of his dream to have a farm, stimulated by the stories of his grandfather, known as Dada Baji, of his farm in Umzimkhulu, in East Griqualand. The family had ended up there when his maternal great-grandfather, who had come from India, moved from Durban. Because he was not allowed to own land, he befriended farmers in the Transkei and became a hawker. His grandfather then farmed land on loan, and continued trading. "But when the river flooded and the farm was destroyed, they decided to move." Plus, the Nationalist government had come into power. "If you were Indian and lived in the Transkei, your children were now not allowed to live with you when they became adults. And so my grandfather looked for someplace else to live." He moved to Stellenbosch; here Indians also couldn't buy land, and the family moved to Strand.

"I would hear stories from my granddad about the farm. It would get to me. I wanted to farm, so I saved 30% of my salary, and when it was enough, bought a farm in the Hemel-en-Aarde Valley." No grapes for him: "I grow strange things, like lavender, rosemary, pomegranates. I'm a weekend farmer, that's my sanity. I'd never be able to afford to farm permanently, it's not a profitable business unless you're prepared to live like a peasant, or to borrow money. You build a farm over the generations. It's not the corner café."

For Karaan, the important philosophical question to ask yourself is: on your deathbed, can you say you have added more to the substance of life than you have destroyed? In terms of this, the wine industry fails: it destroys more than it creates, he believes, and has done so for generations.

Money is poured into wine farms far beyond the returns. One businessman told Karaan he spends 15% of his time on the wine business for only 3% of his income. Groot Constantia, held up as an icon in the wine business, occupies some of the most valuable property in the country. The viticulture and oenology building at Stellenbosch University has just had a R50-million upgrade because this is the only university offering this training in Africa, and hence it was seen as important.

"The wine industry takes money," Karaan says. "It is squandered on image and ego, these are not good values; the downside of the industry is that it destroys human capital, along with its stepbrother, the fruit industry. I used to be astounded at how fellow students justified the *dop* system. And now they are saying wine is good for the heart . . ."

Table grapes are a different story. They don't destroy as much, but labour issues are still pertinent and problematic in some cases. "Of all industries they have created the most economic value in agriculture. However, here too there are problems. The market is at saturation point; and it's a boom/bust industry. It's demand driven and dependent on exchange rates. With Chile and Argentina overproducing, we had a bad time last year. It's a dogfight out there."

The Rural Foundation for which Karaan worked as a researcher after graduating was formed in the 1980s, funded by the KWV (the *Ko-operatieve Wijnbouwers Vereniging van Zuid-Afrika Beperkt*) and supported by farmers. "It covered ten districts, and we found big areas of concern: there was alcohol abuse, lack of access to basic education and services, and the results of mental subjugation over many years. It was worse in some areas, such as De Doorns, Slang River, Rawsonville, the Orange River and the Olifants River. I was locked up in Lutzville because I asked the farmer questions about the *dopstelsel* (*dop* system). It gave me a good insight into the industry. The industry destroys people, and it does it to everyone."

The selling of cheap wine today is tied in with the politics of wine, he says. "All politicians have a romanticism around wine, they're intoxicated with wine. They were going to legislate against *papsakke* (wine sold in foil bags). Nothing happened. Everyone is aghast at the *dop* system, but somewhere the crusade stops with cheap wine. There isn't a logic to wine farming. We produce too much wine, we can't sell it on the world market, so we sell it locally. Production is kept alive. Many co-ops are non-viable businesses."

The fundamental problem facing agriculture, Karaan maintains, is that the two main systems of agriculture in the world are both problematic.

"In the United States, the highly mechanised commercial farmers, with hundreds of hectares of land, are struggling. In China, 230 million people were lifted out of poverty by small-scale farming. A whole family could be supported with food from 700 sq metres of land, but they lived in poverty and fought to survive.

"Both systems are collapsing. The interesting question is, which has the most resilience? Maybe the small-scale sector . . .

"The question to ask an agronomist is, if you had to replant Stellenbosch, what would it be with? Robertson and other areas have yields two to three times greater than here. Why does wine continue to be produced? We have grossly neglected the growing of vegetables, we consume too few and we've not invested in diets in a positive way. The world is running short of vegetables, yet we use good soils to produce vines. Yes, fruit exports are good forex, but there's too much fruit in the world."

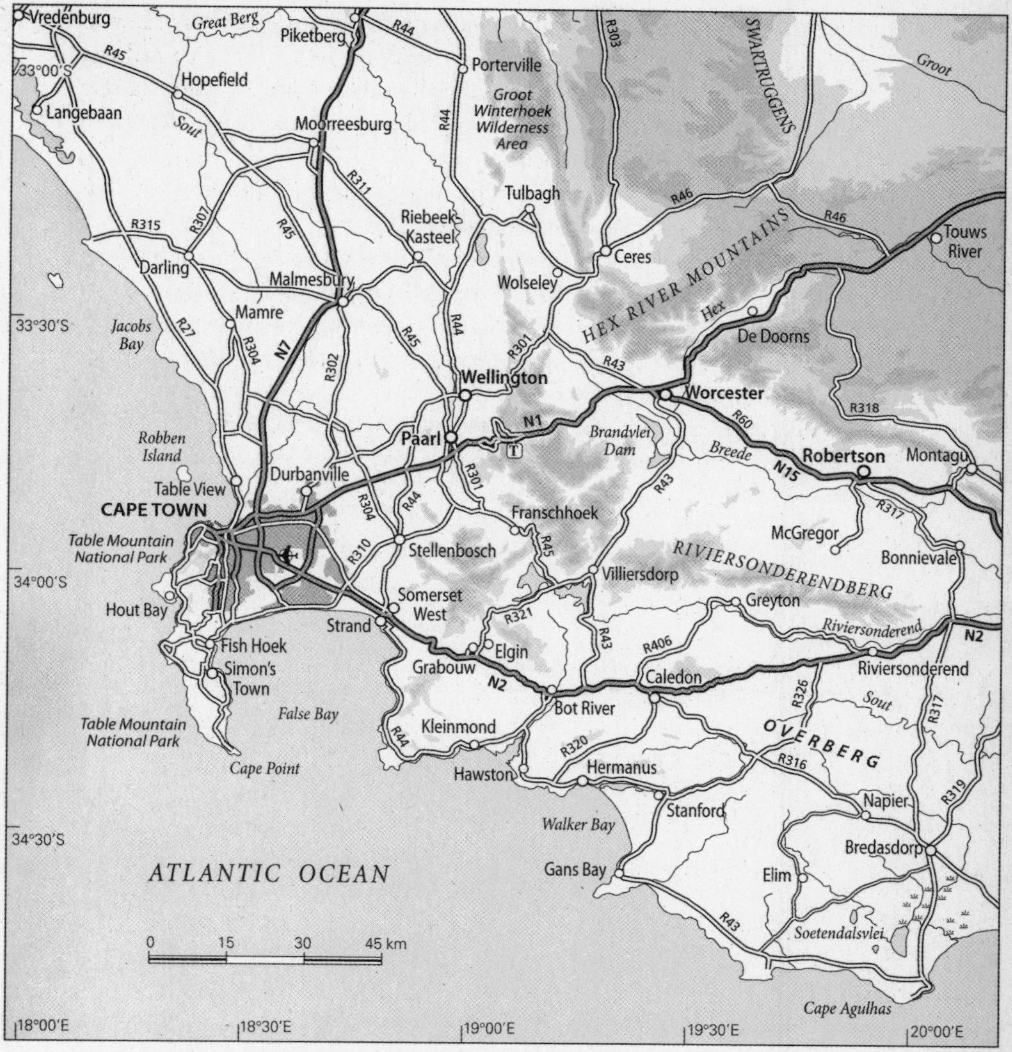

The wine regions surrounding Cape Town

CHAPTER I

Who will work in the vineyards?

"... and in the eyes of the hungry there is a growing wrath. In the souls of the people the grapes of wrath are filling and growing heavy, growing heavy for the vintage."
John Steinbeck, *The Grapes of Wrath*.[5]

Labour, and a steady supply of it, has been a central concern for grape farmers. A constant refrain throughout the history of the grape in South Africa, from the earliest days when the free burghers themselves did the farming until today, has been "there's not enough labour" for the vineyards.

Perhaps, though, it is not a question of a shortage of labour, but rather that people were not and are not prepared to work for what they are being offered.

The story of labour here is not unlike the story told in John Steinbeck's novel *The Grapes of Wrath*, where those dispossessed of their land through drought and a change in farming practices moved to California in their thousands looking for temporary work in the vineyards and orchards, and were inhumanely exploited.

Grape farmers in South Africa have always used both permanent and seasonal labour, as the grapevine demands different care in different seasons. Sometimes this seasonal care was provided by the wives and children of farm workers, sometimes by migrant workers.

And as in *The Grapes of Wrath*, with few rights and desperate for jobs, migrant workers were and are often exploited, having no protection in law, living in poor housing conditions and being paid poorly.

Steinbeck's book hit a raw nerve when it was first published in 1939; it was banned and burned, and the Associated Farmers of California denounced it as a "pack of lies", labelling it "communist propaganda" because they did not like the way farmers' attitudes and conduct towards migrants were depicted.[6] Farm labour is a vexed issue worldwide, migrant labour particularly so. Farm work is hard, physical labour; it is poorly paid and there is not much prospect for advancement.

Table grapes are far more labour intensive than grapes for wine and raisins, both in vine management and harvesting. Grapes are deciduous fruit, dormant in winter, with growth in early spring. Harvest is any time from December in the hot Northern Cape to April/May in the Hex River Valley in the Western Cape. A little pruning is required in winter, a lot of people are needed for thinning a few months later, depending on cultivars and location. New orchards are planted in winter.

Today many seasonal workers are women, either coming from nearby towns or farms. It is hard to come by reliable figures, but Joachim Ewert, professor of sociology at Stellenbosch University, estimates that most permanent workers are still men. "I'd guess at 30% women," he says.

A recent strategy is for farmers and managers to recruit their own seasonal workers, and to get the same workers every year, says Ewert. They will go as far as Victoria West. Others are, contentiously, recruited by labour brokers.

Ewert questions whether there is a real shortage of workers, or just a shortage of those willing to work for the daily rate – of between R40 and R80 a day – a piece worker is paid.

Labour in the early days of the settlement at the Cape

Initially it was the VOC's subjects, the free burghers, who laboured on their small farms. Slaves were few and far between; most of them were owned by the VOC, and many of them worked in the Company's gardens. The first wine farms, Bosheuvel and Constantia, however, did use the Company's slaves for labour. After a few years the authorities realised that the settlement would never prosper without an injection of labour, and slaves were imported in increasing numbers.

They were to become indispensable in the coming years as the settlement grew beyond the boundaries of Table Bay. Those farmers who prospered owned many slaves; most, however, could afford only a few. Slavery at the Cape was very different from that on huge plantations elsewhere in the world, where hundreds of slaves were the norm. From the 350 privately owned slaves in 1690, the numbers grew to 25 754 in 1798, just over 100 years later. These slaves were fairy evenly distributed among burghers. Most slaves lived in small groups of between six and ten on individual farms. On the bigger wine farms in the Stellenbosch and Drakenstein districts, there were more slaves.[7] In 1750, for example, 57% of owners had only one to five slaves; 22% had six to ten. The prosperous wine farmers owned from 11 to 50 slaves.[8]

European labourers, often in a supervisory capacity, also worked on the farms in small numbers. Free blacks, who were often freed slaves, worked where they wished. Although the indigenous Khoikhoi resisted working for the settlers at first, they were gradually forced to seek work on the farms as their social structures disintegrated. While their status was as free people, over time they became little more than indentured labour. In 1809 the "Hottentot Proclamation" was passed, which protected them from gross abuses but also restricted their movements. Khoikhoi servants had to have a fixed place of abode, they were not to move around without a pass and they had to produce one to verify they were not bound to any contracts. If they had no pass, they were classified as "vagrants". This was the final stage in their transition from a nomadic, independent people to landless labourers.[9] Khoikhoi now also had the right to complain about withholding of wages, and masters were compelled to provide servants with the necessities of life.

In 1818 the Khoikhoi formed 8,3% of the Cape population, and 43,4% of that of the eastern frontier. When the oceanic slave trade was abolished in 1807, 40% of the farmers in the Drakenstein and Stellenbosch districts relied exclusively on slave labour, and only 6% employed only Khoikhoi. About 518 farmers used a mix of slaves and Khoikhoi workers.[10]

When the oceanic slave trade was banned by Britain, "prize blacks" (or "prize slaves"), as they were known, were seized from slave ships and brought to the Cape. These slaves, many of them children and mostly Africans, were "liberated" at Cape Town, where they were promptly apprenticed.[11] "In fact, these men, women and children were granted to local farmers and tradesmen and were a little better off than slaves," says amateur historian Patric Mellét. "This 'apprentice' system indentured the freed slaves to an employer for fourteen years. Well into the late 1840s, long after slavery had been abolished, many 'prize slaves' continued to be brought to the Cape. Many of these slaves came from Mozambique, and were known as 'Mozbiekers'." This coincided with the beginnings of indentured African labour being sought from elsewhere in South Africa (the eastern Cape) and from elsewhere in Africa. Between 1879 and 1882, there were 2 400 Mozambican contract labourers recruited. Along with "prize slaves", these labourers were used in the Drakenstein, Malmesbury, Stellenbosch and Caledon areas to do the most menial work.

"When one reads the rather revisionist histories of the Cape Winelands, where it is often claimed that black Africans are recent 'post 1980s' arrivals, it is hard to suppress a chuckle. The wine and wheat areas of the Western Cape is where the majority of the Mosbiekers were sent as labourers," writes historian Christopher Saunders.[12]

People who are forced to work are not good workers. Slaves had no rights, they were possessions, and their resistance in the most part was muted by their powerlessness. Historian Robert Shell has suggested that slaves were in large part kept under control less by violence, and more through psychological means. Living with settler families, they were seen as "members" of that family and controlled through a benign paternalism.[13]

This does not mean slavery was benign. The slaves were the property and personal responsibility of their master, and he could use all kinds of "domestic corrections" or "internal discipline" to impose good behaviour and subordination, writes former economics professor Sampie Terreblanche.[14] "Although severe physical coercion was often used, it is perhaps more correct to say that psychological coercion . . . was more common." There are, however, many accounts of cruelty and extreme violence by masters against their slaves. The court records make for harrowing reading, documenting punishments which were inordinately cruel. These were the more extreme cases.

There were laws which governed the treatment of slaves and owners could not kill their slaves with impunity. The Slave Code of 1754 prescribed how owners should treat slaves, and the slaveowners could only administer the type of punishment a man could apply to his wife and children.

However, farmers did not necessarily adhere to the law; according to historian Wayne Dooling, sustaining a labour regime required a considerable amount of coercion, much of which was violent in the extreme. "Slaves and slaveowners were locked in permanent conflict; slaves surrendered their labour only grudgingly, and were determined to limit the demands placed on them." As a consequence they would routinely be beaten, whipped and deprived of basic requirements for human wellbeing.[15]

The slaves did of course resist, whether blatantly by running away, or in small overt acts such as disobedience or more subtle forms, such as laziness. This in turn would have been ascribed to the behaviour of recalcitrant children, and perpetuated the settler belief that slaves were "like children".[16]

The consequences of resistance were severe, such as extreme violence or even death. Offences such as lifting a hand against a master, absconding and setting fire to property would be punished by the offender being impaled, branded, broken alive on the wheel, and tortured. The bodies of executed slaves were hung up or exposed after mutilation in town and on the farms.

Rural farm slaves were mostly isolated from contact with other slaves. Because they came from ethnically and culturally diverse backgrounds, no shared slave culture developed on farms, and they had no support from others. There was no formal religious life, and in most cases slaves lived with the slaveholding family in their house, or shared with other labourers in outbuildings. In contrast, in Cape Town slaves would have had more freedom to move around and to earn wages, and the growth of Islam among slaves provided a major context for slaves to meet.[17]

Slaveowners could complain to the authorities, although they ran the risk of being punished if their complaints were found to be unfounded.

Farmers' protest, 1831: four days of unrest in Stellenbosch

Amelioration, which the British had introduced to improve the lot of the slaves, had already brought many changes. The first measures, in 1813, had limited the number of lashes owners could give their slaves. The first Guardian of Slaves was appointed in 1826 (in 1830 it became the Office of the Protector of Slaves). George Jackman Rogers was appointed the first Protector and his job was to look after the interests of slaves and adjudicate cases brought by slaves against their owners when they contravened the amelioration laws.

It was these amelioration measures, in particular the requirement that farmers submit *slaven boekjes* (slave books) – a record of the punishment they administered to their slaves – that brought a mob of farmers to Stellenbosch to protest on 11 April 1831.[18] Farmers were now to be answerable for the punishment they meted out to their slaves, and had to record it. They were angry, regarding this as the final straw – under the amelioration laws they saw their absolute authority over slaves being eroded. They were "serious and unruly" in their opposition and the unrest continued for four successive days. They were not going to fill in the punishment books, they asserted. Only 76 of the 3 024 slaveholders in Cape Town and Stellenbosch submitted records, and those who did attempt to submit returns were "hooted and pelted". Then, in 1832, more than 2 000 slaveowners assembled in Cape Town to protest against this order, which they said was adopted without proper consultation.[19]

The authorities quietly overlooked the regulation. It paid to toyi-toyi.

As it turned out, amelioration did not seriously affect farmers' rights to the labour of their slaves, but interference by the British was fiercely resisted and resented by the mostly Dutch farmers. Slaves were often their main property of any value and the most important asset of individual owners, with slaves being readily accepted as security by moneylenders.

False freedom

Isaac van der Merwe, a farmer on the farm Vier-en-Twintig Rivieren, complained to authorities in February 1835 about his four male and two female apprentices, Julie, America, Abel, New Year, Victoria and Lena.

He said: "They forced me to send the wagon for wine for them, whenever I ordered them to do anything they refused, and with insolence – whenever I offered them clothes they refused to take them. I sent the wagon for wine so as to induce them to cut the wheat – I was not sure of my life . . . they were all in disorder and they would not obey my orders. I consider them generally to have been in open resistance to my lawful commands. The cause of complaint has been since 1 December last."

The date Van der Merwe referred to, 1 December 1834, was the day that slaves were emancipated. It was a false start to freedom, however, as they had to still serve a mandatory four-year "apprenticeship". Although there was no organised opposition, there were many acts of resistance, as in the case above. Many apprentices deserted. Others stayed but showed resentment and refused to continue to accept the subordinate roles they associated with slavery. Opposition was different for men and women; men were more likely to desert and women to be insubordinate.[20]

The British had a specific vision of the kind of colonial society they wished to see after emancipation. They saw slavery as not only inhuman, giving dangerous unlimited powers to masters, but also as limiting workers' incentive and productivity. The idea was to replace it with a labour system which avoided direct physical coercion but which also ensured dependence of workers on employers for income and subsistence. Slaves were to be freed from bondage, but not from labour. In this way the flow of colonial produce would not be interrupted.[21]

Apprenticeship implies learning new skills or a trade, but that did not happen.

In reality the apprenticeship period only served farmers, who were given an extended four years of free labour. There was no arrangement for the elderly and infirm, and some farmers used apprenticeship to rid themselves of those workers who were too old to be useful. Others were only too willing to rid themselves of apprentices who were "useless or depraved". Other farmers took resistance further, and with their apprentices left the colony in what was later known as the Great Trek.

Farmers were worried about who would work in the vineyards after emancipation. Economic disaster caused by labour shortages was predicted. In

1837 *De Zuid Afrikaan*, a newspaper sympathetic to the interests of Dutch farmers, urged that action be taken to secure labour in advance of emancipation day: "It is hardly possible to expect that any of these Apprentices (however well they may have been treated) will not fancy they may better themselves by quitting their masters for a while; it therefore becomes the duty of farmers collectively to guard against this evil." The paper argued that workers should be recruited from Germany, India and China, among others.

Farmers agitated for a vagrancy law that would keep workers under control. Otherwise, the colonists feared, they would face continued "impudence and irritating conduct, and the vexations and prevarications to which the Masters are at present exposed" from their current apprentices.[23]

This was not an easy time for the apprentices: there is some evidence that at least some farmers resisted any outside control over their authority and took vengeance on their apprentices. In late 1833 the Acting Governor of the colony noted that many masters, "looking upon the slaves as though they were the cause of the approaching crisis, upbraid them with having, as it were, carried this measure against their masters and transfer to them in ill-treatment no inconsiderable portion of their discontent".[24] Some farmers turned the situation to their advantage – offences such as idleness, insolence, absence and inefficient work were now codified, and recalcitrant labourers were taken to the Special Magistrates. Punishment may even have been harsher than from owners.

Emancipation

After emancipation, some of those newly freed chose to stay on farms and work in return for board and lodging, and sometimes access to a plot of land, or the right to keep livestock. It was early December, just before the grape harvest, and some farmers offered cash inducements for people to stay until the end of the harvest. Some were even able to invoke bonds of loyalty and paternalism to keep ex-slaves as their labourers.[25] Here they did the same work, for the same people, and in some cases lived under more or less the same conditions. They had little or no money or possessions. Whatever social network they had, had existed on the farms and in the immediate areas.

Many, though, did choose to leave the farms, and in 1838 there was a large-scale withdrawal from wine farms. Reports of labour shortages were widespread. Some Cape settlers were shocked to discover that "those very slaves and apprentices who have been best treated, and were considered actually as members of the family, were the first to leave their masters".[26]

However, in some cases farmers welcomed emancipation, believes wine historian Diko van Zyl. "Slavery became a burden to some farmers, who had more capital invested in slaves than in property. If wine prices were good, the farmer could manage. But when not, they still had to feed and clothe their slaves. Grape and wheat farmers also hired out their slaves to each other, as the work was counter-seasonal. This was why many slaveholders did not resist the emancipation of the slaves in 1834. They believed they would be paid sufficient compensation (which did not happen)."[27]

Since the day of emancipation, a group of Stellenbosch farmers complained in 1840, almost all of the apprentices had left their former masters, "unwilling to engage themselves for agricultural labour".[28] This was the main complaint against former slaves in the years that followed. Many freed people went to work on other farms, or joined the seasonal labour market and toured farms during harvesting periods. Some wandered around "in idleness, just as it suited the caprice of the moment",[29] while others who had money settled themselves on small plots of ground outside of towns. Some grew produce. Those former slaves with skills, such as building or tailoring skills, moved to the small towns. Still others found their way to mission stations.

In later years many freed people did return to the farms for various reasons. Among these were higher wages during the wool boom in Swellendam in the 1840s. Laws against squatting were passed in the 1850s, which made it more difficult for freed people to find a place to live and land to farm; and then, from the late 1850s, there was overcrowding at mission stations. Hard economic times forced many freed people to work for farmers in return for food only.

Masters and servants

After emancipation new legislation was needed to regulate contracts between masters and servants on farms,[30] and in 1841 the Masters and Servants Ordinance was passed. The law was the result of many discussions and negotiations over three years on how to accommodate ex-slaves and former free blacks in the new era of paid work. The battle revolved around determining whether every worker was equal before the law, and the extent to which race could be a category which marked workers needing discipline from those who did not. Debates around the ordinance reveal the extent to which settlers, officials in the Cape Colony and the colonial office in England accepted the subordination of a woman to her husband and father. Race as a criterion of whether a person fell under the legislation or not was challenged and abolished; women's subjection to the authority of their husbands, however, passed without comment.[31]

While freed people were now contracted and paid, their conditions of contractual labour as set out in the Masters and Servants Ordinance favoured employers, who were allowed to use certain disciplinary measures, from fines to imprisonment, to regulate the behaviour of labourers, criminalising acts such as insolence, scandalous behaviour, immorality, drunkenness and negligence. Labourers could be fined one month's wages or serve a prison term of up to 14 days with or without hard labour. This Act laid the foundation for later Acts which discriminated against farm workers. For example, Act No. 18 of 1873 made a distinction between farm workers and other servants; the former received higher penalties than their urban counterparts.[32]

Farmers continued to agitate for a vagrancy law, as farmers' difficulties were attributed to the "want of efficient labour, arising from the absence of a vagrant law, of a law properly regulating the mutual obligations of masters and servants".[33] However, freed people continued to come and go as they chose. "What angered farmers most was the indiscriminate way in which labourers could leave their service," writes historian Wayne Dooling.[34]

Freed slaves forced compromise and negotiation on masters. If you paid fair wages, you could get workers. Better wages were paid for day-to-day work than for long-term work. Some farmers allowed people to cultivate plots for themselves as an incentive to stay on farms. Often retail shops were established on farms; many labourers got into debt this way, and debt bondage kept them on the farm.[35] Even today on some farms people complain that most of their wages go to pay their debts at farm shops, often for wine.

Control was tightened with representative government in the Cape Colony in 1853. The revised Masters and Servants Act of 1856 was harsher in its range of offences and the severity of the penalties prescribed for servants.[36] The Masters and Servants Ordinance was only repealed in 1974, after 123 years in existence.

Farm workers today

Today, farm work has increasingly become more skilled, and permanent workers generally find themselves in a better position than seasonal and temporary workers. "In the pre-1994-era viticulture no particular skills were needed, there was no scope for initiative," says Nick Vink, Chair of the Department of Agricultural Economics at Stellenbosch University. "A worker wouldn't dare to make a suggestion: he'd be told '*moet jou nie wit hou nie*' (don't be cheeky). Now it's become more technical, people are more motivated and remuneration is better."

From the 1970s there was some mechanisation and automation. Increasingly, much has been computerised. Irrigation is virtually all automated, and fixed irrigation systems need little labour. Flood irrigation and moveable sprinklers used to require a full-time attendant or a team of six to ten workers to move the sprinklers. Herbicides have changed the way weed control was carried out: instead of manually digging over vineyards, an operator could spray large areas in a day. There is still a lot of scope for mechanisation.

While a basic wage for farm workers is set, farm labour, both here and in most countries, is one of the lowest-paid jobs. This situation holds true as much for the USA as it does for countries such as Chile.

Worldwide over the past 20 years there has been a decline in the number of permanent workers who live on farms in farm housing, and a dramatic increase in the use of casual and seasonal labour (this applies to countries in the North as much as it does to those in the South).[37] Chronic underemployment and low wages put farm workers at a disadvantage in renting houses. Increased casualisation has meant fewer permanent workers and the emergence of a small class of specialised farm workers with better wages and working conditions. Farmers now only provide housing for a small core of permanent workers.

The broader issues facing South African farm workers today are land and tenure rights, says Fatima Shabodien of the Women on Farms Project. And in the even broader social context, pressing issues are alcohol dependence and cultural violence in families, particularly against women and children. The Rural Policing Forum statistics indicate that 78% of victims of violence on farms are women, she says. "It still shocks me that 80% of women report experiencing sexual violence as a child or adult." In Shabodien's view, these problems are linked to the lack of political organisation – farm women have no political voice and influence.

Though farmers and their families initially worked the vineyards themselves, they were soon joined by slaves, later supplemented by displaced Khoikhoi. The slave trade flourished at the Cape, with slaves forming the backbone of the agricultural workforce. In 1838, many freed slaves left the farms, but others stayed on, generation after generation, in a largely feudal relationship. Migrant workers, and more recently casual labour from nearby towns, have joined the mix, but labour remains a challenge.

CHAPTER 2

The roots of the vine

"Mynheer Cloete took us to the wine-press hall, where the whole of our party made wry faces at the idea of drinking wine that had been pressed by three pairs of black feet; but the certainty that the fermentation would carry off every polluted article settled that objection with me. What struck me most was the beautiful antique forms, perpetually changing and perpetually graceful, of the three bronze figures, half naked, who were dancing in the wine-press beating the drum (as it were) with their feet to some other instrument in perfect time. Of these presses, there were four with three slaves in each. Into the first the grapes were tossed in large quantities and the slaves danced on them softly, the wine running out from a hole in the bottom of the barrel, pure and clean. This was done to soft music. A quicker and stronger measure began, when the same grapes were danced on again."

Lady Anne Barnard's description of wine pressing in about 1800.[38]

Richard van der Ross and the people of Strawberry Lane

Below the Steenbergen, in the Cape Town suburb of Constantia in the heart of the Winelands, is a little street off Spaanschemat River Road. Its quaint name may catch your eye as you pass it, but unless you know about Strawberry Lane, you will drive on unawares.

It may seem strange to speak of Constantia as the heart of the Winelands, but it is one of its hearts, in fact its first heart, the place where the first wines, and the first good wines, of the Cape were produced.

Today, as a suburb for the wealthy, it is a far cry from farmland. Not too long ago it was a rural area with wine farms such as Groot Constantia, Klein Constantia, Steenberg and Bergvliet dominating the landscape. But in little pockets here and there and along the Spaanschemat River, people established themselves in small communities. In those days, the early twentieth century, a trip to Cape Town was a major undertaking, especially if you had no money for transport. The flower growers, for example, of the community of Strawberry Lane were poor, and they walked to town to sell their flowers to make a little money to supplement their meagre incomes. Others would walk to nearby Wynberg to hawk the vegetables they grew. One of these was Richard van der Ross's grandmother, who earned money "to buy books for David". David was Richard's father, one of 13 children, and the third coloured man to get a BA degree at the University of Cape Town (UCT). He later became principal of the Battswood Training College for teachers.

"Not bad for a product of a shantytown school off a sandy road, with mainly illiterate parents earning half a crown a day," says Van der Ross.

Richard van der Ross, who followed the family tradition of becoming a teacher (along with all his siblings, apart from one who broke ranks and became a doctor, much to the family's consternation!), went on to become rector and vice-chancellor of the University of the Western Cape (UWC) and later South African ambassador to Spain.

When Van der Ross accepted the job of rector at UWC, people were unhappy, he says, as it was seen as a "bush college" with inferior education. "People said, what are you doing! I said, wait . . . and today UWC is one of six top universities in Africa. It was tough, I sweated blood with the politics of the time."

Van der Ross can trace his ancestors back to the slaves, perhaps those who had worked on Constantia, the huge farm granted to Simon van der Stel.

"Coloured people, my people, were mainly rural," he says. "My father was born in Strawberry Lane. I have many roots, as do all South Africans, with slaves from Java on my mother's side, and St Helena on my father's side. But I must still trace my father's father – he used to say he was a French creole."

Strawberry Lane was a close-knit community of people, white and coloured, Christian and Muslim. On either side of the Spaanschemat River, people grew flowers and vegetables, and a small school was built there in 1889, run by the Dutch Reformed Mission Church. Pupils were taught from grade 1 to standard 5. Any further study required pupils to walk to Wynberg to attend Battswood School.

In all likelihood most of these families were descended from slaves, who after emancipation and the end of the four-year apprenticeship period in 1838 had moved off the farms to make a new life for themselves. Strawberry Lane was a tiny part of the Bergvliet farm, which had been subdivided into smaller and smaller pieces.

Along the Spaanschemat River Road, in the late 1800s Carl Gideon, July Joseph and Jan Joseph, among others, owned land. They too were probably descended from slaves, writes Van der Ross: "They were ordinary, honest to goodness Coloured people who were born at the Cape, who grew up as farm hands . . ."[39] Between 1889 and 1940 the land was sold to Abraham van der Horst, later known as Abraham van der Ross, Richard van der Ross's grandfather. Surnames often mutated through the generations – for some reason, maybe pronunciation, Van der Horst became Van der Ross. "Van der Ross and Van der Horst were two streams of the same family," he says.

Many of the people of Strawberry Lane would have continued to work in the vineyards of the surrounding farms, some as permanent staff, others as casual labour.

People who lived on the east side of Strawberry Lane were classified coloured, writes Van der Ross, but adds: "There is no knowing quite what this means . . . it was a generally accepted term used to describe people descended from colonialists from Europe, who married or interbred with indigenous people."[40] These people have been called, according to the part of the world they are in, mulattoes, chicanos, mestizos, Métis, half-breeds. In South Africa this mingling of people was enriched with slaves from many countries.

"The Dutch called these people *halfslag* (mulattoes), and the next generation *kwartslag* (quadroons) . . . later *bruinmense* (brown people) or coloured." Freed slaves, and those who came to South Africa as exiles or convicts or simply to seek their fortunes, were called free blacks.

In the early days many free blacks, especially women, were absorbed into white society. Anna de Koning, daughter of a slave and at one time owner of Constantia, was one of these. More on her later.

"But most of the people remained poor," says Van der Ross. "Most were menial workers – messengers, labourers, servants, artisans, and in 1838, when 39 000 slaves were set free, numbers swelled. Many worked on farms where they had become experts in viticulture, making wine and bottling it. Some were coopers."

Jacob Pieter Cloete owned much of the land in Constantia at this time, and his daughter Miss Bonnie Cloete would collect rent from the tenants of the four cottages they owned.

Van Der Ross's tribute to the people of Strawberry Lane, published in 2007 as *Buy My Flowers*, has been largely reconstructed from people's memories. "But the main purpose has been to show that this part of Constantia valley was occupied by Coloured people who had in the main emerged from slavery. They were landowners and tenants, hardworking, proud, law-abiding, religious and self-respecting . . . they were poor, but dignified."[41]

Farm workers always have been and are still marginalised, he says. "But poverty is a relative thing. When is a man poor? When he's poor materially?

My grandmother was poor materially, but her 13 kids never went to bed hungry. By the grace of God, they will tell you. School, church, home were all-important. She walked to Wynberg to sell the vegetables she grew, barefoot (she kept her shoes for Sundays), because "*David moet 'n boek hê*" (David must have a book).

Education was crucial – the ability to read and write often went together with being admitted to Christian churches, which provided schools and played a central role in people's lives.

By the late nineteenth century the literacy levels of the people of Strawberry Lane were very mixed, ranging from being illiterate to having a fair ability to read and write Dutch.

The tragedy of this close-knit community was that it was broken up under the Group Areas Act in the 1960s. Even though the local Group Areas Act committee advised that the community not be removed, the recommendation was ignored. People's houses were demolished, and they were scattered to all parts of Cape Town. There is a land claim on the area, but Van der Ross says it will not be resolved in his lifetime.

The miracle is that people of Strawberry Lane, and now their descendants, still gather four times a year to discuss the business of the Constantia Funeral Benefit Society founded in 1878. Abraham van der Ross was one of founders, and it came about because there were those in the community who were poor, and there was concern that when a person died there would be no money to bury him or her. "And so when one of the community died, every householder gave half a crown, and something to the family. It's the oldest coloured organisation in existence," says Van Der Ross. He laughs: "My Uncle Kenny amused me, he used to say, coloured people want two things – a big wedding and a big funeral."

Funeral societies were established on many farms where people had no savings for a funeral. In some areas people were not permitted to be buried on the farm. Spatz Sperling of the farm Delheim, near Stellenbosch, tells how, when he and his wife Vera heard his labourers were giving their dead a pauper's burial in Bellville because they could not afford coffins, they established a graveyard on the farm where anyone working or living on the farm could be buried. "We buried Vera's father here," he says.

The area where the people of Strawberry Lane lived was part of the original Constantia, a huge farm the size of Amsterdam, which was granted to Commander (later Governor) Simon van der Stel in 1685 as a reward for his work at the Cape. Van der Stel was appointed as commander of the Cape settlement in 1679, after Jan van Riebeeck, and knew a lot more about wine and viticulture than his predecessor who was, in his defence, a doctor.

A little known fact about Van der Stel's grandmother, Monica Da Costa (the surname means "of the Coast"), is that she was an Indian woman; in our peculiar South African parlance, he would have been a "coloured". "Simon van der Stel was a mestizo – *maar hulle praat nie daarvan nie*! (they don't talk about it)" chuckles Van der Ross. Few pictures of Van der Stel survive. In the days of apartheid, where skin colour assumed such importance and history was whitewashed, it would not have been prudent to admit that the father of viticulture and the man who established farming in Stellenbosch had not been "white".

"In the beginning (at the Cape) race wasn't a factor," says Van der Ross. "When Jan van Riebeeck arrived, there were 100 men and eight women – there you are.

"At emancipation, 39 000 slaves were set free. They were thoroughly mixed, most were born here, and they were referred to as Coloured. By and large there was a big category of poor people, most of them Coloured, and they were fishermen, hawkers, gardeners. And the rich were white. And then different things crept into the fabric. With sex being a sin outside marriage in the Dutch Reformed Church, those born out of wedlock, children for example of slaves and masters, were tainted by 'sin'.

"There was even a *plakkaat* (proclamation) issued that forbade farmers from coming into the kitchen at night, where the slave women slept," he says. "Coloured blood became seen as bad blood, evidence of illegal sex and sinful relationships."

In Van der Stel's time, however, skin colour was of little concern, believes Van der Ross. Simon was educated in Holland after the death of his father Adriaan, who had been in the VOC's service, when he was seven. There is no record of what happened to his mother Maria Lievens. Simon grew up to be "a man under the medium stature, and of a dark complexion, with an open cheerful countenance," writes historian George McCall Theal.[42]

Van der Stel seems to have been a good governor, and Constantia was granted to him in spite of VOC employees being prohibited from owning land. He was both enthusiastic and knowledgeable about viticulture and winemaking and in 1695 he set out the Constantia estate, planting the vineyards according to the established norms of Europe, as an example to other farmers.

There have been many divisions and subdivisions of Constantia since Simon van der Stel was granted the farm. He lived there after his retirement in 1699, and after his death in 1712 Constantia was divided into three and sold. Two of the parts were called Bergvliet and Klein Constantia (also known as De Hoop op Constantia), while the part on which the Van der Stel farm buildings stood was called Constantia (later Groot Constantia).[43]

The first vines, the first slaves

Van der Stel was not the first to plant vineyards.

Soon after Jan van Riebeeck had arrived at the Cape, on 27 February 1652 while walking towards Mouille Point, he came upon "the most beautiful land for sowing and for grazing cattle that one could desire . . . for which we require some married Chinese and other free Mardijckers or even also Hollanders". The next day he set out in the opposite direction towards Salt River and the valley of the Liesbeek River: "Even if there were thousands of Chinese or other tillers they could not take up or cultivate a tenth part of this land. It is moreover so fertile and rich that neither Formosa (Taiwan) which I have seen, nor New Netherland (New York and Albany) which I have heard of, can be compared with it."[44]

Seven weeks later he wrote to the authorities in Batavia requesting "some slaves for the dirtiest and heaviest work". These were not forthcoming. After two years of struggling, on 2 April 1654, he noted in his journal: "It would be very much cheaper to have agricultural work, seal catching and all other necessary work done by slaves in return for plain fare of rice and fish or seal and penguin meat alone, and without pay." His request was repeated three weeks later. However, slaves were slow to arrive, and initially came in ones and twos.

The first known slave at the Cape was the stowaway Abraham of Batavia, on board the *Malacca*, who arrived on 2 March 1653. In December 1654 the slave woman Eva, aged about 30, and her son Jan Bruyn, about two years old, were bought from Madagascar. A few more followed. Angela and Domingo (a woman) van Bengalen arrived in November 1655, bought on the ship *Amersfoort*. Angela died in 1720 as a prominent member of the local free-black community. Her daughter Anna was to become the first woman to own the farm Constantia.[45]

In spite of instructions that the garden settlement remain confined to providing for the Company's needs, in 1657 Van Riebeeck released nine Company servants to become full-time farmers on their plots of about 11,4 ha near the fort and further inland. They were the first free burghers.

A tough birth for viticulture

While Van Riebeeck encouraged farmers to plant vineyards, vines were not attractive to the free burghers. In 1658 he wrote to the authorities: "They (free burghers) are also very indifferent about planting vineyards, primarily because of the expense and trouble. But as at present the vines are thriving excellently and we had already in January last tasted some of their new fruit, and so many have grown that in September next (the best planting and pruning time), thousands of slips may be planted on favourable spots, it is a pity that no more fanciers can be found here, as the cultivation can in a short time be developed in an extraordinary manner. We accordingly request you to furnish us with some information regarding pressing . . . as well as some tools necessary for the same, and if possible, two or three persons understanding the business, for the prospects of an abundant growth of vineyards appear to be exceptionally good . . ."[46]

But viticulture was slow to take root. Vines took three years to produce fruit, while wheat and vegetables were not as costly to grow and offered more immediate results. Farmers also faced many setbacks: gales battered the settlement and destroyed newly planted vines, birds ate the berries and locusts destroyed crops. Farmers were barely able to feed themselves, let alone passing fleets, writes historian Wayne Dooling.[47] Profits were elusive, as loans to the Company had to be serviced. The Company fixed agricultural prices and monopolised the market. The majority, then, lived in dire poverty. Many decided to abandon agriculture – by 1678 not even a third of the free burghers continued to farm. There were profits to be had in cattle trade with the Khoikhoi, but this was illegal.

"It was a reluctant settler class – by 1707 some 40% of the 570 burghers whose fate is known had given up independent existence," notes Dooling. "They either returned to the Company's service or stowed away on passing ships. Some sought work as artisans or established boarding houses . . . "

Labour was a huge problem for the new settlement. Khoikhoi were reluctant to work, and Company servants were too expensive.

Then, in 1658, a significant number of slaves arrived: 228 slaves from the coast of Guinea and 174 from Angola. More than half of the settlement now consisted of slaves.[48]

The Company had declared the Khoikhoi a free people who could neither be conquered nor enslaved, and Van Riebeeck had to devote much of his ten-year tenure to intricate diplomatic manoeuvres designed to win the goodwill of at least some Khoikhoi. But there were many trade disputes and charges of theft between Dutch and Khoikhoi, who feared they would be deprived of their pasturage and watering places. In 1659 the Khoikhoi mounted a series of rapid and successful raids on free burghers' herds. The first Khoikhoi-Dutch War lasted a year, with few deaths.[49]

Van Riebeeck planted vines at his own farm in Wynberg (Wine Mountain), which he acquired in 1658, the same year some new slaves arrived. In his diary he wrote: "With the aid of certain free farmers and some slaves, as the moon waned, large parts of Bosheuvel were planted with rooted vines and cuttings."[50] In four days in August, 1 200 rooted vines and cuttings were transplanted. However, a few months later an attack by Khoikhoi ruined the young vines. The next year more vines were planted on the same land.

Then, in an historic entry in his diary dated 2 February 1659, Van Riebeeck wrote: 'Today, praise be to God, wine was made for the first time from Cape grapes, namely from the new must fresh from the vat. The grapes were mostly Muscadel and other white, round grapes, very fragrant and tasty. The Spanish grapes are still quite green, though they hang reasonably thickly on several vines and give promise of a first-class crop. These grapes, from three young vines planted 2 years ago, have yielded about 12 quarts of must, and we shall soon discover how it will be affected by maturing. The return fleet will thus put in here annually just in time for the new must and well-matured beer, when various fruits are also at their best and fully ripe . . . "[51]

In 2009, therefore, the South African wine industry was 350 years old.

Although the early farmers were dirt poor and struggling to survive, it soon became apparent that vines did well in Cape, unlike some other crops. Slowly viticulture began to flourish. With long sunshine hours and winter rainfall, the Cape's climate seemed ideal for growing the hardy grape. Poor soils can produce good wines because grapes are not fastidious about soils. Vines also benefited from the Cape Doctor, the southeaster, which dried out any moisture on the leaves and bunches of grapes, preventing fungal diseases, whereas wheat suffered.

By 1660 the farmers were so successful with grape growing that they began to neglect wheat, to Van Riebeeck's displeasure. Vines were even planted on Robben Island. When Van Riebeeck left the settlement in 1662, the farm Bosheuvel reverted to the Company.

Good wine, bad wine

The wine trade was not lucrative; Cape wine was primarily made for domestic consumption, stored and sold in casks, but decanted into glass bottles or flagons for use in taverns and households. The wine trade was leased to contractors, who had to supply wine to the Company at low prices, and had a monopoly to sell wine to tavern keepers in the port city; hence farmers could not retail their own wine.[52]

Lack of storage space meant wine had to be drunk before the next harvest, so wine prices were low. And while Constantia wine (also known as Vin Constance or Vin de Constance) became world-famous and much sought after, most wines made locally were awful. Wine from the Cape was once described as tasting and smelling like bad potato. Because it was so bad and not to European tastes, there was no export market for it. In addition, wine, unless fortified, did not travel well.

Why the poor quality of wine? Initially farmers lacked knowledge and the right tools. They knew nothing of the basics of winemaking. Storage containers were difficult to get, if not impossible, as Cape timber was unsuitable for cooperage. The barrels that came on ships were filled with arak (a coarse spirit), beer, meat or salt pork and the taste they imparted to the wine was horrible. Until cold fermentation was introduced in the 1950s, temperatures were just too hot and the wines would ferment too heavily, explains wine historian, Diko van Zyl. "Brandy was used to suppress fermentation, (making what are called fortified wines) but because the brandy was of such poor quality, the wine was dreadful. The Cape brandy was the worst spirit ever made, made from the leftovers after winemaking, including the stalks."

Although Van Riebeeck referred to them as his *Spaansche drywe* (Spanish grapes), researchers have identified these first vine plants as French rather than Spanish. It is possible that the "Spanish grapes" were Hanepoot, known in France as Muscat d'Alexandrie. Steen vines, the French Chenin Blanc, were probably also introduced at this time.

Weeding, harvesting and treading grapes

" ... *the myriads of injurious insects to which that farm (Constantia) is subject more than any other here necessarily demands incessantly, before even the vineyards show their first buds, and until the grapes are cut and brought into press, a large number of slaves to search for them and thus save the grapes from destruction.*"[53]

With the emerging viticulture came the need for labour. Grapes are grown and wine is made by human hands, and it was the people who worked in the vineyards and cellars who made Vin Constance, and later other wines, famous.

The early vines required intense labour. The European way was to plant vines closely together, which meant it was not possible to till with animals, so digging by hand was the only alternative. For this, slaves were needed. In colder countries good results were achieved this way, with shoots fixed to upright stakes. In hotter areas, lack of moisture in summer is often a restricting factor, and without irrigation, a better yield results from wider spacing. However, the inexperienced Dutch spaced their early vineyards close together, and treated them like vineyards in cold countries. According to the oenologist Professor CJ Orffer, the narrowly spaced vines "had an important political consequence, namely the complication of the race problem because slaves had to be brought to the country from the East, Madagascar and Central Africa."[54] From his particular viewpoint, writing in 1968, Orffer saw this as a "complication". With other eyes, slaves were the only way to ensure the prosperity of the growing colony; far from a complication, they were to be the backbone of the wine industry.

Apart from tilling, slaves were also needed to weed, harvest, tread grapes and clean and prepare the wine casks. Picking grapes is backbreaking work. Birds were a particular problem, which the slaves scared away with whips. Some farmers decided to pick the grapes while still green to avoid this, resulting in wine "strength" being poor. In 1695 the Cape was visited by a plague of lice and locusts, and the only solution was to have slaves catch locusts in order to keep their numbers down. Slaves cleared the insects from the vines by hand, planted thousands of new vines, cleaned the casks, harvested and trampled the grapes, worked in the household, made clothes, built the gabled buildings.

Goat's blood and a bucket of wine - Constantia wines

"To prepare Constantia wine one takes a rinsing basin filled with sheep or goat's blood, and a bucket of wine from a cask, mix these together and pour the mixture back and forth until it foams."[55] – Lambertus Colijn, early 1800s

Constantia wines were special wine, in demand the world over. They were the only Cape wines to receive any acclaim overseas, and were sought out by royalty: King Frederick the Great of Prussia, King George IV of England and King Louis-Philippe of France, as well as Napoleon Bonaparte, all loved Vin Constance. They were the first, and for a long time among the few, good wines made at the Cape.

The original vines planted at Constantia were probably imported from France and planted by Simon van der Stel on Groot Constantia and the neighbouring De Hoop op Constantia. Compared to what is allowed by law today, the wines were high in sugar, more like a liqueur or sweet wine.

Constantia wines did not just come from the farm Constantia, later to be called Groot Constantia; in fact, it was the wines of Johannes Colijn of Klein Constantia which began to draw attention overseas and first became known as Constantia wine. These were further developed by Hendrik Cloete, who no doubt learned a great deal from Lambertus Colijn, Johannes's son.

As any winemaker will tell you, good wine starts in the vineyard: the quality of wine has as much to do with the terroir as with extended ripening on the vine, and the special care and craftsmanship of its winemakers. Constantia grapes received extra manure, and vermin and weeds were eradicated. The harvesting, pressing, preparing and preserving of wines were very labour-intensive activities on this farm. The grapes were cleaned of stalks and sand, the pips removed. The warm weather meant the grapes could stay on the vine until the skins started wrinkling, ensuring a high sugar content. Vats were well cleaned . . . they were rinsed, washed, dried and sulphur was burned in them, to destroy bacteria. Then they were filled with water, and rinsed again.[56]

Hildagonda Duckitt, who lived at the farm Groote Post near Darling from 1839 to 1905, was related to the Cloete family. Her great-niece Mary Kuttel wrote *Quadrilles and Konfyt – the Life and Journey of Hildagonda Duckitt*, and from Duckitt's diary she quotes: "The greatest care was always exercised in making the famous Constantia wine. When the bunches of grapes had ripened their stalks were twisted but they were left on the vine till almost raisins and then gathered to be pressed. No rotten berries were ever allowed to be pressed . . . "[57]

Lambertus Colijn of the farm De Hoop op Constantia, who wrote about the goat's blood in the excerpt from his manual quoted above, continued: " . . . this is then poured into a cask from which it is drawn off at the bottom and again poured in at the top, until one notices that the blood lies at the bottom. This is left for eight days. Then a clean cask, aired the day before, is taken, the treated wine placed in it . . .[58]

Lambertus's father Johannes was probably the first after Van der Stel to refine the winemaking process in the 1730s. Johannes was the son of Maria Evertsz, also known as Zwarte Maria (Black Maria), and a Dutchman, Bastiaan Colijn. Colijn apparently owned nothing, while Maria owned 60 morgen in what is today Camps Bay – the very successful daughter of two freed

Guinean slaves. Johannes married the coloured widow Elsabe van Hoff, who had inherited Klein Constantia from her first husband.[59]

It was, however, Hendrik Cloete Sr (who acquired Constantia in 1778) who made Vin Constance into the most famous wine from the "younger countries" – his was an unfortified wine made from a blend of mostly Muscat de Frontignan, Pontac, red and white Muscadel on vines originally bought from Persia. They had a thick skin and tough flesh, took a long time to ripen, and the yield was relatively low.

We know a lot about Cloete, and a little about his slaves and those of his son and successor Hendrik Cloete Jr. This was one of the few large wine estates, and Cloete and later his son had a large workforce. In about 1800 Lady Anne Barnard, writer, artist and wife of the Secretary to the British Governor at the Cape, described slaves pressing wine at Groot Constantia (see the quotation at the start of this chapter). She noted that there were four wine presses in the cellar, with each press worked by three slaves. Having trampled the grapes, the slaves sifted the pulp and skins. This process, she wrote, produced a full-bodied wine.

Hildagonda Duckitt wrote in her diary about a visit to Constantia, the home of her mother's uncle and aunt: "The winemaking in my young days was done in the classic way of 'treading out the grape' and the world-famed Sweet Constantia took the first prize at many a French and English exhibition. Mr Cloete imported the choicest varieties of grapes and it is to them the Colony owes the delicious 'Saschelas', a delicate pale-pink grape for eating; the Hermitage, a beautiful bluish-red grape which makes a sort of claret and other endless varieties. The enormous vats, filled with the wines of different vintages, were made of teak wood, beautifully kept and almost polished; they always impressed me with a sense of the neatness and order which pervaded the whole place."[60]

Owing to their high quality and scarcity, these wines were ten times the price of ordinary Cape wines and not available on the open market. The VOC, as well as the British government after 1795, however, claimed a high percentage of the production of Constantia wines from their owners for local and foreign high-ranking people at much less than the market price. This was financially detrimental to the Constantia wine farmers up to the 1830s, and a constant source of irritation to Hendrik Cloete Sr.

Sadly, the phylloxera outbreak in 1886 saw an end to these wines. Then, in the 1980s, Duggie Jooste and his son Lowell, the present owners of Klein Constantia, decided to make Vin de Constance again.[61] With the help of the late Professor Chris Orffer, an oenologist, the Joostes began to research and experiment in order to produce a wine faithful to the original vintage. They selected small-berry Muscat de Frontignan, which had been identified as one of the original cultivars, and planted just over 2 ha of vineyards. After almost 100 years, this sweet wine of world fame was being made again.

Daily lives of slaves on a wine farm

While the wine industry in the Cape was built on the backs of slaves, we know little about their lives. There are few slave narratives from which one can glean what they thought or felt, or how they survived their lives of servitude. A slave was sole cellar master at Constantia from 1759-78, but nothing is known about his identity. Piecing together what it was like for a slave on a wine farm gives a patchy picture only. Historian Thys van der Merwe, who researched Groot Constantia's history, says: "As members of the working classes of the Colony at that time, slaves' specific histories were not documented. Instead, the presence of slaves at Groot Constantia, as elsewhere on Cape farms, is refracted through lists of slaveowners' possessions, estate transfer documents and court cases."

Van der Merwe explains that there was little information on slaves until he came upon the slave registers, which were mandatory between 1816 and 1834. "It's the first time we get a detailed picture of what was going on," he says. "I worked through the whole lot of them. And they are not complete. I followed Groot Constantia slaves from owner to owner. Slaves' places of origin, many of their names and their medical treatment are mentioned. But while I called my thesis 'personal histories', it was nothing but data, age, origins, mother and father and owner. For personal narratives, there's nothing. Which illustrates the point that slaves were possessions and nothing else."

Hundreds of slaves were managed from Groot Constantia and distributed among local farmers. They were mobile and moved as needed. Some slaves were highly specialised, tradesmen from the East, or they were taught here. Religion was not likely to have been encouraged on Groot Constantia; the Dutch had decreed that no religion other than the Dutch Reformed one could be practised at the Cape. But many slaves would have brought their religions with them, especially those from Indonesia. In 1712 some 23 slaves attempted to escape from Groot Constantia, led by an exiled imam Santrij from Java, who lived there. As an imam, Santrij no doubt shared his teachings. The slaves gathered at Groot Constantia, but the plan was foiled, and Santrij was executed for leading the rebellion.

Van der Merwe notes that there are indications at Groot Constantia which suggest more than one religion was practised. "It's just theory, but in the kitchen at the Jonkershuis there were two rows; architects suggest the hearth was placed to accommodate more than one religion, such as Islam."

Constantia's first slaves belonged to Simon van der Stel, who bought his first slave Jan van Oldenburg from Bengal in 1680 from a Company official who was leaving the Cape. From 1680 onwards he bought more slaves from other estates and from English ship's captains. By 1688 he owned 22 slaves, who worked mainly at Constantia. This was not the norm for the free burgher farmers, however, who seldom had more than a few slaves working for them.

Historical records reflect the slaves' varied origins. Some of them were children. In 1693, Van der Stel bought from the Danish ship *Charlotte Amalia* two children, Mange and Motta, who came from Trancquebare in Madras, India. From an English ship he bought George, aged ten, who came from Madagascar. In the same year he sold the three-year-old Revan, also a native of Madagascar, to the Prince of Madagascar, Dain Majampa.

Sixteen slaves whom he bought in 1695 came from India, Bali and Madagascar. In 1698 he bought from an English ship's captain 12 slaves who came from Temetard in India, and from the captain of a Danish ship three slaves who came from Cape Verde. Others came from Brazil, the Canary Islands, China, Ceylon and Batavia. Some had been born at the Cape. By 1709 Van der Stel had 60 slaves.

Slaves on wine-producing estates would have worked throughout the year in large groups controlled by *mandoors* (foremen). This system was used on the farms well into the nineteenth century. Usually the farmer or one of his family members acted as supervisor, but on farms like Constantia, VOC employees known as *knechten* were also employed to supervise the slaves.

Living conditions for slaves varied. A wealthy farm like Constantia had separate buildings used as slave quarters, namely the original Van der Stel outbuildings that were turned into slave quarters and stables. Slaves also ate separately. On Groot Constantia an ox or fat *hamel* (ram) was slaughtered weekly for the slaves. They usually had bread with butter or herring for breakfast, meat at midday and vegetables for dinner. The slaves also consumed up to 560 litres of wine monthly: their daily wine allowance was a tot (125 ml). There were also a few Khoikhoi workers on Groot Constantia, and they were paid quite well. But once again there is little information on them, says Van der Merwe.

Most house slaves were women. They did domestic work and worked in the vegetable gardens. After emancipation a lot of slaves left, and many returned, but how many we do not know. "There's no way of knowing what happened to them, as they could have moved anywhere," says Van der Merwe. "What I do know is that there was a labour problem, and it was huge. Jacob Pieter Cloete told Anthony Trollope (the British novelist) in the 1870s that if they could get labour, they could turn it (the farm) into a paradise again."

It is interesting to note that on Groot Constantia there was a crèche for children. But according to Van der Merwe, "we don't know whether the child minders (slaves) were literate, or what they taught the children."

Larger than life – Hendrik Cloete Sr and his able workforce

Perhaps the best documented of the Constantia farmers was the larger-than-life Hendrik Cloete (1725-99), who was responsible for developing, along with his many slaves and servants, the farm Constantia and the quality of its wine to the full. He was a very successful farmer and wine merchant, and owned many farms in Stellenbosch. He bought Groot Constantia two days after his 53rd birthday, in 1778.

Cloete owned 12 slaves even before he took over at Groot Constantia. By 1818 his son Hendrik Jr had 85 working there. Documents from the years 1814 to 1817 show that the slaves were given the best medical attention. Like his father, Hendrik Cloete Jr employed Khoikhoi men and women as labourers, but on a small scale. They numbered ten in 1818.

Around this time we begin to get details of the people who worked the farm. When he bought Groot Constantia, Cloete Sr paid an extra 30 000 rix-dollars for "moveable goods". Slaves were considered goods, and often were not even mentioned by name in sales. However, the 16 male slaves he bought in one sale are named: April, Salomon, Toontje, Jan, Schipeon, Februarij, Maart, Jaco, Chrispijn, Manes, Casper, Onton, Reppa, Julij, October and Baatjoe.[62]

The list is a reminder of how slaves lost their own names when they arrived at the Cape – five of them are named after months of the year, probably the order in which they arrived here. They lost their former identities, along with their homelands, their families and anything familiar to them. Some were given European names, or nicknames to make it easy for the settlers to remember them. Often names came from the Bible or classical mythology. Guinean slaves, for some reason, kept their names and this gave them certain limited identity and individuality, names such as Jajenne, Houwj, Gegeima, Cattibou.[63]

Children born to slave women seem to have been named after their European fathers at times, such as Anna de Koning, but there was seldom acknowledgment of paternity. To further identify slaves, their names were followed by the place they came from, or perhaps the place they were shipped from.

And so, while these names are useful in identifying a general area of origin, they are not accurate as to the person's homeland. "Van de Caab" after a name meant they were born at the Cape.

Soon after buying Constantia, Cloete saw that 16 slaves were insufficient for his needs, and in 1780 he wrote to Hendrik Swellengrebel: "Sir, 16 slaves were not sufficient to bring order to this neglected farm, I had to add another 16, with whose help I have made great changes."[64]

Cloete became one of the Cape's largest slaveowners, owning at least 50 at Groot Constantia alone. He was not, however, happy with the cellar man he inherited from the previous owner, whom he described as "not only a most ignorant person, but he had little or no knowledge of winemaking".

He was replaced by April van de Caab, who so pleased Cloete that he left April 100 rix-dollars in his will "in return for faithful services", and the choice of freedom at the estate's expense, or the choice to live with one of the heirs with a monthly allowance of three dollars.[65]

Cloete seems to have treated his slaves well, albeit in a paternalistic way, seeing his slaves as children and, always, as possessions. But he was nevertheless self-indulgent: a late eighteenth-century drawing depicts a slave with Groot Constantia's owner, Hendrik Cloete Sr. The slave, named Jacob, supports Cloete's long clay pipe. Cloete was also woken each morning by his slave orchestra playing outside his window.

Two other slaves were equally rewarded in his will: the *mandoor* Titus (an overseer) and the coachman Philip were given 100 rix-dollars as reward, and the choice of being emancipated or living with an heir. In his will he provided for Jephta, also known as Kleintje, to be rewarded, but not freed. The elderly were looked after: Nero of Malabaar no longer needed to work, and would get one dollar a month; all slaves who reached 60 years or more could not be sold, and could choose which heir they wished to live with.

Some of the other slaves at Groot Constantia, and their occupations, were Meij of Nias, a tailor of women's clothing; the wagon drivers Leander of the Cape, Amor of Madagascar and Bacchus of Madagascar; domestic servant Jonathan of the Cape, and carpenter Bacchus of the Coast.

In Cloete's will of July 1799 he also states that he "emphatically desires that none of his male slaves having relationships with his female slaves shall be separated from them; even less should the children who are not yet twelve years old be separated from their mothers". At this time slaves were not allowed to get married, and they could easily be sold away from their children and partners. Cloete, although patriarchal, had a strong sense of responsibility towards his dependants. Like most farmers, he did not encourage his slaves to attend church – according to a register of parishioners of 1786, none of his slaves, male or female, was at the time a church member at Stellenbosch.

Cloete was also prepared to work very closely with his slaves: "I do not leave the cellar for a moment, no longer is a midday pause taken. Kleintje is in the vineyard picking grapes, the shirt is off and in gauze trousers, I stand here all day minding the pressing vat."[66]

Wine farming and winemaking, especially the way Cloete did it, was labour intensive: in his memorandum on essential expenses at Constantia in 1788, he includes "30 labourers; servant's pay for keeping wild buck out of the vineyard and to guard the farm against all kinds of evil; a cook and helper for my slaves; 3 boys routinely occupied with the preparation of wine casks and other work in the cellar".

Along with his huge workforce he made many improvements to Constantia, building a new cellar, and improving the exterior of house. He also planted 13 000 to 14 000 new vines, which required heavy labour as trees had to be removed and soil prepared.

Cape farmers of the time did not have the freedom to market or export their agricultural produce; the Company had preference in the purchase of vegetable and animal products from farmers. It had the monopoly in import and export of many goods, including wine, and both directly and indirectly fixed prices.

Hendrik Cloete Sr was often frustrated by the Company's monopoly on the wine trade and petitioned the authorities to allow him to trade freely – his wine was sought-after and expensive to produce, and the Company was paying far below market value for wine and then selling it at ten times the cost.[67] But the VOC largely maintained its position, taken from the start, that all commerce at the Cape was subject to its trading interests. There was, however, some private wine selling going on and the VOC often received less wine than it ordered; producers claimed they had less to give, blaming climatic conditions, plant diseases, pests and other setbacks which had affected their harvest. It is very likely that they retained some wine for private sales.[68]

After the death of Hendrik Cloete Jr in 1818, his wife Anna Catharina Scheller became the second woman to own Groot Constantia. In February 1823 her son Johan Gerhard Cloete bought part of the estate, which became known as Klein Constantia. On 3 December 1824 Jacob Pieter Cloete bought Groot Constantia from his mother. It is from that date that the farm became known officially as Groot Constantia to distinguish it from Klein Constantia.

New problems loomed for Jacob Cloete and Lambertus Colijn, with increasing competition from their neighbours, the Van Reenens of High

Constantia. Many visitors who previously came to Groot Constantia and De Hoop op Constantia began to frequent High Constantia and from about 1840 Jacob and Sebastiaan Valentijn van Reenen were in fierce competition, even lowering their wine prices at times to encourage sales.

In 1885 Groot Constantia was sold to the Cape government.

The Constantia Valley was the first area where the settlers established viticulture. Although the Cape wasn't intended as a wine farming area, grapes thrived. Wine making, however, took a little longer to develop into the fine art it is today, and with a few exceptions, the wine was dreadful. Constantia was one such exception: with great care taken in the vineyards and some winemaking expertise, a sweet wine from these vineyards gained world fame and was much sought after. Constantia provides us with a rare glimpse, albeit incomplete, into the lives of slaves; it was also home to many of the freed slaves, who lived in areas like Strawberry Lane, before being moved away. One of the oldest wine-producing areas, it is also one of the richest in stories.

CHAPTER 3

Beyond the settlement – the place of the "Hottentots"

For a few years after the European settlers arrived at the Cape, the small settlement at Table Bay was enough for their needs. But it did not contain them for long, and soon there were explorations towards the Hottentots Holland mountain range. Five years after his arrival, in 1657, Jan van Riebeeck wrote in his journal:

> In the vicinity of a very beautiful river, on the sides of which bitter almond trees grew in profusion and in such fine, fertile soil, . . . [we] found two native encampments numbering 500 or 600 people . . . who . . . called this place their Fatherland or Holland, to give our men an idea of the abundance of food and the excellent pasturage to be found there.[69]

Thus was Hottentots Holland named, the home of the "Hottentots", as the various groups of Khoikhoi were known. It is still the name used today for the mountain range that separates the Cape Flats from the mountainous interior. This area was indeed home to the indigenous people, the Khoikhoi and the San. In the mood of the time, however, land was there for the taking, and the finer points of habitation and possession were not considered.

The heart of the Winelands has always been the Stellenbosch and Drakenstein areas. Settled after Table Bay, this region was later to become the centre of the wine industry, where a few wealthy wine farmers prospered and made fine wines. It is not easy from today's vantage point to think of these farms as being anything other than gracious wine estates with vineyard after vineyard covering the slopes of the mountains here.

But a mere 350 years ago this was wilderness, used by the pastoral Khoikhoi to graze their livestock. They encamped along the rivers, setting up their kraals. The Dutch knew that Khoikhoi and San lived here – when Abraham Gabbema visited the Drakenstein area in 1657, he described kraals all along what he called the "Groot Berg River". Early maps show *kraalen* – usually circles of huts – near the farms, never on them. Colonial maps were drawn up to reflect the ideology of the time and historian Gavin Lucas[70] notes that

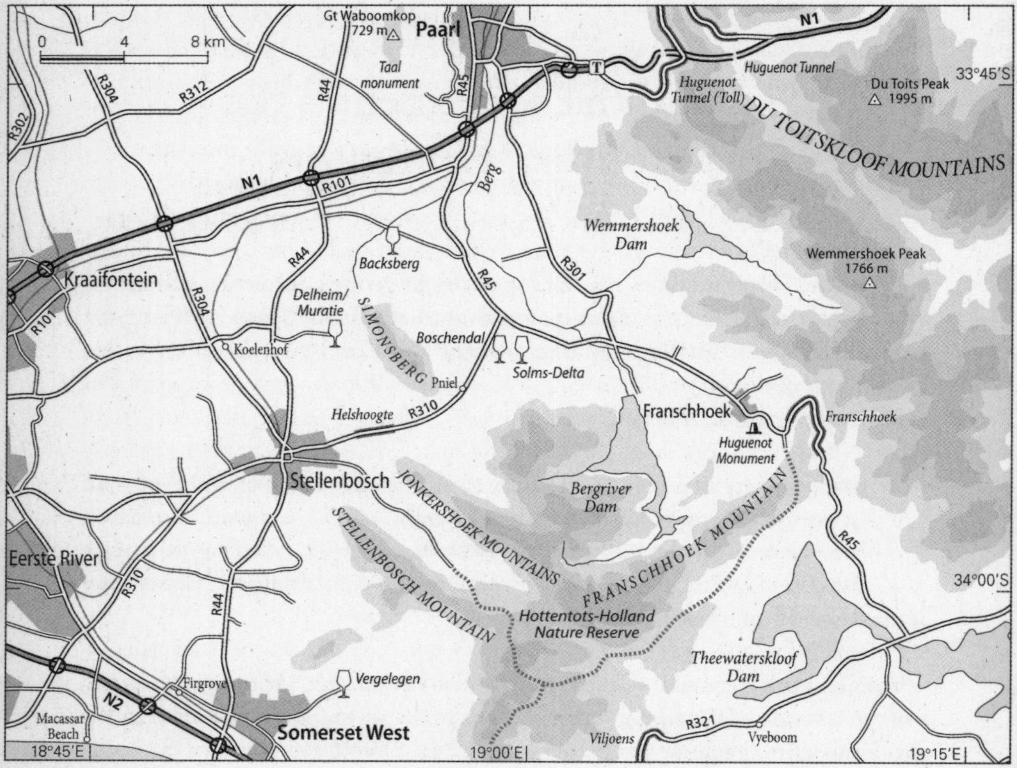

A present-day map showing Stellenbosch and Drakenstein, the areas first settled beyond Table Bay, where many Khoikhoi kraals were present. These are major wine-growing areas today.

Khoikhoi settlements were named generically after their tribal or regional ascription, while the settlers were given personal and individual names.

There was no doubt about whose land this was, and who was living here when the Europeans arrived. Interesting archaeological work at Solms-Delta, a wine farm in the Drakenstein area, has uncovered not only the ruins of a seventeenth-century dwelling, but only a metre away a prehistoric site with Stone-Age artefacts, dating back to 5 000 years ago, on a plateau overlooking the Dwars River, where Khoikhoi would have lived. There are also many traces of the San, a collective name for different groups of hunter-gatherers, who also lived in the Drakenstein area, and rock paintings have been found in Wemmershoek nearby. This is something that usually escapes the Winelands history books.

More than 30 years after Gabbema's visit, a map of the Stellenbosch area of 1690 shows the kraals of the "Gonnemase Hottentots" clearly marked. Gonnema was a chief of the Cochoqua. As Gavin Lucas comments, the fact that the nomadic Khoikhoi are depicted on this map is interesting precisely because they are represented in the same way as the European settlers, as fixed settlements. Other accounts refer to their mobile lifestyle.[71] This is still being debated by historians.

Khoikhoi groups moved seasonally to where the grazing was good, and although they had no sense of ownership of land, as in the European tradition, with title deeds, different groups used certain areas and everyone who came into them was expected to treat them with respect. What is not widely known, is that between Khoikhoi and San relationships of hierarchy and servitude existed long before the Europeans arrived. The Khoikhoi, "the real people" or the "men of men", called the hunter-gatherers Soaqua, Sonqua or Sanqua, abbreviated to San, meaning "the others" – those of lower status. The relationship was complicated, marked by co-operation at times as well as violent disputes over hunting and watering grounds.[72] Between Khoikhoi groups there was also frequent raiding of cattle.

Different Khoikhoi groups used the area named Stellenbosch. The Khoikhoi had been moving their herds around from about 500 AD when Khoikhoi pastoralists first inhabited the southwestern Cape. They burnt patches of bush at their grazing grounds in order to clear the tall, impenetrable fynbos and stimulate the growth of fresh grasses. When farmers first inhabited the valley, it is highly likely that they used these established clearings and routes as a basis for their dwellings and fields. Interesting stone artefacts found in Ida's Valley near Stellenbosch indicate that it has been a human habitat for at least 700 000 years.[73] These were also the traditional hunting grounds of the San.

When Simon van der Stel visited the area and recognised that the valley called Wildebosch was good farming land, he renamed it after himself – Stellenbosch. He offered freehold grants of land on a first-come-first-served basis along the Eerste Rivier, and in 1679 the first free burgher had settled in Stellenbosch. The settlers who were allocated land were a mixed bunch: among them were many former VOC employees, some free blacks (people either born free and exiled to the Cape, or former slaves), and others who were willing to work hard at farming in the "wild" interior. Company servants came from the lowest social classes of Europe. After Europe's Thirty Years' War (1618-48), peasants from all over Europe travelled to Holland to find work. The only work available for the unskilled was as soldiers or sailors; they had to serve the Company for five years, exclusive of the voyage to the Cape.[74]

Van der Stel, of mixed parentage himself, encouraged free blacks to populate the new frontier, as he believed, from his experience of plantations in Mauritius, that they were harder working than European settlers. He also asked for Chinese to be sent out in large numbers at one stage, but that did not happen. Some free blacks established themselves as farmers but not many were successful.

The farms were relatively small, a problem that even today makes it difficult to make a wine farm economically viable. With the market far away in Cape Town, and a tough road to travel on across the Cape Flats, land suitable for arable agriculture was mostly used for grazing. Wheat and vines were the main crops grown. Farmers had to sow six morgen of corn for every one morgen of vineyard, one tenth of which was to be delivered to the Company, to prevent farmers from giving too much attention to vineyards and neglecting corn.

In 1687 Van der Stel granted more land along the Upper Berg River Valley, on a more selective basis, in Drakenstein. Initially, the Company had not been keen to expand any further – it wanted to keep control of the colonists and more importantly, ensure a steady meat supply from the Khoikhoi. Furthermore, Van der Stel had a poor opinion of his free burghers. In 1699 he advised his son Willem Adriaan, who took over from him as governor, that "the free burghers were nothing but lazy idlers who would indulge in illicit trade with the Khoikhoi and make insatiable demands for land unless they were closely controlled".[75] Prophetic words.

Ansela van de Caab and the early wine farmers

The farms of the interior were a far cry from the wine estates of today. Most of the farmers were poor, and struggled to make ends meet. Wine was a minor product. Very few farms had more than five or six slaves; few even had separate buildings for slaves.

Into this early settlement came Ansela, a former slave, who married Lourens Campher, a German soldier, in the late 1600s. They were the first owners of the farm De Driesprong, today the farm Muratie (and parts of Delheim) near Stellenbosch.[76]

Today the wine made from the farms in this area are world renowned – Muratie, Delheim and Kanonkop, to name a few. Indeed, the area in front of the Simonsberg mountain has arguably the best terroir in the country for growing grapes for certain wines.

"You can feel the history here," says Annatjie Melck, owner of the farm Muratie, where she lives. "When Ronnie (her husband) and I bought the farm (in 1988), I wondered what the stories here were all about, and we asked Helena Scheffler to research the history."

At the time she had no idea that the story of Ansela would emerge – and what a wonderful story it was. "It was incredibly valuable and strong. I like yesterday, you can't build today and tomorrow until you know yesterday," says Melck.

Ansela and Lourens's story is a romantic one, although there was little romantic about the lives of the early farmers in Stellenbosch, where survival was a struggle. Ansela van de Caab was born in the time of Jan van Riebeeck's commandership.[77] She was the daughter of Martha, a slave of *volle kleur* or *heelslag* (unmixed parentage) from Guinea or Angola, and an unknown European father. Her name, Ansela van de Caab, tells us she was born locally; like most slaves, she had no second name, and was owned by the VOC.

While working in the Company's Gardens she met the German Lourens Campher, who was probably a soldier or seaman and hailed from Mohrow in Pomerania in northeastern Europe, and they began a lifelong relationship. Ansela lived in the Slave Lodge, where all the Company's slaves lived, a grim place, barely fit for human habitation. It was not a healthy environment, and slaves regularly became sick and died. The roof leaked, the wind blew rain in. Morale was low, there was no privacy, and all the slaves lived in one large room and slept on the floor.

Lourens would visit Ansela at the Slave Lodge, but there was nothing stealthy about his visits. It may have been against the law for Europeans to have sex with slaves, but it happened nevertheless. At 8pm every night there would be a roll call, and once all the slaves were accounted for, the doors would be locked. At 9pm they would be opened, briefly, and the visiting soldiers and sailors let out. The VOC unsuccessfully attempted to forbid them from entering the lodge by issuing one proclamation after another, but they appeared to have been to little avail, for in 1718 the Council of Policy, the political arm of VOC, was forced to recognise that sexual relations between slaves and soldiers were commonplace, and that many soldiers had in fact fathered children by slave women. Carl Peter Thunberg, a Swedish traveller to the Cape in the 1770s, noted that junior Company servants, "ruined themselves by connexions with black women".[78] However, the average soldier and sailor from lower socioeconomic classes in Europe paid little attention to differences in class, position or colour. Mingling between people of different geographical origins in the early days of the settlement was to an extent acceptable.

The Slave Lodge was not a romantic place to court, and an unlikely place to establish a lasting relationship. But happen it did, and Ansela and Lourens formed a close attachment in spite of her slave status and, at that stage, little hope of her being manumitted (freed). Her three children, fathered by Lourens, were automatically slaves, belonging to the Company. The children were baptised – it was Company policy to baptise the children of slaves, even if the slaves were not Christians. Ansela's first baby, Cornelis, was christened in the Castle in 1686. Campher's name was not given in the church register, according to the custom at the christening of "Company" babies. A child born of a slave belonged to the owner; maternity was known, paternity not acknowledged. The birth of a slave child was regarded as an economic gain to the Company. Lourens and Ansela's second child, Agnietie, was christened in 1690 and their third child, Jacoba, in 1692. She was noted as being a *kastijse*, or a quadroon, three-quarters white.

Ansela herself was baptised three years later on 19 June 1695, no doubt in preparation for marrying Lourens. This was one of the conditions of marriage; a freed slave had to be baptised, be able to speak Dutch, profess the Christian faith and be a member of the church. The man had to be trustworthy and honourable and in a position to keep a wife. Ansela was freed nine days later, on 28 June 1695. The interesting part of their story is that Ansela and Lourens were some of the first farmers in the newly opened Stellenbosch area. And as a "mixed" couple, they were not unusual for the time. It was common for burghers, as the German, French and Dutch citizens were known, as well as former VOC employees, to marry freed slaves. Many of the Cape's early families were of mixed heritage; the *stammoeder* ("mother" ancestor) of the Basson family, for example, was the free-black woman Mooi Ansela, who married Arnoldus Willemsz Basson (whose family owned

Meererust and Eensaamheid). And there are many, many more examples. Women were very scarce at the Cape; those here married young, were frequently widowed, and married often.

Ansela, as a freed slave, would have been accepted in Stellenbosch society of the time, such as it was, writes researcher Helena Scheffler: "Extramarital relationships and births as well as intermarriage occurred frequently in the early years at Cape, and did not cause raised eyebrows."

At Muratie, the first title deed to the farm De Driesprong is mounted on the wall of the cellar. The farm was granted to Campher on 28 February 1699; the title deed is signed by Willem Adriaan van der Stel.

Lourens had already moved to Stellenbosch, at that stage just a hamlet, by the time Ansela was freed, and had been living there for many years as a free burgher. He would visit Ansela regularly in spite of the long and difficult road to the Cape, about 64 km away. The journey was a slow one, by ox-wagon or horse, across the sandy plains of the Cape Flats. When a strong southeaster blew, the road could disappear under the sand and the route become almost impassable. For a farmer to take his wine to the Cape by wagon, drawn by 18 or 20 oxen, would take more than an hour for every kilometre across the sandy road.

This was the journey that Ansela, Lourens and their children Cornelis, now nine, five-year-old Agnietie and three-year-old Jacoba undertook in 1695 on their way to their new home. The farm is nestled below the Simonsberg, next to a river. "De Driesprong" means the place where three roads meet. The farm covered 30 morgen and 410 sq roods, with two legs running almost parallel to each other. The title deed allowed him to plant crops, keep livestock and cut timber, and let or sell the farm. All trees cut down had to be replaced by young oaks or other timber trees, and a tenth of the grain harvest had to be assigned to the authorities. When the farm was granted, Lourens had already been farming the land for three years, and there are indications he had already been there 14 years, since 1685.

We cannot know how Ansela felt as she approached her new home, but it must have been a welcome sight. From De Driesprong you can see Table Mountain in the distance; Simonsberg lies behind it. This was one of the first mountain farms in the Stellenbosch area – others were along the flat banks of the Eerste River. The simple house, which still stands, was built on a rise near the mountain stream, beyond the reach of floodwaters, but near enough for fetching water. It is a small building with a pitched roof, probably thatched in those days, and simple upright end gables, with a door in the gable wall nearest the river, characteristic of rural farmhouses of the time. What is thought to be the original window fitting in one wall remains; next door was the stable, and an open-topped kraal, which would have protected their small livestock. There are numerous holes in the walls made for chickens to roost, sloping backwards so the eggs would not fall out.

"My dream is to restore Ansela's house. The historic people stop me, they're anxious I'll spoil it. But I have such an appreciation for the past . . . " says Annatjie Melck.

The year Ansela joined Campher on the muster roll, they are listed as owning two heads of cattle and 150 sheep. They sowed three muids of wheat. From the muster roll of annual returns between 1716 to 1734, Scheffler builds up some picture as to how the Camphers fared. They were not well off, and they never owned slaves. This was probably not for ethical reasons – many wealthy freed slaves did not hesitate to buy slaves themselves. But slaves were expensive, and many farmers simply could not afford them. The Camphers also never employed a farmhand, and Lourens and Cornelis had to plough, sow and reap in the vineyards and press the grapes themselves.

The Camphers always had trekoxen; and Cornelis owned one horse. Lourens and Cornelis each had a flintlock and a sword, and Cornelis had a brace of pistols. The Camphers' vines varied year by year between none to 8 000, and the number of leaguers of wine they produced varied between a quarter and three leaguers. The average was about one leaguer a year – 575 687 litres. This was very little compared to others. In 1716 they had 7 000 vines while other farmers had 20 000 to 30 000, and sometimes up to 70 000 vines. Returns year after year tell a story of hope and disappointment, writes Scheffler. If the corn harvest was good, livestock increased. If bad, they owned nothing. They farmed sheep between 1719 to 1722, owning 50 to 80.

Farmers struggled from year to year with the high production costs of corn and wine. At this stage there was a limited market for wine and what there was, was controlled by the governor. Farmers often sat with a surplus. But at this time there were already a few wealthy farmers, such as Adam Tas, who was to lead a rebellion against Governor Willem Adriaan van der Stel's monopolistic actions. Van der Stel succeeded his father as governor at the Cape in 1699 and soon gained extensive land holdings in Hottentots Holland, which was against Company policy. He farmed on a large scale at Vergelegen, and prospered by illegally using Company slaves and *knechts*. Farmers also had grievances about the way the wine and meat *pachten* (what we would call tenders today) were awarded by the authorities. When Van der Stel became a threat to local farmers, they rose up against him. One of these was wine historian Diko van Zyl's *stamvader* (ancestor), Willem van Zyl, who was originally a gardener at Rondebosch. "He was one of those toyi-toying against Willem Adriaan van der Stel," Van Zyl says. "He fled to Vier-en-Twintig-Rivieren until Van Der Stel was expelled from the Cape."

The early farmers struggled because they had to pay off their debts from loans for farm equipment and materials. In 1720 Lourens Campher gave up farming, perhaps because it was just too hard, or he was getting old, and he died between May 1729 and May 1730, probably aged about 75. His only possessions were a flintlock and sword. His son Cornelis went on farming for about five years before Ansela sold the farm. Cornelis died in 1736, aged 50, and Ansela would most likely have lived with one of her other children. The value of the farm when sold was 2 500 guilders, the equivalent of the salary a soldier or seaman would have earned over 23 years.

It would be nice to say that De Driesprong was a prosperous farm, and that Lourens and Ansela's descendants thrived there. It was not, and they were not alone. Many farms in the area did not bring prosperity, as is still the case today.

In its 310-year history (1699 to 2009), De Driespong has passed through 21 owners. "There were some interesting women here; Ansela was the matriarch of the farm and it was a beautiful love story, showing strength of character, perseverance and love," says Annatjie Melck. "Others were Trienkie Beyers, very well known in this community; Annemie Canitz, a tiny woman, who rode huge stallions; in her time she was the only woman winemaker in the industry. The Stanfords were four daughters and a mother. After paying a social visit to their neighbours, the Beyers family, who were Afrikaans, they decided they were culturally acceptable, and they could play bridge with them. One of the Van der Byl's names is inscribed on the window of the room I sleep in – Wilma, 1905, she was born here.

"I love the warmth of this house. This house is kept alive by the people who lived here. It's got the truth. If you sit up at the end of the farm, you can see Table Bay, and you can imagine the story that played out here."

On a naive map drawn around the time Ansela and Lourens settled at De Driesprong, there are two kraals close by, writes Scheffler. To the south are drawn lots of little hills, stretching off the map. We know very little about settler and Khoikhoi interaction in this area because there has been little archaeological work done. Early contact with Europeans took place in the 1650s and 60s, when the Khoikhoi bartered livestock with the Dutch for copper, tobacco and tobacco pipes.

Uncovering the past

When you stand in front of the slave wall at the Museum Van De Caab on the farm Solms-Delta, it takes a while to take it all in. There are over 200 small blocks of black marble, most with names on, but some blank, representing the slaves who worked on the farm Delta (as it was previously called) in the years between 1690 and 1838, when slaves were emancipated. Their names include many with the months of the year; many are Van de Caab, meaning they were born at the Cape. It is a graphic way of showing their lives lived as possessions. It is sobering.

Tracey Randle, an historian who undertook research for the Solms-Delta Museum, worked closely with owner Mark Solms to unearth the early history of the Dwars River area. The archaeological dig was part of Solms's way of untangling the past and understanding the problems he inherited when he bought the farm in 2002. Seven families lived there then.

"Normal relationships with people were impossible," he says. "We couldn't have a conversation: they were despairing, sceptical and suspicious. If there's a problem, as a psychoanalyst, I want to know where it came from. It looked impossibly tangled and I wanted to understand. So we started with oral histories and digging up the place. Everyone was involved in the museum."

What was revealed was startling. Not only were the foundations of the first house built on Delta found, but within a few metres on a small mound, a Stone-Age site, dating back between 6 000 and 4 000 years ago, was uncovered. Here San people would have sat chipping away at pieces of rock to make the tools that would catch the food to ensure their survival.

"We know about Cape Dutch architecture and porcelain and glass, but we had no idea that there was all this other stuff going on," says Randle.

Opening up history and acknowledging what was here before, she says, has helped to build relationships as the history that involved people living on the farm was uncovered. As farm resident Ampie Pietersen commented to Solms: "Our people were here before yours."

Randle's research on the many owners through the years found that the first owner, Christoffel Snyman, was the first Snyman in the Cape, and then it was discovered he was the son of a slave.

Of her research, she says: "I was surprised. The history was more complex than I thought . . . the Khoikhoi enslaved the San, there was hierarchy and power. They were called clients, but they were so impoverished they had to work for Khoikhoi and were pushed out of areas by them. There were very few indigenous San when Jan van Riebeeck arrived. I was also surprised at how open and fluid the society was in terms of mixed marriages, at how accepted it was on all the farms around us. Nearly all the men were married to slaves or descendants of slaves. Christoffel was the exception in that he was the son of a slave who married a Huguenot – usually it was the men who married former slave women.

"And I found that slaves weren't all virtuous. What's also been interesting is how people living on the farm related to the uncovering. Sanna Malgas, when we pointed out she was related to a slave who had worked on the farm (Van Malagasy), said we were being unkind. But slowly she came round. However, people are more willing to connect to their slave history than to Khoikhoi ancestry."

There was contact between Khoikhoi and settlers, and anecdotal evidence suggests conflict from the beginning and an uneasy relationship. On 21 May 1702 Daniel Hugo from the farm Sion in the Drakenstein burnt down the hut of Chief Jan because the Khoikhoi cattle had damaged his vineyard. In 1700 Armand Veron was assaulted with sticks and stones by eight Khoikhoi from Ovequa kraal because he refused to transport them on his wagon. He fled.

In 1702 Abraham de Villiers, who farmed in Oliphantshoek (the area now known as Franschhoek), lodged six complaints against a Khoikhoi called Kleine Kaptein: for killing his dog, stealing a lamb, heifer, pig and ox, and finally for threats of arson and theft. In return, Kleine Kaptein accused De Villiers of burning his houses and shooting his livestock. Kleine Kaptein had to pay the costs of the case – three calves – to the landdrost (magistrate). In the same year De Villiers moved to the Dwars River Valley, buying a farm there, perhaps to avoid further trouble.

Silent violence – losing land, losing livelihood

The Company decided in the early 1700s to change its policy on expansion as it wanted to end its dependence on the Khoikhoi for meat, and it was hoped colonists allowed to go beyond the boundaries of the settlement would eventually be able to supply its requirements. Willem Adriaan van der Stel made two decisions that were to have serious repercussion for the Khoikhoi and San over the next 100 years, leading to the destruction of their culture and independence.[79] Firstly, he opened the Land van Waveren (the Tulbagh area) in July 1700 to farmers to graze their livestock on the loan-farm system, whereby they paid a rental for the land and were granted grazing licences. Secondly, in the same year, he opened the cattle trade with the Khoikhoi to the colonists. Thereafter settlers expanded north along the Berg River and to either side along tributaries until 1717, when the policy of issuing freeholds was changed.[80] By 1710 Wagenmakersvallei (Wellington), the Swartland and the Land van Waveren were all settled.

But not without fierce resistance. The story of Allesverloren, a long-established wine estate near Riebeek West, is told like this on the estate's website:

> In the Swartland, about 100 km northeast of Cape Town, lies the Allesverloren estate, the oldest wine estate in the district. The history of the estate dates back to between 1696 and 1704, when the governor of the Cape left it to a widow named Cloete. This courageous woman was one of the first settlers who ventured into the inhospitable Swartland region. The early settlers were simple people, with only the most limited agricultural equipment and basic necessities with which to support themselves.
>
> In order to purchase tools or attend church, they had to undertake a long and arduous wagon journey along primitive roads to Stellenbosch. It was on their return from one such journey in 1704 that the settlers found their house burnt to the ground and the farm destroyed. Hence the estate's sad name, "Allesverloren", which means "all is lost".

Why was the farm burnt to the ground? It is not explained on the website for the wine estate, but with a little probing into the history of the area, it becomes evident. There is little doubt the Khoikhoi or San (known collectively as Khoisan) would have been responsible, and whether it was a private feud or general retaliation for the incursion into Khoisan lands, we will never know. But burning farmhouses was a common form of Khoisan attack, as was stealing livestock, often in retaliation for having their livestock stolen by the trekboers (as the stock farmers moving into the interior in search of more grazing were called). With the initial expansion of settlers into the Land van Waveren, fighting broke out immediately. Allesverloren was just one of the many, many skirmishes in the guerilla war that took place as the trekboers moved northwards into Khoisan land.

Khoisan resistance was fierce and unrelenting. The trekboers, however, and later their offspring, many a result of marriages to Khoikhoi women, were an unstoppable force, armed with weapons and the arrogance of their belief in their superiority over the indigenous people. The Dutch VOC, and later the British, probably gave them support, although there were also attempts by authorities to curb their excesses and cruelty.[81]

The Khoikhoi conceded land and water holes rather than losing livestock. They refused to trade their strongest and healthiest cows – this was their livelihood. Losing their livestock was more dangerous than moving away, and so many moved northwards or eastwards. There were some brief battles, but as the Khoikhoi slowly lost their grazing, so too did they lose their wealth and power.

Those who did not move away were forced to work for the farmers, probably on a seasonal basis, and this led to a further disintegration of their society as they were displaced in almost "silent violence". "Their story is very hard to recover," writes historian Gavin Lucas. "Work on post-contact groups, especially the Khoekhoe, is almost non-existent – as if they themselves no longer existed after 1652."[82]

Settlers were not allowed to trade with the Khoikhoi, but they did. By the end of the 1690s the farmers had built up their own herds and competed for, or monopolised, the same grazing and water resources the Khoikhoi used. In the early years at the Cape the VOC preferred not to employ Khoikhoi labourers, who most of the time preferred not to work for them anyway as they valued their independence.

But free burghers had less choice, as labour was in short supply. Farmers, especially pastoral farmers, depended the most heavily on Khoikhoi, but even in arable districts such as Stellenbosch, Khoikhoi labourers formed 30% of the workforce.[83] Migrant groups of Khoikhoi men moved from farm to farm harvesting grapes. In the early days farmers in the rural districts owned relatively few slaves – in 1695 there were only 48 slaves in the whole Drakenstein district.

Some Khoikhoi would do casual work on farms in exchange for tobacco, food and wine, while remaining livestock owners, and initially had the choice not to do hard manual labour for the colonists. At first only the men worked on the farms; women and children stayed home in the kraals. However, by the late 1600s the women and children too moved to the farms. By the 1700s more and more Khoikhoi worked on farms in order to give their dwindling herds access to the grazing and water now controlled by the new settlers.

The Khoikhoi's expert knowledge of animal husbandry meant that they were usually employed to guard herds, or as guides, wagon drivers or to work with the oxen used to plough the fields. As they became more assimilated into the culture of their new masters, they were also sometimes employed to help catch runaway slaves and take part in the commandos (to retrieve stolen cattle, and raid other Khoikhoi bands). Women were usually employed in the home to do laundry and as maids.

By 1705 the Khoikhoi were so impoverished that there were only two kraals left between the Berg River and present-day Klawer (283 km north of Cape Town). In 1713 a smallpox epidemic at the Cape greatly reduced the numbers of Khoikhoi, and although this has been seen as pivotal in their destruction, historian Robert Ross says the epidemic disasters which struck them more heavily are likely to have been "those affecting cattle, such as the foot-and-mouth disease ... (in) the years after 1713 ... and the loss of grazing land under the pressure of the superior force of the whites ... that explain the transition from pastoralist tribesmen to farm labourers, in a condition comparable to bondage, a deterioration of their social status which the Khoekhoe suffered".[84]

By the 1720s there were few independent Khoikhoi to be found within a distance of 50-60 Dutch miles of Cape Town.

What made a successful farmer?

The history of many wine estates has been told in detail in glossy books and self-published manuscripts. Certain family names endure – the Myburghs at Meerlust, with eight generations still farming, is one such case. But they are an exception to the general rule. Farms frequently changed hands, such as Muratie above. Historian Wayne Dooling traces the gentrification of wine farmers in his fascinating study *Slavery, Emancipation and Colonial Rule in South Africa* (2007) and tracks the waning fortunes of many farmers.[85]

What made a farmer successful seems to have been extensive landholdings and enough slaves to farm them. Women often held the key: partible inheritance under the Dutch law gave them control over property, landed and human. One reason for the failure of many farms during that time has been ascribed to this system of inheritance, which meant that a widow inherited half the estate, with the other half divided among the children. While this was a fair way of dividing wealth, it made it very difficult for families to keep land together, unlike the British system where the oldest son inherited everything. This system did mean, however, that widows did not stay unmarried for long – marriage was a lucrative proposition for men in their quest for land.[86]

An interesting question is, what happened to the free blacks as farmers? Success in farming, particularly the wine farming of the eighteenth century, hinged on many factors. But did their colour or status play a part in their demise?

One free black who was a successful wine farmer was Willem Stolts, a former slave. At the time of his death in 1750, Stolts was a prosperous slave-owning farmer who owned two farms, Wolwedans and Hoornbosch, and produced ten leaguers of wine from 10 000 vines. His farm Hoornbosch was overseen by a white *knecht*. Stolts started off with very little: he was the slave of the former *heemraad* Jan Botma and his wife Stijntje Christoffel de Bruijn, who owned the farm Welgevallen on the edge of Stellenbosch village.[87] When De Bruijn died in 1724, her will stated that Willem and his fellow slaves should be freed and be given a wagon, eight trekoxen and two fishing nets with which to earn their living. It is not clear how he broke into land-ownership, writes Dooling: "Colour was clearly not an absolute barrier to success in the first half of the 18th century. He raised capital by raising mortgage loans from senior VOC servants; the first was from Hendrik Swellengrebel, and the second from Willem van Kerkhof."[88] Initially Stolts must have done much of the farm work himself, as he owned only one male slave in 1731. In 1735 he owned five slaves (four men) and had 11 slaves at his death. After his death his estate was auctioned, and the proceeds went to his wife and children.

Another successful black farmer was Jacob van As, son of a freed slave, Mooi Ansela (from Bengal), who farmed in the Dwars River area. Mooi Ansela was freed in 1666 and Van As was possibly the son of Johannes van As from Friesland.[89] In 1669 Mooi Ansela married ex-VOC soldier Arnoldus Basson who had two freeholds, one in his name and one in that of his stepson, Jacob van As. Van As became a wealthy burgher and the owner of Nieuwendorp, as well as loan farms to the north. His wealth was based on livestock, wine and wheat, and he owned 11 slaves. Jacob went on to marry Maria Clements, a Swedish immigrant. Jacob accumulated all the farms nearby – those of his parents and halfbrothers – and consolidated them into Nieuwendorp.

As an example in dynasty building, it is interesting to compare Van As to Abraham de Villiers, a French Huguenot who sought refuge at the Cape. De Villiers was one of three brothers from a wine farm in Burgundy, who settled in Oliphantshoek (now known as Franschhoek), one of the few French refugees who had any knowledge of winemaking. The myth of the Huguenot influence on winemaking is one that prevails today, but it is a myth. "The majority of French Huguenots had no knowledge of winemaking or viticulture," notes historian Tracey Randle who does research on the area. "They were tailors and bakers, and they were allocated land on condition that they had to develop it. So of course they said yes. They practised mixed farming because they had to survive, there was no town nearby and they had to be self-sufficient." Hard workers they were – but not good winemakers. "In fact, I've found complaints about how poor wine was," she says.

When the De Villiers brothers arrived, they took three adjacent farms: Champagne, Bourgogne and La Bri. Abraham moved to the Dwars Valley and bought up many farms here – Meerust, Boschendal and Lekkerwijn. He became the largest landowner in the valley, with 500 acres. In the De Villiers family, properties were kept within the family and helped to sustain an emerging family dynasty which continued to dominate farms in the valley and beyond. In 1724 De Villiers bought Nieuwendorp from Van As, doubling the family landownings. He now owned nearly half the Dwars Valley.

The shifting of property between family members was common in the eighteenth and nineteenth centuries. Attempts to keep property in the family through the female line (as said before, widows inherited half the property and the other half went to children) is suggested to be the reason why an elite was able to emerge and maintain their positions. While both Van As and De Villiers had large extended families, one chose to remain in the valley, the other to move away. The Van As family dispersed as new opportunities arose. There is nothing in the research to suggest that the Van As family was treated any differently from the De Villiers family in the society of the time.[90]

Other free blacks formed part of the growing grape-community of the Winelands, often acquiring land through marriage. There are plenty of examples of this. One such was Christoffel Snyman, the son of Groote Catrijn, or Catharina of Palicatte, who was banished to the Cape for murdering her lover. Company soldier Hans Snijman was his father. Christoffel's mother died when he was 13; his godmother was Mooi Ansela who, as mentioned above, was married to Arnoldus Basson. Christoffel was the second owner of Zandvliet (now Solms-Delta) and married Marguerite Thérèse de Savoye, the daughter of a French Huguenot, Jacques. Hans Silverbach, the first owner of Zandvliet, was also married to a woman of slave descent, Ansela van de Caab (not the same one as the Ansela who married Lourens Campher).

Other Huguenot settlers, the Cordiers, had two of their sons marry sisters who were freed slaves. Amongst the French Huguenots was Jacob Etienne Gauch, the son of French parents, but born in Switzerland in 1684. He came to the Cape in 1691 and settled in Franschhoek under the name Steven Gous. In 1718 he married a 13-year-old freed slave girl, Catharina Bok. They had seven children. When the widow Catharina died in 1767, she was able to bequeath her youngest son the farms Berg en Dal and Klipheuwel, plus 12 000 guilders in cash.

However, free blacks in the area did not all turn to farming. Many learnt a trade, while some were employed by farmers and worked for a wage as *knechten* (overseers). One of the early free blacks at the Cape was Evert van Guinee, one of Van Riebeeck's slaves, who may have worked on one of his farms in the orchards and vineyards, at Uitwijk or Bosheuvel. The farm Lanzerac in Jonkershoek just outside Stellenbosch, originally known as Schoongezicht, was granted partly to free blacks Manuel of Angola, Antonie of Angola and Louis of Bengal in 1692. They also owned slaves. The nearby Oude Nektar (originally Jan Lui) was owned by the freed slaves Manquard and Jan of Ceylon in 1692. Jan of Ceylon also owned other properties in Jonkershoek.

But most free blacks did not do that well as farmers. Whether this was just because farming was difficult, or because of their mixed heritage, we do not know. Historian Richard Elphick writes:

> Colonists and officials could very easily stop the free blacks from rising beyond a certain point by not extending credit, by not granting licensing privileges ... however no evidence for such discrimination has yet been found. Whatever the reasons, the retreat of free blacks to Cape Town ... was of crucial importance in the shaping of the entire colony. For the free blacks were left behind in a society which came to be dominated by agriculture and intercontinental commerce, where Europeans normally ruled over a black labouring force and where European settlers soon owned virtually all the land and possessed most of the great fortunes.[91]

According to historian and novelist Karel Schoeman, while there was little overt prejudice at first in the farmlands, with the increase in the number of free blacks after 1700 the tendency arose to see the "black"(colour) in free blacks rather than the "free". He refers in particular to the free burghers' official account of the agitation against Willem Adriaan van der Stel. "While it never becomes a significant issue, a marked awareness of colour runs through the account."[92]

Patric Tariq Mellét, an amateur historian, believes that under the leadership of Dutch farmer Adam Tas in the agitation, a clear fissure based on class and colour developed. "A petition was drafted by Tas and signed by 14 other white farmers (not all farmers were willing to sign) demanding codes that entrenched distinctions and privileges between white farmers and any person of colour; Free Black, slaves, indigenous Khoi, and even people of colour who were intermarried with settlers. The petition, by today's standards, was a 'hate-speech' diatribe of fear mixed with loathing of the Khoi, regarded to have murderous intent," writes Mellét. "Of likewise character, the petition identifies 'slaves, caffers, mulattos, mestizos and all that black brood amongst us, and related to European and Christians by marriage'. The document lashes out that these are allowed to advance in Cape society and warns that the blood of Ham is not to be trusted."

Within this atmosphere, speculates Mellét, free blacks clung to the safety of Table Bay and turned their hands to more subsistence endeavours. Others made their way to the Gariep/Orange River area on the wild western frontier and beyond, assimilating into the Oorlams Afrikaners under the leadership of Jager Afrikaner, and the Basters who later became the Griquas under Adam Kok.[93]

Another factor which might have contributed to the fall in fortunes of free blacks around the mid-1730s, suggests Mellét, was the legal convention that after death they were regarded as minors, and the family of their former owners, or free burghers who petitioned a sound claim, could inherit their property or goods. "In the case of the farms owned by Free Blacks Manuel of Angola, Antonie of Angola and Louis of Bengal, they were all incorporated into the neighbouring farm Schoongezicht, owned by Isaq Schrijver. (These farms are all part of Lanzerac today). Leef-op-Hoop, owned by Louis of Bengal, was merged on his death, and added to the farm of Antonie of Angola, whose property on his death went to Schrijver. This farm is Klein Gustrouw today."

Another reason for their demise was that the descendants of many freed slaves who had married Europeans were assimilated into the white population. "The most famous of these was the very wealthy Swarte Maria Evertsz. Her grandson was Johannes Colijn, a wine farmer in Constantia," says Mellét. (This is the same Johannes Colijn mentioned in connection with Constantia in Chapter 2.)

Although the Khoikhoi fiercely resisted when farmers settled beyond Table Bay, they were steadily pushed off their traditional grazing grounds. Many moved east or northwards. The new farmers found farming in Stellenbosch, and then Drakenstein, tough going. Farms were small and farmers often owed the Company money. Labour was scarce, and slaves were expensive. The social milieu of this time was fluid, and women were much in demand for marriage. There were many "mixed" marriages, with freed slaves marrying farmers. Free blacks also took up farming, but few were successful. A small number of successful farmers ended up with extensive landholdings in an area which slowly established itself as the heart of the winelands.

CHAPTER 4

On a mission - the people of Pniel

Pniel, meaning "the Face of God", lies in the Dwars River Valley, below the Drakenstein mountains. The earliest road built to get there was over the Helshoogte Pass which runs from Stellenbosch to Franschhoek, a steep, winding pass which probably had its origins in a Khoikhoi cattle path.

The town of Pniel started as a mission station a few years after the emancipation of slaves in 1838, with humble dwellings and a strict behaviour code. It was the first home for many of the former slaves who had worked on the farms in the area, the first opportunity for a family life, and the possibility of an education.

Pniel's history is a window into what happened to one group of former slaves who left the farms and took up their freedom to start a new life.

The community has come a long way from slavery until the present, and today you will find doctors, lawyers and professionals living in the town, as well as successful businessmen, among them giants in the fruit transport business. Old Pniel families such as the Myburghs, the De Wets and the Williams family can trace their roots back to the very early days of Pniel, when their forefathers and -mothers would grow and sell their own produce, as well as excess produce from the farmers. Starting as *smouse* (hawkers), selling small quantities, they slowly built up their businesses, and could afford bigger and better transport. Today they operate 36-ton trucks, and their large transport companies make millions in turnover.

Although it is difficult to trace where Pniel's first residents came from, in all likelihood most of them would have been freed slaves, invited to join the mission station from surrounding farms.

Pniel was one of many mission stations to give emancipated slaves a place of refuge, a secure home and a place to belong in an uncertain time. It has been a stable community, with property staying within families for generations. Land was owned by the church, and there were strict rules around alienating property.

Mattie Cyster, a retired headmaster and lifelong resident, who has co-written a book on the town *(Pniël en Sy Mense* – Pniel and its People), believes that Pniel was for a long time the perfect model for a successful community, based as it was on church, sports and a strong social network.

Pniel is full of stories, we are told: some of them are to be believed, others not. Stories are fragments of truth which have made their way down through the generations, and now form part of the mythology of a community.

When two farmers made land available for Pniel to be established as a mission station by the Apostolic Union in 1843, was it an act of philanthropy arising from compassion for the needs of recently freed people? Or was it out of a need to maintain the labour on nearby farms that was so desperately needed now that slavery had been abolished? That is a matter for opinion and conjecture.

"We tell two stories," a Pniel resident says, "one of philanthropy – and one of social construction."

Pniel resident and amateur historian Quinton Fortuin believes the farmers' agenda was to keep their labour force close by, a sort of labour pool. Mattie Cyster believes it was probably a combination of philanthropy and social engineering, as these were God-fearing men. Another suggestion is that with the growth of Islam among freed people in Cape Town after emancipation, the Protestant churches stepped up their efforts to "save souls", one answer being to set up mission stations for freed people and others. Excavations in the area have uncovered an Islamic artefact – a star-and-crescent badge – at the Silvermine settlement above Pniel of 1745. Here about 50 people lived on the slopes of Simonsberg, in search of silver (which did not materialise). The artefact may indicate the presence of Muslims in the area, says historian Gavin Lucas, although in the eighteenth century the symbol had wider currency than just as an Islamic symbol, but it is nevertheless a "provocative artefact".[94] Anyone living on the mission station would have had to embrace Christianity.

There is a story in Pniel, mischievous perhaps, that the farmer De Villiers was making provision for some of his illegitimate children by establishing Pniel.

Whatever the reasons, after the slaves' apprenticeship period ended in 1838, many former slaves had moved off the farms and farmers were struggling to keep their labourers. Without homes or money, these people would have had to find a place to live. No doubt there were people already living in the area as farmers were complaining of vagrancy.

In *Pniel and Its First Missionary Superintendent*, author Christian Silberbauer quotes from an appeal for funds for the new mission in 1842, from a document belonging to Pniel's first pastor JF Stegmann: "The Parish churches are in most cases far distant from the Farms of a great part of the People . . . the coloured Population is left entirely without Instruction, a prey to Sin and Satan."[95]

Pniel was ostensibly founded, then, out of a need to give a religious home to people. Because of the distance to the parish church at Paarl "we have no provision for the Instruction of the Poor and the Heathen", the appeal continues.

The Apostolic Union of the time was open to all Protestants of any denomination and had close ties to the Scottish Presbyterian Church. It was based in Bree Street in Cape Town at St Stephen's Church, which had been founded for the benefit of "emancipated slaves and other coloured people".

A large part of Silberbauer's book is an account of a court judgment in 1911, written by Justice Hopley. Here, the objectives of the Pniel Mission Institute were set out as a "mission intended for the benefit of the coloured people of that neighbourhood, the object being to educate them in the Apostolic Faith, to give them an ordinary elementary education, and also to train them in agricultural pursuits with a view to making them useful labourers easily available for the owners of the neighbouring estates"[96]. For the judge there was clearly nothing unequivocal about the intention of the founders, but remember this was almost 60 years later, and only his reading of the matter. Pniel was at that time still governed by directors and ministers "all of pure European descent", in other words, white.

The farmers seeking funds, Pieter Isaac De Villiers and Paul Retief (brother of Voortrekker leader Piet Retief), donated the land by registered Deed of Gift for a school, parsonage and church, and transfer was eventually registered on 6 July 1843. In December 1843 the farm Papiere Molen was added to Pniel.

Before this, however, there were already a schoolhouse and a small church on the land. Pniel was administered by three local farmers (the above-mentioned Retief and De Villiers as well as JJ Haupt), two laymen in Cape Town, one minister of the Apostolic Union, and one of the Presbyterian Church.

Freedom? Or a new paternalism?

John Frederick Stegmann from the Apostolic Union was only 20 years old when he was placed in charge of the Pniel Mission, where he remained for the next 65 years. He was pastor, schoolmaster and administrator of the institution. Residents had to abide by the station's rules.

Stegmann was the new patriarch: paternalism on the farms was exchanged for another paternalism – that of the church. Indeed, the mission's aim was to inculcate "respectability" in this new working-class population.[97]

According to historian Pamela Scully, "(t)he mission was regarded as the setting in which to inculcate their ideals of the nuclear family among the former slaves. The family was seen as the key context for shaping the behaviour of former slaves, for 'civilising and humanising' them. At the head of any model family was the father."[98]

The conditions for living at Pniel included that there was to be no public house or canteen, no liquor licences . . . and no dancing parties. The church had definite ideas about morality, and the board could eject anyone "notoriously practising gross immorality".

The freed people were seen to be in need of moral instruction; prevailing ideas were that people not of European descent were at a "lower" level of development. The idea was to make "decent" people out of the freed slaves; the family was seen as the vehicle to do this, not only providing a curb on the supposed "hypersexuality" perceived to be a hallmark of former slave women (and men), but also encouraging the European idea of the separation of spheres – man working, woman staying at home, children at school. That is not quite how it worked out, however. Families were formed as former slaves married, consolidating relationships that had gone unrecognised before, and many women did stay at home and children did attend school. But women and children also engaged in casual or seasonal work on the farms, out of economic necessity. Men earned 9d, not enough to cover the stipend of one pound 16 they were required to pay at Pniel after 1856. Wages went up during harvest season.

Women and children therefore had to work, especially during the busy fruit-harvesting season. Women also did domestic work on farms, or casual work such as laundry. Many men, however, had to move to distant farms for work, especially wheat farms, which are counter-seasonal to grapes, sometimes for up to two months of the year. The "head" of the house's role was thus reduced to an economic one, and women soon took on the primary responsibility for maintaining the cultural values and ethics of the mission community.[99]

Pniel in 1849

Estimates are that nearly 6 000 of about 25 000 freed slaves found a place at mission stations. Already by 1839 Elim and Genadendal were reported to be full.[100] Governor George Napier, who saw the government's task as being to induce the "emancipated classes . . . to spread over the country and become the tenants of the farmers", said the problem with mission stations was that the labouring population could "by the cultivation of a small portion of land and the grazing of a few head of cattle satisfy their subsistence needs", making them unavailable for labour. That just would not do in colonial eyes.

Some historians have argued that not much changed for slaves economically after emancipation. Indeed, the freed slaves living in Pniel were recorded as working on farms nearby like Delta, Boschendal, Lekkerwijn, Meerust/Eenzaamheid and Bellingham.

The difference was, however, that they could now choose where to work and live. Many women left domestic work on farms, and farmers complained that their wives and daughters now had to do the work. Freed women continued to labour to help support families, but now it was on their own terms.

In 1849 a report was drawn up on the Pniel mission station by the resident magistrate based in Paarl, K van Breda, and Justice of the Peace JE de Villiers Louw.[101] The report was written with a particular agenda, it seems, which was to ensure farmers had sufficient labour. The British authorities were worried about making "honest workers" out of the former slaves; the freed people no doubt were not so keen to become servants to their former masters.

"The farmers complain loudly against the people of the Institution on account of their idleness and insolence . . . " the report noted, and the former slaves were not willing to work for them.[102] Mission stations were seen as offering freed people an alternative to farm work, and since it was the grape-pressing time, and labour was much needed, farmers had complained bitterly.

The 1849 report found that Pniel had 49 "adults", five who could read the Bible, and 15 found in the service of the De Villiers brothers; and 53 "women" on the station, four who could read the Bible and 15 at work with farmers. Of the children over 12 years old, 54 out of 66 were said to be working for farmers. That women were not considered adults says much of the status of women in post-emancipation times. Women were minors and men the head of the household, although this may not have matched the reality of their experience. It must have been quite an adjustment for them: as slaves, women were often in charge of running farm households, while men had less power as labourers.

The magistrate at Paarl doubted the accuracy of what he had been told the first time and returned to Pniel with the justice of the peace, visiting 31 farms in one and a half days, to check the situation for themselves. On this day they found 37 adults (men), six women and only six children, out of 66 above 12 years old.

The second report said of the Pniel residents that "very few rose from their seats when we entered" and on passing them where they were at work, "they seemed to consider whether they would salute us or not – the invariable practice in the colony being to salute in some one manner or other". This confirmed their insolence.

The report went on to say that people grew their own food – maize, pumpkins and beans "insufficient to support their numerous families a fortnight" – and that there were 20 houses. Stegmann told them that child labour was not encouraged – children were required to be at school until the age of 15, and before that no one had the right to engage them to any farmer before getting Stegmann's consent, which he granted only occasionally.

The report spoke of 308 people being employed by farmers at the time, 21 from Genadendal and Groenekloof (Mamre) and only 42 from Pniel. Farmers, it said, had "ample employment" for 111 more, which could easily be supplied by Pniel "if they felt inclined to help the farmers upon such an urgent time as this".

The report has a tone of condescension and peevishness, and criticised the Institution for making money, rather than being non-profit: " . . . it will appear . . . that if the influx to the Institution continues as it has taken place of late, the Institution will be totally out of debt within four years; and it is our thorough belief that if no provision is made with regards to such Institutions, the whole of the colored (sic) population at Drakenstein will flock to that Institution, and the farmers will be deprived of their services, and the profit which the Institution will derive hereafter will be incalculable, to not only the detriment but the total ruin of the adjacent farmers."[103]

Stegmann's measured response to the report paints a different picture: he described the report as "characterised by such a spirit of enmity to the missionary cause in general, so full of such illiberal views, and so opposed to the liberties of Her Majesty's subjects . . . "

In response to the report's statement that "it is not customary for the people to go and work with the farmers – they are idle, insolent, did not go to assist at the late pressing season, nor at the late harvest", he wrote that if the magistrate had visited all the farms around the station, he would have found more.

"The people on the station are not idle; as proof, the magistrate himself declares that when he passed, the people were at work, too busy to rise up and bow before his worship. Twenty-two were lawfully engaged in building their houses, their own property." Stegmann provided detailed lists of labourers showing with whom they were working, where, during what period of time and their wages.

In response to the statement that only nine of the 49 adults and 53 women could read, Stegmann said: "The magistrate does not know what the word adult means, and therefore states incorrectly. There are about 200 men and women having their home on the station – the majority, from age and circumstances, are beyond learning to read; however, upwards of 30 adults are able to read Bibles well."

And, he pointed out, if it was true that people were short of rations, "it would prove that people trusted to obtain food by labour; but if the magistrate had asked to see what provision had been made for winter, it would appear sufficient and to spare."

He was vehement about allegations of profit making: "Not true – missionary receives nothing from the people, and never has. The people pay to contribute to purchase money of institution; they aim at self-support, ie when the place shall have been cleared of debt, the congregation will support their minister."

The Pniel Mission offered people lodging, but not ownership of their houses. The greater part of the Pniel area was subdivided into 99 holdings. Each had a building site and a share in a garden site, separate from the house. Today, along the *tuinpaadjie* (garden path) there are still plots for gardening. There were 13 families at Pniel in 1843; by 1849 there were more than 200 men and women.

Tenure was regulated by Stegmann, and those he accepted into the community were known as erf-holders.

Eleanor Damon, a teacher born in Pniel and a co-author of *Pniel en Sy Mense*,[104] believes people were chosen to come to Pniel, they did not just arrive. "The pastor in charge, Stegmann, had to choose; for references, he went to farms, and invited the more 'reputable' people," she says. Each paid 3s rental a month until they had paid 18 pounds in total. After 1856, 1s 10d had to be paid "monthly and for all time" to support the minister. Houses could be transferred, with Stegmann's approval, and certain laws of succession were understood: the youngest son took over the house, and houses largely stayed within families.

The first residents most likely came from the surrounding farms after emancipation; some from further away. Others may have been free blacks living in the area, some of whom may have been people banished to the Cape for political reasons by the VOC. And there may have been some Khoikhoi living here.

One area of Pniel was known as Mozbiekvlei, where, it is said, Stegmann placed the black freed slaves. Was there segregation from early on, albeit subtle? "That doesn't hold true," believes Cyster. "There are stories that go around, be very careful, there are lots of stories in Pniel. Pniel is a rainbow nation. And in Pniel we are all related." Yet residents commonly refer to it by this name.

"Mozbiekvlei? It's a story told by locals, but I'm sceptical. Skin colour wasn't important for ex-slaves, it didn't matter," agrees Fortuin. "Perhaps in the 1950s colour became a divide, but only then."

But still, stories are told about this family and that family, who lived in Mozbiekvlei, who were very dark skinned. People refer to the "lighter-skinned" and the "darker-skinned" residents; in later years when the Group Areas Act was enforced, some lighter-complexioned people moved out, and were reclassified "white". With skin colour playing such a huge role in the apartheid years, it would be strange if Pniel had escaped the prejudices of the time.

What's in a name?

One of the freedoms that emancipation offered was the freedom to choose a name.

As mentioned before, slaves were most often known by only one name, and that often a name given to them. Sometimes this was followed by a toponym to indicate the country they came from, or where they were sold from, such as 'Van Bengale'. Those born at the Cape, as we have seen, were known as 'Van de Caab'. But by the time of emancipation many of these toponyms had fallen away. The magistrate's report of 1849 on Pniel referred to above, as well as the marriage registry at Pniel, which dates back to 1844, confirms that many of the first people to marry here did not have a second name. The first step to forming a new identity was to choose a name, and this is a rich source of stories in Pniel.

Pniel's marriage registry

The marriage registry of Pniel tells fragments of people's lives. At first no one's occupation is registered; the majority of people are listed as coming from Groot Drakenstein. Then in 1847 Clara Esau appears, from Paarl; in 1848 Orange Abrahamse from Banhoek (just up the pass) marries Sophia.

In 1850s there is movement from further afield – Gabriel Speulmann comes from Cape Town. Also in 1850 the first people listing Pniel as "home" get married – Samson Roman and Catharina Peterus, on July 15. Barend Van Beek is the first tailor mentioned, and he marries Jacoba Europa in 1847. They are the foreparents of the Mullers, who owned the garage in Pniel. The Van Beek family tailoring tradition is carried on – in 1851 Simson David Primo, a shoemaker from Stellenbosch, marries Wilhelmina Johanna van Beek, a clothesmaker from Pniel.

Trades were often carried from generation to generation.

Names sometimes indicate the different origins of the people living in Pniel: Mandilie Dambosie and Aharie Matloewalosie are two "Mozbiekers" listed. Pniel could have been home to some white working-class people, who were also members of the church; a photographer, Herman Gustav Adolph Brensing from Worcester, married Helena de Villiers from Groot Drakenstein here in 1896.

In 1897 Clara Blankenberg, a teacher from Pniel, married Apollos Willems, a seed planter. A carpenter from Cape Town, Henry Charles Meeder, married Sarah Cyster in 1909.

The marriage registry mentions occupations like worker, pruner, shoemaker, ironer, needleworker, tailor, painter and gardener.[105] Former slaves would have brought these skills with them. Later came the teachers; Tant Mina Davids was probably the first teacher, although not formally trained.

It is not easy for people to trace their ancestry too far back, however, because of the absence of surnames. Sometimes, after a generation, people's first names became surnames. For example, resident Abraham Lakey is mentioned in an 1848 report on Pniel, aged 26, as married to or living with Delia Arends, aged 45, and their 10 children. They settled in Pniel at the beginning of 1847. A male slave called Lakey was registered in 1816 under the ownership of Carl Albrecht Haupt, who owned nearby farms Languedoc and Rhone, and a portion of Goede Hoop. Abraham Lakey, if related, was probably his son.[106] Later Lakey changed to Lackay, a family who owned a plot on the western side of the mission, but also a house in the eastern part.

Some freed people did, however, arrive with a surname.

One story in Pniel tells how Stegmann changed the surnames of those freed people who called themselves De Villiers to Willemse (later anglicised to become Williams), to break the connection with their servitude. And also their paternity, said to perhaps have been that of one of the many De Villiers brothers, wealthy landowners in the Dwars River area.

Where is the truth in that?

It is well-known that many slaveowners did have children by their female slaves. One case in point is Philida,[107] whose story is also told at the fascinating Museum Van De Caab on the farm Solms-Delta near Pniel. Sexual relations between masters and slaves were not uncommon, especially between adolescent sons and their father's domestic slaves, and often resulted in pregnancy. Philida claimed all four of her children had been fathered by her owner's son, Frans Brink. We know about Philida from the court records, because she complained to the protector of slaves that she was being sold to break her connection with Frans, whom she said had seduced her with the promise of buying her freedom. She was rebuked for her "wantonness" and, along with two of her children, sold to a farmer in the Tulbagh district. Her complaint was made just after the birth of her fourth child – and shortly before Frans got married to the daughter of a wealthy military auditor, Maria Magdalena Berrange.

How much choice slaves had in these sexual relations is impossible to know; perhaps to speak of choice at all is ill-advised: slaves were property, and slave women had no power to resist sexual advances. It would have been difficult, if not impossible, to refuse the advances of an owner or his son. Even "consent" would have been coupled with promises of freedom or other rewards. Historian Pamela Scully talks about slave women suffering sexual abuse and rape from owners, part of their rights as masters, and says masters had an incentive to sire children who would add to their workforce (a child born of a slave was also a slave).[108]

The strange situation then arose that children of slaveholders on farms would grow up with their half-brothers and -sisters, worlds apart in terms of status. A half-sibling could even grow up to "own" his or her brother or sister. Johan Christian Roode was a case in point: a slaveowner, he admitted to the assistant protector of slaves at Worcester that he had two children, Adriaan and Hendrik, with his slave Clara. Clara had hoped that having Johan admit paternity would secure their freedom, which it did not. Although Roode said he wanted them to be "made happy", his mother-in-law's will meant the two children remained slaves and they became the property of their half-sibling, also Johan.[109] Evidence suggests that slaveholding society condoned but did not encourage sexual relations between masters and their slaves.[110] Where they were discussed, they were seen as the result of the "promiscuity" of slave women, not the domination of slaveholders.[111]

Often slave women would name their children after their owners, who may or may not have fathered their children. They would either give them their surnames, or use a patronym such as Davidsz or Davids. The "sz" in Dutch meant "son of", so for example Jacob de Villiers Abrahamsz meant Jacob de Villiers, son of Abraham. In slave registers only maternity was recognised. With paternity denied, or not being registered, most slaves had no claim on their slaveowner fathers. Perhaps slave women were asserting their children's paternity, and their very limited power, by naming them in this way? However, these names did not always indicate biological paternity, but rather perhaps a social connection, writes Scully.

Even when it came to naming children, a slave did not have rights. In 1831 the slave Goliah complained that his master Van Zyl had named his child Aaron, contrary to the wishes of himself and his mother, who wanted him named Goliah. At issue was the right to name, which signified who had control of his child. Goliah thought it important enough to take it up with the slave protector, who suggested that Van Zyl negotiate with Goliah.[112]

Many surnames, then, at the Pniel mission station in the early days are the first names of many of the De Villiers clan, one of the largest landowning families in the district at the time, names such as David(s) and Hendrick(s), perhaps coincidentally, perhaps not. Quinton Fortuin was curious about this story of Stegmann changing the De Villiers name to Willemse. "Eighty per-cent of people in Pniel are related to the Williams family," he says. His mother Dorothy was a Williams, his father was Edward George Fortuin. "I'd heard the story from different people that Stegmann changed it to break ties with an unpleasant past. But I decided to find out more, and this story didn't fit." What Fortuin found was that there were indeed connections between the De Villiers and Williams family; folklore was right, but it was not Stegmann who had changed the names.

Fortuin did some genealogical research, based on a story an old teacher of his told, of Sofie Beyers, a white woman in nearby Simondium, somehow related to the Williams family, who came to visit her cousin in Pniel and sold chickens. There was also a white man, a Dr De Villiers in Paarl, who owned a farm in Simondium and who referred to the Williamses as "family". Sofie, it turns out, was related to Alida de Villiers, whose half-brother was Adriaan Willemse, said to be the illegitimate son of Dawid de Villiers of Lekkerwijn farm (near Pniel). Fortuin's conclusion is that Adriaan Willemse was Sofie's uncle, and that family ties were maintained despite his illegitimacy. Who Adriaan's mother was, is not known. Fortuin has a picture of Adriaan Willemse, a bewhiskered man with light-coloured eyes. It is difficult to determine the hue of his skin, and its only relevance is that skin colour became all-important in later years when the Population Registration Act of 1950 came into being. Many families were torn apart when one sibling was registered as "white" and another as "coloured" under the absurd categories of the apartheid law. However, being lighter skinned, wrongly or rightly, was seen as desirable in Pniel and many other such communities where different groups came together, mingling and marrying and creating the uniquely named (in South Africa) "coloured" people.

Eleanor Damon

Eleanor Damon was born a Cyster, one of the first families in Pniel, which grew to be a prominent and influential one. Her father Gerald is one of the descendants of the slave Karel Cyster, who, according to oral history, she guesses was born in Madagascar, and Sara Willems, said to be a *Duusvrou*, a Dutch woman, from Drakenstein.

Eleanor Damon

Eleanor has done extensive research into her genealogy, and is doing research for a doctorate on the Cyster family. Her interest started with her auntie's stories; aunts seem to be the repository of the family records. One aunt in particular, Aunt Madge, who never married, "adopted" her brother Gerald's children as her own.

"I would go down there all the time. To visit the Cyster house was to have tea, and over tea, stories were told. I loved the stories she told, but I became confused, so I began to write them down and then construct a family tree." This was in Pniel in the 1960s, a small Boland community near the heart of Afrikaner Nationalism, Stellenbosch. The

Population Registration Act, the Mixed Marriages Act, the Group Areas Act were all impacting on communities. "My Aunt Madge would whisper in my ear about the Kannemeyers and the Cysters." The Kannemeyers were her paternal grandmother's people; they came from the mission town of Suurbraak near Swellendam, and Eleanor is sure, from their appearance and location, that they were descendants of the local people of the area, the Khoikhoi.

"The Pniel people often have an Aisan look, sharp noses and black hair. The Kannemeyers had curly hair and different features."

On the Cyster side, her great-grandfather was Oupa Jan (youngest son of the original Cyster in Pniel, Karel) who married Ouma Dinah, from Cilliers Siding. Cilliers Siding was near the farm Babylonstoren, next to the station. Eleanor has a picture of them, and Dinah has a strong broad face and curly hair.

Many years later, qualified as a teacher and living and working in Atlantis, while studying further for her BA degree in Afrikaans and history, history came alive, says Eleanor. "It's grown on me, and I've been doing research for more than ten years." Her genealogical research, which started as a hobby, developed into an idea for a doctoral thesis.

When the Cyster and Williams family trees were displayed in Pniel recently, the family connections were a revelation to many, and some of the gaps were filled in. "It was amazing, people were shouting, 'Oh my God, I didn't know'."

It confirmed what is said in the village: "In Pniel, we are all related".

Eleanor's mother was Martha Maria Jacoba Smith, from Calvinia in the Northern Cape. "We'd travel to Namaqualand by train, the *ambakhaya*, to visit them – until my dad got a bakkie." She never met her Calvinia grandmother, a Cloete: she and her sister had died while trekking from Leliefontein to the Richtersveld, of cholera.

Eleanor then, has ancestry from many groups: the Smiths, from the 1820 British Settlers; the Cloetes from the Northern Cape; the Cysters from the Boland, and the Kannemeyers from Suurbraak.

In genealogy there is always a bit of guesswork; records are not always accurate, and sometimes they are missing. Where, for instance, is Karel Cyster, the slave, in the 1849 report on Pniel that was mentioned earlier? "I've taken a guess that he was born in 1814," says Eleanor. "But neither his name, nor Sarah's (his wife), is on the list of residents compiled by Pastor Stegmann for the report." There is a Cyster Cysters (written thus), 14, and a Hendrik Cyster, 12, listed as working for farmers. There is a Cyster Bahouss, but Eleanor does not believe that it is him. Perhaps Karel was too old to work. More research needs to be done.

The couple may have come to the mission station as a de facto married couple, as did many others. Shortly after Pniel was founded, there was a "mass" marriage on 26 February 1844, legitimizing existing unions.[113]

Karel Cyster, brother of Klein Jan, in 1885 married Roza Jason, said to have been a Scottish woman. The descendants of "Die Wilde Cysters" (the wild Cysters), as they were known, were later reclassified "white". They bought land from a local farmer Hoeft, and today the area is still known as the "Cystergronde" (Cyster land). Being classified white had many privileges and advantages. This did, however, isolate them from the community – and the rest of their family, says Eleanor. "They even had their own graveyard, I stumbled on it when I was very small." Today it sits overgrown and strangely placed between two houses in a newly developed part of Pniel.

Growing up in a small community required you to conform. "Growing up in Pniel, you had to belong," says Eleanor. "You belonged to Sunday school, to the various groups. It was protective." And along with that came the idea that it was better to marry within Pniel. "You knew the people, their habits, and there were no strange things lurking

Oupa Jan and Ouma Dinah Cyster

in the family, like a murderer. Why break the network?" This idea also tied into inheritance, and keeping property ownership within the original families, as the youngest son inherited the house.[114]

In *Pniël en Sy Mense* residents talk about "*ondertrouery*" (intermarriage) being common from early times, an unwritten rule being that you marry "*jou eie gemors*" (your own rubbish) rather than a stranger. Intermarriage between cousins was not unusual in this small community. It happened, albeit mistakenly, as outsiders were regarded with suspicion, and it took a while to belong.

"Born in Pniel, I thought it was the world. Interlocked by mountains, my vision was blocked. We had only one church. Then I went to high school in Stellenbosch – Luckhoff in Ida's Valley, and I learned – you can travel. And then further afield, to Bellville to study teaching." She worked in Atlantis, the "truly very lost city", but returned, teaching at Luckhoff, Pniel, Macassar, Kylemore and Upington. She has taught in England, and worked in Franschhoek on the Berg River Dam project. Today Eleanor's wandering spirit has taken her far from the small town of Pniel, and she teaches in China.

"Troublemakers"

Pastor Stegmann was by all accounts well respected, and any dissatisfaction with the running of the mission seems to have been kept under wraps.

Until 1905, that is, a few years before his death in 1910.

When his health began to fail, the directors of Pniel took a more active role in its management. In Justice Hopley's 1911 report, he noted that "folk for whose benefit the mission had been started were beginning to be somewhat unruly and troublesome" and " . . . some of the flock which he (Stegmann) had tended so carefully became recalcitrant" and questioned the authority of the directors.[115]

The erf-holders held a meeting with the directors, where they contended they were the owners of the estates they had "paid" for, and elected themselves as directors. They were told they were only tenants, and the meeting "broke up in discord and discontent". The discontent seems to have been put on hold until Stegmann passed away, and two erf-holders, Garnaat Cyster and Stefanus de Wet, on behalf of the community, challenged the authority of the directors to manage Pniel. They approached the Supreme Court in 1911 and asked that it declare them legal directors and trustees of all Pniel's property. The directors opposed this.

Eleanor Damon's great-grandfather was a cousin of Stefanus de Wet and brother of Garnaat Cyster. "They took on the *predikant* (minister) and began a split in the community which remained for a long time, with arguments and no-go zones and no relationships across the divide. They lost the case, but they stood up for themselves."

As the authors of *Pniël en Sy Mense* say: "This was a worthy and brave step, as descendants of a group of former slaves dared to challenge the authority of the day."[116]

Justice Hopley's findings in the case illustrate the patronising attitude to what was a strong challenge to authority: "I am convinced that it would be extremely unwise to accede to the wishes of the plaintiffs," he wrote.[117] "The men . . . are no doubt worthy men in their own station in life, and are possibly well able to manage some of the affairs of such a community." These included water supply, building repairs and management. Justice Hopley, however, felt "certain it would not be safe to leave to them the entire direction of the spiritual ministrations or the educational requirements of the place. Though some of them are fairly educated, they have not yet reached a high standard of public life. Paltry ideas, petty jealousies and strife would be sure to arise."

Justice Hopley did not dismiss their desire to have a voice in their own affairs, but said the inclusion of erf-holders in the management would have little chance of success. "The attitude which they have adopted towards the (directors) . . . makes it impossible for me to think that anything but strife, possibly ending in deadlock, would ensue."

The defendants (directors) were "unanimous in condemning any attempt at a mixed board . . . This does not arise . . . from any rooted and insuperable dislike to co-operate with the inhabitants on the ground of their race or colour; but because of their antagonistic attitude and somewhat bumptious assertion of their position . . . "

The order of the court was that a body of eight trustees would run the Institution Pniel, "all such Trustees being men of European race or descent, and of the Protestant faith." The first four would be the defendants in the court case; three of the other four would be elected by erf-holders, and one by members of the congregation of the church.

Gavin Lucas writes: "The judicial hearing is interesting because it reaffirms that paternalism was still very much alive as an ideology among the white population. The liberal tradition which swept Britain and the colonies in the 1820s and 1830s was already on the wane by the 1840s, giving way to harsher imperial ideology and the strident racism of the late 19th century. Paternalism in the form of infantilisation of the ex-slave community was still employed as rhetoric for keeping people in their place."[118]

Around the time of the court case, farming was undergoing rapid changes.

Cecil John Rhodes, who had left politics for farming, had bought many of the grape farms in the area, which had been devastated by phylloxera, and converted them to fruit farms. In 1898 he commissioned the renowned architect Sir Herbert Baker (who also designed the Union Buildings) to design the agri-village Languedoc for workers to live in.

In 1915 Pniel fell under the Department of Native Affairs. In 1916 the law governing mission stations changed, and a council of local people was appointed. The chairman was supposed to be the local magistrate, but according to minutes, that did not often happen as he did not come to meetings.

The first meeting of the Pniel Village Management Board was held on 27 October 1916: "This was an historic event, with slave children managing their own town."[119]

Under the Mission Stations Act of 1909, the community had to decide "to which church or denomination, to which spiritual care Pniel Mission Station shall be confided". This caused a deep divide in the community, with families fighting each other, and even a brother stabbing a brother. In the end the majority vote was to move to the Congregational Union. During the vote 36 people walked out of the meeting. In 1917 Pniel's church became part of the Congregational Union of South Africa.

The church was in all practical senses in control of the town and community until the 1930s. When this began to change, the council at times took decisions the church was not satisfied with. Council members most often were also members of the church, and so church and governance were closely related. But slowly the council exerted its autonomy, and came into conflict with the church. Talk was of "church" and "anti-church" and these deep divisions affected all aspects of life in Pniel: children were taken out of school and moved elsewhere, babies were taken to the church in Languedoc to be baptised; even sporting events were affected.

It's been many years since Pniel outgrew itself and had to find place for its children; in 1898 four families purchased a section of Rust en Vrede, a farm forming part of Zorgvliet, from Arthur Harrington Kyle for land for their families. It was called Kylemore. Johannesdal was bought by Carel Cyster. Meanwhile an Apostolic Church was built in Kylemore.

Kylemore, while being governed by the Mamre Misison, was in effect closely linked to Pniel; their complaints were accepted at Pniel and heard by

Pniel management boards (which also fell under the Mamre Mission's administration). Kylemore was subdivided in the 1980s and in that process existing boundaries were taken as real boundaries – somewhere in the process land was "lost", claim some residents.

By 1943, administration had passed to the community, who elected members of its own to manage its affairs; from 1944 Pniel came under the Department of Social Welfare, under which all "coloured matters" and mission stations fell.

In 1968, Pniel was declared a "Rural Coloured Area" in terms of the Group Areas Act. At much the same time, Johannesdal and Kylemore were similarly declared in terms of this Act.

During apartheid, after the Mixed Marriages Act of 1949, many people left the country – "mixed" marriages meant some couples had to leave if they were to stay together. Others left for economic reasons, or a better chance for their children.

It was only in December 1995 that the first Pniel erf-holders were given title deeds to their land. This marked the end of an era and many were concerned that it would also mark the end of the tight-knit community. It did, however, free people up to improve their properties and get bonds for new ones.

In 2000 Pniel became part of the greater Stellenbosch municipality.

Today the church still dominates the small village, imposing in its size and whiteness on the slope. The church, as a building and an institution, has played a central role in the life of Pniel, the centre of many activities.

The village maintains a distinct identity, but development pressure is changing the face of the town. A new road is being built to replace the winding, single-lane road that weaves through it. Against the slopes of Simonsberg behind Pniel, mansions are being built; when some residents finally got title deeds to their homes, they were free to sell to the highest bidder.

The Sir Herbert Baker designed-Languedoc agri-village, originally housing workers from the Rhodes Fruit Farms group, has been expanded to accommodate workers from surrounding farms. The Good Hope farm is being developed into the Founders Estate, a luxury housing complex with 18 smallholdings selling at a premium. The next phase is a retirement village, residential homes and a hotel at the Boschendal Estate.

The social fabric of Pniel is changing rapidly with the new influx of people.

Farming is the first love of Pnielers, according to the authors of *Pniel en Sy Mense*. Many came from and worked on nearby fruit farms, and they knew agriculture well. Today Pnielers are known far beyond the borders of Pniel as fruit handlers and entrepreneurs. And for their rugby teams, as sport plays a central role in community life.

Mattie Cyster is very proud of Pniel and its history.

"I was born and grew up here – my dad was a *smous*, a fruit merchant, who bought from farmers and sold to the market. This is an entrepreneurial community – at both ends of the business, both grower and the merchant.

"I used to go pick fruit and pack it, and couldn't understand this relationship between farmer and *smous*. There was a good understanding between my father and the farmer, we'd go to certain farmers regularly. But we'd have to address them as *baas* (boss) and *jongbaas* (young boss). I was in my 20s, and I couldn't stand it."

Cyster was the second person from Pniel to go to university – the University of the Western Cape (UWC) – where he obtained a BSc degree and a postgraduate education diploma. "I was bought up in apolitical surroundings. Nothing touched us here. At UWC we heard about Mandela, we took part in rallies and boycotts during the 60s. That was so different from in Pniel, where we were taught to shut up and listen." Cyster went on to become a school principal, first the vice-principal at Luckhoff (in Ida's Valley in Stellenbosch), then at the local primary school.

In 1993 Cyster organised the erection of the Freedom Monument of Pniel to commemorate slavery. Then, in 2007, he was involved in organising the Ubuntu Monument, which honours slave heritage. Part of it is a rock from Robben Island, and he tells the story of waiting in anticipation for the rock to be delivered. When it arrived it was much smaller than expected, he laughs.

"Until fairly recently, talking about slave ancestry was taboo," says Cyster. "The old people didn't want to remember, they were ashamed of their slave ancestors."

But that too is changing, and as people become curious about their roots, they are reclaiming their slave ancestry.

Islam and farm workers

Before the emancipation of the slaves, a small Muslim community lived at Mosterd Bay, now known as Strand, a town next to the sea on the northeastern shore of False Bay. After emancipation its numbers swelled as freed people sought refuge at the sea, from where they could make a living, and in a religion which offered them an alternative to that of their former owners.

Kalamodien, a free black, belonged to this community. His wife

Kandaza and his sons Leander and Jacobus, however, were the registered slaves of a Willem Morkel, of the farm Voorbrug in Somerset West, which adjoins Strand.

These were the forebears of Ebrahim Rhoda, who today lives in Firgrove, not far from Strand. Slaves were not allowed to marry legally before the early 1800s and Christian churches would not perform these ceremonies. "The imams would marry slaves, which presented an alternative to them," he says.

Finding his slave ancestry was a high point for Rhoda. A former principal of Strand Moslem Primary School, he was one of seven participants who attempted to trace their slave roots in the Cape Slavery Community Research Project.

Rhoda grew up in Strand; he went on to do an MA in history (without prior degrees) at UWC at the age of 68, in 2006, and was awarded a distinction. Rhoda says he has long been interested in history, and had asked his aunt Gadija Wentzel, née Rhoda, to tell him about his grandparents. When he began his research, then, he had some names to go by. Wentzel told him about the two slave brothers, Leander and Jacobus.

"I started with death registers, using the brothers' Muslim names, and looked at slave registers on farms in Hottentots Holland from 1816, when it was compulsory to keep a register of slaves. I hoped to find a record of when the brothers died, and their ages, so that I could work out approximate dates of birth."

After emancipation, Kalamodien probably brought his family to Mosterd Bay, although Rhoda does not know when. His sons became fishermen and embraced Islam. Their names were changed – Kandaza became Jaria, Leander became Faggedien and Jacobus Samodien.

Rhoda found that Faggedien Rode was born in 1819 and died in 1912; Samodien was born in 1824 and died in 1911. Samodien's death notice revealed that his parents were Kalamodien and Jaria Rode. Kandaza, he discovered, was first registered on 5 December 1816, aged 25 years old, born at the Cape. She was probably born in 1791, says Rhoda. "Kandaza probably worked as a domestic, and would have slept inside the house."

Voorbrug was one of many farms owned by Morkel. The Lourens River passes though it, as does the road leading to Sir Lowry's Pass. Rhoda also found that Kandaza, her sons and 17 fellow slaves were offered as collateral for a loan of 16 000 rix-dollars . . . she was appraised as being worth about 90 rix-dollars, as was Leander, and Jacobus 75 rix-dollars.

"Samodien Rode was my great grandfather. The Muslim Rhoda family (he has also traced Christan Rhodas to the farms Vergelegen and De Bos) was most probably united at Mosterd Bay before 1849 because Faggadien's eldest daughter Momena was born at Mosterd Bay in 1849."

Ebrahim Rhoda was born in 1938, a mere 200 metres away from the site of his great-grandfather Samodien's thatch house. Rhoda says his ambition since childhood was to become a teacher at the community school, which he fulfilled in 1959. His grandfather Lulu Rhoda had a barbershop in Market Square.

"I used to earn pocket money by helping clean fish, and I paid for my schoolbooks. I learnt to swim at the jetty, now in disuse. During apartheid it was reserved for whites only."

The Mosterd Bay (Strand) community started when Abdus Sammat from Semerang and five compatriots settled there in 1822. Before that Sammat, a free black living in Cape Town, had moved to Stellenbosch and then Hottentots Holland in 1820, where he worked as a *knecht* on a farm in the Somerset West area. By 1825 the Mosterd Bay community had grown to 19 free-black males, seven Khoikhoi women and a young girl of 11, living on Crown Land near the beach.[120] Between 1822 and 1840, 28 free blacks, mostly from Java, came to settle with Sammat. He died in 1838, the year the slaves were freed.

By 1842 there had been a big influx of people into the area: people set free needed to sustain life so they came to the sea, says Rhoda. By 1851 there were 160 families, mostly Malay; by 1879 there were 800 people, and 75% were Muslims.

Although there was little freedom of religion before the British arrived at the Cape – a *plakkaat* (statute) of 1642 had forbidden the practice of any religion other than Dutch Reformed in Dutch colonies at the risk of forfeiture of property or death – there had long been a Muslim presence. Some 200 Muslim political exiles spent time at the Cape between 1652 and the end of Company rule. As mentioned earlier, Santrij, a slave who led an escape of 23 slaves from Constantia, was an imam (he was put to death for his role in the revolt).[121]

Slaves on farms had little access to religion – in 1770 a *plakkaat* (statute) was issued that Christian slaves could not be sold, discouraging farmers from baptising them. A direct consequence was growing opposition of slaveowners to Christian mission work among slaves.[122]

Within a few years the benches reserved for slaves in the Groote Kerk in Cape Town were no longer needed.[123]

Some slaves brought to the Cape would have brought their religion with them, and many of them were Muslim. Some slaveowners encouraged their slaves to become Muslims, not least because of Islam's prohibition on the drinking of alcohol and other social vices, which made slaves more reliable workers and better servants[124]; many owners of wine estates, it is said, preferred the sobriety of Muslim overseers and wagon drivers, who did not drink wine.

The phenomenal growth of Islam which took place during the first half of the nineteenth century, mostly in the urban areas, caused alarm to Dutch Reformed missionaries, as more slaves had converted to Islam than to Christianity in the early nineteenth century. At the beginning of the nineteenth century, Stellenbosch slaveowners had about 10 000 slaves, and they became the focus of Christian missionary efforts.

The growing Muslim community was not welcomed by the Christian church. In the mid-1870s Methodist Reverend JH Tindall, reflecting the prejudices and misconceptions of his time, reported: "Nearly every Church has had to grapple with this foe, but has had to confess itself beaten. Mohammedanism has a great attraction for the carnal mind. Its merry holiday keeping, its noisy festivals, its vaunted sobriety, and its loose morality, give it a stronghold on the passions of people."[125]

In 1864 the authorities reported that Muslims were not coming to school – a madressa had been opened in Strand; and in the 1870s a mosque was built.

While many rural slaves were drawn to Christian mission stations after emancipation, others joined the Muslim faith, forming communities such as that at Mosterd Bay.

The story of Pniel is just one example of what happened to freed people after Emancipation. There are many other mission stations – Mamre, Genadendal, Wupperthal, to name a few – where former slaves could seek a new life. Each has its unique story, but all were communities where religion played a strong role. These communities fostered strong family ties, emphasised education and provided an alternative to living under a farmer's control.

CHAPTER 5

"To market, to market" – making wine, selling wine

While wine and grapes are major contributors to the agricultural economy of the Western Cape, making wine has never been easy money for farmers. Wine prices have fluctuated wildly through the 350 years of production, affected by preferential tariffs, wars, drought, boycotts, grape diseases, such as phylloxera, and regulation – or the lack of it.

As farmers say, it's easy to make wine from money, but not money from wine.

The idyllic picture painted for tourists of beautiful wine estates, a gracious lifestyle and prosperity is a compelling one. But behind this lies the hard facts of economics, the high cost of land, and labour. Today, many wine farms are for sale, and that is not unique to these times: through the centuries wine farms have changed owners regularly. Few farms have stayed in one family through many generations. Production costs and labour costs are too high to make much of a profit, especially from good table wines.

"You need a lot of money to make money," says Joachim Ewert, professor of sociology at Stellenbosch University. "You probably need at least R25-million capital, plus knowledge and technology. And it's labour intensive. The margins are paper thin for growing grapes for basic wine." It takes three generations.

The story of the wine industry is one of a constant effort to market wines in a competitive world, and often the struggle to survive. Many farmers, then and now, had other sources of income. Many estates add value with a restaurant, conference centre or accommodation, and wine tourism adds value to a farm. Wine, sometimes combined with golf, housing estates like De Zalze between Stellenbosch and Somerset West are becoming more popular, using the "romantic" perception of wine estates to sell a lifestyle of leisure and luxury.

"Success in the wine industry is built around a person or a brand," says Professor Mohammed Karaan. "Eighty percent (of producers) work very hard, but they don't get to the top." Referring to some well-known Western Cape wine producers, he notes that "value doesn't come from the estate itself –

Jan 'Boland' Coetzee was a rugby player. Beyers Truter is 'Mr Pinotage'. Paul Cluver is a brain surgeon . . . "

Some family-owned farms still prosper – Backsberg has been in Michael Back's family for three generations and he is preparing to hand it over to his son. Meerlust has been in the Myburgh family for eight generations; and there are others.

Making money from wine, says Beyers Truter who co-owns the farm Beyerskloof, is "a 300-year walk through history, your sons' sons reap the benefits".

"It's all about the brand, and building a brand takes a long time," Truter explains. "We started with nothing and selected wines from other areas, knowing what we wanted, and sold it under our label. Today we're at the stage that we can sell wines at the top end of the market (R300 and upwards), but it took 20 years of building to get there."

Making a wine farm profitable requires many skills, and since deregulation of the industry in 1997, that includes savvy marketing. No longer is it a case of producing wine, of varied quality, to sell to the co-op. Of the 550 wine farms, the top third is lucrative, the next third marginal and the last third won't make it, says Professor Nick Vink, chair of the Department of Agricultural Economics at Stellenbosch University: "The politics around the grape industry is always about the growers. Like any other commodity that was deregulated, you get big or you get out. If you're not a good manager, you won't make money. If you're earning R300 000 a year, there's not an easy way to get out of it. You may have assets in your land, but that's dead money."

A 2002 report on the deregulation of the wine industry states: "It is almost impossible to generalise sensibly about the profitability of wine grape farming. Farms differ in terms of the mix of products produced, the mix of white and red wines, and of cultivars produced, the yields and quality levels achieved, farmers' expectations of a realistic return on their effort, different wage rates in the different regions, different prices paid by buyers, etc."[126]

Farms like Kanonkop and Vergelegen produce small volumes only. The co-ops still produce over 70% of the wine volume. Here growers sell to the co-op, and it is all put in one tank. Producers are paid according to volume. Surplus wine is used for distilling.

Marketing is important, but, says Vink, "in the end, even with the best of marketing, you can't fool the consumer. You have to improve intrinsic quality, and you need precision, hands-on vineyard practices to get it right."

Why wine?

To return to a question asked in the Introduction: why, then, have farmers continued to grow grapes? The answer, says wine historian Diko van Zyl, is that the Cape's climate offers little alternative. With the Cape's wet winters, poor soils and gale-force winds, vines thrive here and, as the early farmers found, many other crops do not.

But that may not be the whole story. "Europe didn't need wine," says Karaan. "Some say it was for the farmers' and other colonists' own consumption. The economy of the Cape derived from Europe – whatever happened here added to the colonial coffers. Early farmers were told what to plant, all in the service of the Dutch East India Company. These were not investment decisions, but political decisions to save the mother country." Political decisions, such as the imposition of excise taxes and supporting the manipulation of the market, have shaped the wine market over the 350 years of winemaking.

One incentive for the wine industry was the demand from war: the more wars the British fought, the more fortified wine was needed. Wars in the late 1700s and 1800s pushed up demand to supply passing ships and their soldiers, remarks Vink.[127] In the Second World War, demand for brandy solved the KWV's immediate problem of surplus disposal.[128]

In the late 1800s, when diamonds and gold were discovered in the interior of the country, new markets for brandy opened up. Pubs were the focus of community life and the demand brought high prices for wine and brandy. Brandy production rose from 431 000 gallons to one million gallons between 1865 and 1875.[129]

Another reason for wine's persistence was that wine became a habit, notes Vink. Once something works, it keeps on going. There is a path of dependence – Elsenburg Agricultural College was established in 1898, different research councils were set up (now under one umbrella at the Agricultural Research Centre), and Stellenbosch University started a viticulture department. There were incentives to encourage research and an industry structure developed.

There is no pat answer to the question, "why wine?". The answer offered by Michael Back of Backsberg is: "I honestly don't know . . . "

Being in the wine business is not about making a fortune, says Lebogang Rangaka, whose family has only recently established M'Hudi Wines. "What we've found is that there is some money to be made in wine, growing the wine brand and developing the farm, but all the money we make we reinvest in the farm. This is about a lifestyle. This is not going to make money in our generation, but maybe our children's. Our job is to lay the foundation."

Today, those who buy wine farms are often people who want a certain lifestyle and do not need to make money from it. There has been a huge influx of both foreign owners and people from elsewhere in South Africa. Status and the snob value of your own wine label add to the appeal.

Selling wine

Making good wine and selling it became a whole lot easier after deregulation in 1997 when the KWV's quota system was abolished. New areas of wine production opened up, and farmers were free to experiment and explore.

Between 1992 and 1999, the number of wine-producing cellars grew by 52% as new wine producers entered into the market.[130]

"Come democracy, everyone wanted to support our wines, but all they could do was buy bucket-loads full of cheap wine," says Su Birch, CEO of Wines of South Africa (WOSA), which promotes exports of wine. In the mid-1990s, South Africa was not at all competitive. "Of our South African wines, 85% were white, popular cultivars were limited. Wine producers had to become competitive on the world market very quickly." WOSA was formed in 2000: 40% of vineyards have been replanted in the past ten years, new intellectual capital has come in, and supermarkets have raised the standards required. Exports grew from 50 million litres in the 1990s to 395,6 million litres in 2009, with 49% of the wine produced, exported. The production of wine contributed R3 650 million to state revenue in 2009, up from R 1 612 million in 1996.[131]

While open markets may have stimulated creativity, they have also made trading a challenge in a competitive market where there is a surplus of wine and local and international wine consumption has decreased. Consumers are also faced with a wide choice when it comes to wines, with little brand differentiation.

A brief history

It is one thing to make wine, another to sell it. South Africa has a very small wine-drinking population. Only 11,4% of the population drink natural wine, compared to the 65,5% who drink beer (including traditional beer).[132] In 2010, South Africa ranked 30th in the world for per capita wine consumption, at 7,5 litres a person a year (2006 figures).[133] In 1997 that figure was almost 10 litres, similar to that of 1991.

The history of good table wine in the Cape is less than 15 years old, says Su Birch of WOSA. That may come as a surprise to anyone under 50. Wine routes, wine tastings and wine festivals seem to have been around for a long time, but are relatively recent events.

In fact, surprisingly, before the 1960s there were very few good table wines around, and the table-wine-drinking public was very small. One wine, Lieberstein, sold very well and became the biggest-selling table wine in the world in 1964. Other wines also did well: Tassenberg was launched in 1936 and a few wines, like Grünberger Stein, received awards. But fortified wines such as sherry and port, and spirits such as brandy, were still preferred, along with a few medium-priced slightly sweet wines. Only a few wine estates, such as Meerlust, Delheim and Kanonkop, made good drinking wine.

Winemaking was only revitalised after 1994, and then there was an exponential improvement in wine quality, says Birch.

Creating a wine-drinking public

Creating a wine-drinking public in South Africa dates back decades: it was a concern for the writers and readers of *Wynboer* magazine[134] from as far back as 1949, says historian Tracey Randle in her fascinating dissertation on wine tourism. Part of her research was to look at back issues of the magazine. "On the eve of 1950, debates raged over whether the South African wine and liquor industry should publicize its products in a collective campaign. It was believed the problem lay with 'the majority of the population [being] ... non-wine drinking', where wine at the dinner table was not custom as it was in France and Italy." In South Africa, winemaking was not "an ancient and honoured craft which is intimately connected with the customs and the history of the people" and in fact the wine industry was seen as just another industry.[135] Wine and the drinking of wine were not seen "as part and parcel of [man's] civilized life, a part of man's history".[136]

South Africa's first wine route opened in 1972, thanks to the efforts of three innovative Stellenbosch wine farmers: Spatz Sperling, Frans Malan and Niel Joubert. Sperling, now 80 years old, writes in his unpublished memoirs: "Devising ways of getting people to buy more wine filled my days during the '70s." South Africa was definitely not a table-wine-consuming society: it liked a *stywe dop* (stiff drink), sherry, port and brandy.

"If you have no relationship to wine, then the most basic problem you have is to quench your thirst, and beer is easiest. I can't see people taking a bottle of wine to rugby," says Sperling.

South Africa has never had a strong wine-drinking tradition. Even now, in 2011, most South Africans have not tasted wine (about 60%). Until the 1960s, wine could not be sold by the glass in restaurants, and only in very limited quantities from wine farms directly. Very few people drank wine with meals. "In fact the wine scene was so lacking in vibrancy," writes Sperling, "that . . . back in 1954 there was just one bottle store in Cape Town that sold table wine: namely the Van Ryn Wine & Spirits in Claremont. And the wine? A white called White Leipzig, made by liquor wholesaler Sedgwicks from grapes grown on the farm Aan-de-Doorns near Worcester."

"The reason for this serious lack of wine interest can be found in the origin of the settlers from Holland and the UK, and the Cape's distance from the traditional winelands of Germany and France," he says. "By contrast the local Coloured population . . . were the biggest wine drinkers."

According to Sperling, completely new territory had to be created for people to accept European-styled table wines and that was difficult in the climate of government regulation, which prohibited the tasting of wines at vineyards and estates before people bought the wine. Furthermore, a "farmer's licence" stipulated that one could not sell less than one case (12 bottles) of wine to one person. Not everyone wanted to buy in bulk. In the 1950s the Sperlings were selling about ten cases of wine a month off the farm, and desperately needed supplementary income.

Marketing wine on a larger scale presented a problem. "We couldn't ship wine to the continent, bulk transport from the Cape to Europe was too exposed to spoilage. Only fortified wine could be exported, and you can't drink a lot of that. My generation saw the vacuum, and developed a highly sophisticated wine industry." His ideas included wine auctions, tasting tours outside the Western Cape, the wine route and wine festivals.

It was a difficult milieu in which to operate. The KWV had been formed in 1918 to direct, control and regulate the sale of wine and fortified wine by its members, and to secure for them an adequate return. This it no doubt did, and the KWV was initially a lifeline for farmers who had struggled inordinately with overproduction in the years before it was formed.

But over the years it became an all-powerful body, enabled by legislation, controlling who could grow vines and make wine. Most producers had little incentive to improve the quality of their wines and every reason to irrigate land, increase yields and stay with their tried and tested varietals. Production of quality table wines remained confined largely to Constantia, Stellenbosch and Paarl.[137]

In 1924 the Smuts government passed the Wine and Spirit Control Act, empowering the KWV to fix the minimum price to be paid to farmers for their distilling wine. It could also fix production quotas and control what could be planted and where. At first membership had been voluntary, and many Stellenbosch farmers refused to join, but in 1924 the law required all producers to join the organisation. In 1940 the Wine and Spirit Control Act required that "wine production now required a permit obtained from the KWV and all transactions between producers and sellers had to be sanctioned by them".[138] In 1978 it had 5 000 members.

One of the biggest obstacles to the acceptance of wine at the dinner table and at social occasions was the strong Temperance Movement in South Africa that heavily influenced the 1928 Liquor Act. The KWV argued determinedly against the campaign: it wanted to expand the market by liberalising liquor licences and lifting the prohibition of sales to Africans. It also wanted to extend the *dop* system – providing wine to farm workers – in the Transvaal and Natal.[139]

For the first half of the twentieth century, the wine industry predominantly produced distilling and fortified wines, and subsequently switched to the production of sweet table wines initially. By 1953 table wine exceeded fortified wine production for the first time in South Africa.[140] Selling wine at grocery stores was only allowed in 1966, at Checkers in Springs.[141]

The KWV, say some, strangled innovation and stifled creativity. It also limited entry to the business of viticulture of those who did not belong to the "*boeremafia*" (farmers' mafia). "We were very limited by the political situation," says Sperling. "You couldn't get into the business without being seen in the Dutch Reformed Church on Sundays. There were two forces – Sperling (known as "*die blerrie Duitser*", the bloody German) the non church-goer, and Frans Malan, of Simonsig, a good Afrikaner. But Malan was close to the directors of KWV . . . " he laughs.

The wine route started with an idea: Sperling recalls how one day in 1971 a rather excited Frans Malan returned from Europe and proclaimed: "Sperling, the French have a Route de Vin. We must also establish one, just here in Stellenbosch to begin with."

"So, that's what we did, together with Niel Joubert of Spier." In 1972, the Stellenbosch Wine Route was formed.

Wine routes are now a familiar tourist attraction, with 15 wine routes as well as a brandy route, and wine tourism is a big income generator in the Western Cape.

Spatz Sperling - pioneer

Michael "Spatz" Sperling is a Cape Winelands character of note, always outspoken and frank, and one of the pioneers of good wine in South Africa. Sperling came to the Cape as a young man after the Second World War when his Prussian family had lost everything; his father had been killed the day after the war ended. His mother knew there was no future for him in post-war Europe and sent him to work for her cousin Del Hoheisen, married to Hans at the farm then called De Driesprong. (part of the farm originally owned by Ansela and Lourens Campher, whom we have already met.).[142]

At that stage most farms still practised mixed farming – Hoheisen had fruit, tobacco, vegetables and wine grapes. Whatever wine was produced was mostly for own consumption. A cellar was built in 1944 by Italian prisoners of war whose skills working with sand and stone created concrete tanks so outstanding that these same containers are still used today. Half the grape crop was sold as distilling wine, a little was made into drinking wine.

Hans Hoheisen was in most part absent from the farm, leaving it up to his wife and the young immigrant Spatz to make a go of farming. They barely survived, selling chrysanthemums and vegetables at the Mowbray market on Saturdays, helped by Abraham Jephta who assisted in preparing and sorting the vegetables.

As Sperling explains in his memoirs, he had no experience, and at first made the wine himself by trial and error. "In the 1950s there was no proper viticultural and oenological training in these areas in South Africa. The technical know-how of winemaking in those days resided in Germany/Austria. Trained German winemakers and viticulturists emigrated to South Africa as they saw no future in their Heimat if their family did not own a vineyard. I survived . . . by 'stealing' knowledge wherever readable. I befriended the first group of German-speaking students from the then South West Africa (now Namibia). Among them was a chemical engineer called Peter Kolbe, who advised me on titration methods to determine the acidity of a wine. My 'lab' was one half of Tante Del's laundry.

"Driesprong was a difficult farm, with its steep slopes, winds and mountain storms causing regular crop losses. Bottles we bought from a second-hand dealer in hessian bags, 12 dozen to the bag. My first Kieselguhr filter I picked up on the rubbish dump at Stellenbosch Farmers' Winery. I spent hours and hours trying to upgrade what was already an outdated model, and it never worked! A few years later we bought our first sheet filter and I had to go to the KWV to ask how the 'bloody thing' worked. We could only afford a second-hand basket press. It cost me the huge amount of R500. Only after three years did I scratch together enough savings to buy a two-speed mixer. Before that, I used a long stick which was lowered into the concrete tank through the bunghole and laboriously twirled around until I thought the wine had been properly mixed. Which was, of course, not always the case, as some dangerous instability in the bottled product would show.

"My first harvest, in February 1952, consisted of about 18 tons of grapes from which we made some 13 000 litres of wine. About 60% was distilling wine and dispatched to the KWV," he recalls. "We also sold wine in one gallon (4,5l) glass jugs – the traditional demijohns with two 'ears' – on the Mowbray market."

The KWV limited creativity, and helped if you were lazy. You could use the law to help you get by, he says. If you got a licence, you could produce 100 tons – everything else went to the central distillery. "It was useful. Now you let surplus go down the drain."

Sperling, along with Frans Malan and Sydney Back of Backsberg were responsible for getting the Wine of Origin system in place. "We 'Three Angry Men with a Cause', as we became known throughout the industry, went on to fight a protracted battle with legislators, as well as the large producer wholesalers such as Stellenbosch Farmers' Winery (SFW), Gilbey's and The Bergkelder (Distillers), to give some real meaning to the term 'Estate'."

The Wine of Origin certification scheme was a control system for wine produced in South Africa. "I have to say that we should have been ashamed that in the 1950s and early 1960s no such system existed which guaranteed the contents of a bottle of wine. Ultimately, I suppose, the impetus for such rules to guarantee origin, variety and vintage came as a result of increased interest in exporting wine, which meant meeting strict European Union regulatory requirements."

Wooing the new market

The challenge today is to create new wine drinkers and the focus is on the black market, where traditionally wine has been unknown, or frowned upon. Marketing wine to black consumers today presents similar challenges to those of 50 or 60 years ago: how do you get people who have never tasted wine to become wine drinkers?

The Soweto Wine Festival was started in 2004 and has been held each year since in September, targeted at those who have little or no knowledge of wine or wine-tasting experience.[143]

Lebogang Rangaka of M'Hudi Wines (the story of the Rangakas' wine farm is told in Chapter 11) says there is a family joke that black people like to drink wine, but they do not like to pay for it.

"They flock to the Soweto show, but wine sales are not great," is her experience. "And they're not supportive of black-owned wines, questioning the credibility of the brand. They think we don't have the expertise, don't know much. We have to prove ourselves. We may as well call ourselves *Sarie Marais*."

The black market is still small, and growing, but it has yet to graduate into serious or real wine, Rangaka believes. People still like semi-sweet wine. In her view, there is an arrogance and pretentiousness around wine that needs to be broken down to make wine more accessible to people.

A few producers have been making inroads into this emerging market[144] and Distell is reported to be the most successful so far, especially in establishing the Nederburg, JC le Roux and Graça brands. Nederburg Baronne has changed its image and is colloquially known in the Soweto area as the "Coca-Cola wine".[145] Van Loveren have also done well in this market: they launched their Four Cousins brand to appeal to young people such as students, first-time wine drinkers, the female market, the elderly, and the cider market.

Jacob's Quest

Today there is a whole new market of wine drinkers being created, and they live far from the Winelands, physically and culturally. They are young black people, and wine is a new beverage for them.

Jacob Peu knew he would make a mark on the world. In his own words, he is "stylish" and has always been curious about the finer side of life. And so he was drawn to wine. Something about it, the image probably, fitted in with his quiet sense of style and his way of being in the world, he says.

As a young black entrepreneur, he spotted a gap, and started promoting wine to the emerging middle class in Johannesburg. Then he met the businessman Desmond Green and an idea was born: how about Jacob having his own label? Absurd as it seemed, since he lives in Johannesburg and had never visited a wine farm, a plan was hatched. This was no idea from a high-flying ad agency. This was down-to-earth Jacob and friends working on creating a wine that would appeal to people and sell. It had to be an entry-level wine, low in alcohol and appealing. The target market was to be women: the creative juices flowed and they came up with a light white and rosé sparkling wine. It was not a rosé, it was not a champagne – in fact, it is hard to categorise. Called Jacob's Quest, it is made and bottled at Riebeek Cellars in Porterville, in the Malmesbury wine region.

Jacob's Quest was launched in May 2008, and slowly it is gaining popularity in the taverns and clubs of Johannesburg and Soweto. While he is not sure that he is at the end of his quest, Jacob is very sure he is still on a journey. A wine label today, who knows what business venture is next. A wine farm? He laughs. Maybe, if that is where it takes him.

Meanwhile, on visits to a little farm in Porterville in the Western Cape to meet his business associates, he is learning how wine is made in an old cellar dating back to the 1700s. Garagiste winemaking is a family affair, and is increasingly becoming a popular hobby. When I meet him, Peu is bottling red wine from two years ago, tapping it from the oak barrels. The newly harvested grapes have been destalked and crushed and are sitting in the fermentation tanks, in which bottles of iced water keep the temperature down. Everyone is helping out: children are corking the bottles, packing the crates. This is winemaking at its most basic.

Questions of quality

By now we are used to our wines and brandies winning awards internationally, but as said before, until a few decades ago wine from the Cape was mostly of a terrible quality, described variously as "villainous", "wretched", "miserable trash", "horrible" and "filthy", amongst other unsavoury descriptions.[146] "The wine sold here is a sour rubbish which cannot be sold in town before it has been distilled as brandy or vinegar. The farmers however drink it as it is . . . " Swedish traveller Anders Sparrman reported in the 1770s.[147] The exception was the sweet Constantia wine, and some Muscadels.

The wine was so bad because farmers had little knowledge of winemaking. Wine was made in the hot weather, they had no capital to age wines properly, and they stopped fermentation with sulphur dioxide or local brandies, which were horrible. In 1825 dealer John Collison refused to use Cape brandy to fortify wine for export because it "poisoned" the wine.[148]

Exports were very limited, and wine was increasingly used for making brandy. The Dutch were world leaders in distilling brandy and the VOC prohibited all local distilling under Willem Adriaan van der Stel's governorship, so that only imported brandy could be legally bought.[149] But local farmers produced their own brandy, the Cape Smaak, or Cape Smoke as it came to be known, which was described as "intolerable nastiness" and gained the reputation as a drink "only for the intrepid or the desperate". The desperate included those who travelled northwards: wine did not travel well but brandy did, and one cask of brandy equalled seven to ten of wine in terms of alcohol.[150]

Brandy, then, was to play a major part in the lives of wine farmers. Early farmers survived on mixed farming, of which vines were just a part. In the first decade of the 1700s a wine surplus built up, as there was a limited local market for wine. As has been mentioned, increased shipping around the Cape increased demand at times, but it fluctuated wildly. This was to be the pattern for the next 200 years, with booms and busts in the wine trade. It is fair to say that before the KWV was established in 1918, wine farming was a rollercoaster ride. With every upturn and downturn, the lives of thousands of slaves and labourers were also affected.

Boom time

When the British reoccupied the Cape in 1806 (after a brief interlude earlier), they promised to free the colony from the restrictive practices of the VOC and to incorporate it into the world's most dynamic economy of the day. The colony needed to pay for itself in the face of a severe trade deficit, and it was realised this could only be addressed by increasing agricultural output. Wheat failed to become the export the colony sought and attempts to get wool production off the ground were unsuccessful. "It was in wine that the Colony found salvation."[151]

In 1812 the office of the wine taster was established to help farmers improve the quality of their wines. In 1813 duties on wine imported into Britain were reduced to a third of former tariffs, and wine production expanded rapidly. Wine output increased by 151% between 1809 and 1823.[152] By 1817 Cape wine was selling well; in 1821 wine exports amounted to close to 63% of all exports and by 1822 Cape wine represented 10,4% of all wine consumed in Britain.

With the boom came a new entrepreneurial English merchant class, who bought wine directly from farmers, invested in storage warehouses and promoted the cause of Cape wine in London. Very small numbers profited from the wine boom, writes historian Wayne Dooling. The bulk of production was controlled by a small number of colonial families – in 1825, 19 families controlled around 41% of wine production.[153]

The wine boom could not have taken place without intensified exploitation of slave labour, and wine farmers came to own numbers of slaves disproportionate to those of other farmers – on average 16 slaves (as opposed to the average of eight). Slaves became more expensive because of the abolition of the transoceanic slave trade and the increased demand for slaves. More than 40% of slaves were sold between 1816 and 1826, many of them transferred from Cape Town.

"A marginal increase in the size of the slave population; an absence of alternate sources of labour or advances in wine production technology . . . meant that a virtually stagnant and aging slave population bore the brunt of the state's answer to the colonial trade deficit," writes Dooling.[154] It is calculated that the average adult male on wine farms in the Cape district produced 2,9 leaguers of wine in 1823, compared to only 0,6 leaguers in 1814, a more than 400% increase. He would have had to tend more than double the number of vines.

. . . and bust – wine woes

Then, in 1825, the British government suspended preferential duties on Cape wine. The wine industry collapsed, the economy was plunged into crisis. Between 1828 and 1834, the annual wine output declined by close to 25% in the Cape district and nearly 50% in Stellenbosch. Wine farms, and slaves, lost as much as two thirds of their former value.[155] It was no less an uncertain time for slaves. Many were sold to new owners. Farmers were unable to move slaves to other profitable employment.

There were widespread bankruptcies. Farmers were aware that slavery was disintegrating around them. In lean years slaves were expensive to feed and clothe, and for some farmers the compensation for slaves promised at emancipation was welcome to liquidate debts that had been taken on to underwrite expansion of earlier decades. Nervous creditors started calling in loans; slaveowners were faced with insolvency.[156]

In 1838 slavery was abolished and 1 247 000 pounds' compensation was paid to farmers. It was less than expected, and there was a discrepancy between appraised value and what slaveowners received.

The injection of money did contribute to a minor economic boom but the wine industry entered the era of emancipation in a state of recession. Farmers were faced with produce they could not sell and wine farms' value fell, depreciating by almost half.[157]

This was a period of considerable economic difficulty for former slave-owners. "Not one wine farmer has been enabled to make both ends meet unless they have had other resources . . ." it was noted in March 1843.[158]

Many slaveowners suffered real distress; the gentry and those unencumbered by mortgages benefited. Dooling explains that "the great bulk who had to satisfy local and merchant creditors, suffered most. A wine elite began to emerge. Historians who have downplayed the detrimental economic consequences for slaveholders and overstated the beneficial effects of compensation have invariably confined analysis to too short a time-span and ignored the importance of the mobility of former slaves, mortgage indebtedness and fluctuating interest rates and land values."[159]

Land, however, stayed within the farming families: local lending and surety standing between neighbours and families militated against the passage of land into the hands of outsiders. Extension of credit was guided by a strong moral code – most importantly, that interest not be charged at more than 6%; those who charged higher rates were considered "as little better than atheists". Advocates of "free trade in money", however, were arguing that interest should be determined by risk, and a Bill to allow it would do no more than open the market to the "respectable capitalist, the man with a conscience".[160]

Many farmers then, in large part, were already struggling in the mid-1800s. Worse was to come. In 1861, Great Britain, now at peace with France, lowered tariffs on French wine imports, another blow to the wine industry. Exports dropped and overproduction became a serious problem.

Also in that year the vineyards were struck with *oidium tuckeri* or white rust, which destroyed the wine crop of 1862. This coincided with the worst drought in memory.

Widespread bankruptcy among farm owners meant hunger for labourers as farmers could not employ them. The mission station at Pacaltsdorp reported in 1863 that the "poorer classes in the Colony were reduced to very great distress. At this place it was but too plainly visible in their emaciated countenance and their general feebleness of health".[161] At the mission station of Zuurbraak (later known as Suurbraak) the population was reduced almost to a state of famine.

Unlike the 1840s, complaints about the price of labour hardly feature in reports of those who went insolvent. Labour was for once plentiful, and the civil commissioner of Caledon wrote in 1866 that "many, very many, of the coloured classes have been reduced to extreme want, and have been ready to work for merely their food."[162]

Wine prices remained low; locals could not compete on the British market. "In 1868 every wine farm is overstocked with wine . . . prices offered will not cover outlay for labour."[163]

These were years of great hardship and poverty. Free trade in money had been introduced, causing bitter political disputes, and farmers partly blamed it for their inability to get themselves back on track. Interest rates (previously limited to 6%) were now set freely.

The discovery of diamonds at Kimberley in 1870, and then gold on the Witwatersrand in 1886, gave some relief to farmers as a new market for brandy (and food) opened up. So too did employment opportunities, and higher wages drew many farm workers away to earn more on the mines and the expanding railway system.

The labour commission of 1893 wrote: "Great employers of labour in mines, public works and towns are under stress and compete strongly against each other. They thus fix high rates of wages beyond that which farmers could pay. Farmers too have to compete against each other, especially in critical times, under pain of losing a . . . harvest or vintage . . . which will not wait."[164]

Between 1878 and 1896 labour shortages continued, as did the recession.

And then phylloxera arrived.

Phylloxera vastatrix is an aphid which lives off the roots and leaves of vines. American plants had become immune to it, but the European vine was not resistant. In the early 1860s American grapevines reached France and 75% of the European vineyards were wiped out. Phylloxera finally reached the Cape in 1885 and within a few years devastated the Cape vineyards.

There was, however, a good stockpile of wine during this time, and the Cape Town Wine and Export Syndicate was formed in August 1889 "for the purpose of finding an export for the surplus production of Cape Wine". Lower wine production also boosted prices; many farmers had diversified and planted fruit orchards. More wine was made into brandy to meet the strong demand in the northern parts of the country.

The Cape vineyards were replanted with phylloxera-resistant imported rootstock, and the industry revived. However, wine exports were negligible and a large surplus once again accumulated.

The problem of overproduction – and the resultant low prices for wine – led to one of the most important developments for the South African wine industry: the co-operative movement, with the first in Tulbagh in 1906, and the formation of the KWV in 1918.

In 1925 the Stellenbosch Farmers' Winery (SFW) was formed by William Charles Winshaw and Susanna Elizabeth Krige. Distillers Corporation was formed in 1945, and merged with SFW in 2000 to form Distell.

Winemakers

Winemaking was until fairly recently the preserve of men, mostly white. German and Italian winemakers brought their talents to the Cape in the middle of the last century, and a great deal of experimentation went on in the quest for making good table wines. It is difficult to say when the first black winemaker came onto the scene, but in cellars across the Cape coloured people would have been very able assistants to cellar masters over the years. Like the slave who was a winemaker at Constantia, there are no doubt many more unnamed winemakers.

In a book celebrating 50 years of the Klawer Wynkelder, there is a picture of Alfred Malife sitting next to Piet Matthee, with two trophies awarded to the Klawer Wine Cellar in 1977.[165] Malife has a grey beard, not a young man, and was no doubt much valued for his skills as assistant winemaker at Klawer Co-op. But he could not bring his wife here because of the Group Areas Act – the Cape was a coloured preferential work area – and families were not allowed to join black Africans who did find work here. And so Malife left, lost to the wine industry, to become assistant lighthouse keeper at Dassen Island, where his family could join him. As an island it was somehow exempt from the laws of the day.[166]

Malife would have had on-the-job training in Klawer. More recently, many have studied at university level to become winemakers.

Ntsiki Biyela

Ntsiki Biyela, winemaker at Stellekaya, studied BSc Oenology at Stellenbosch University and is probably the first black woman winemaker who cannot speak Afrikaans. (The first black woman winemaker was the "coloured" Carmen Stevens, in 1995.) Stellekaya is a small winery and as the winemaker, Biyela is involved in every part of the process. When we meet, she is sticking labels on bottles

Biyela comes from rural KwaZulu-Natal, a village called KwaVuthela. She tells me that she did not choose oenology. "I was recruited by

Jabulani because I did well in science, and he said there were bursaries available. I hadn't ever tasted wine." (Jabulani Ntshangase heads Thabani Wines, a young company based in the Cape Winelands with a soon-to-be-built boutique blending cellar in KwaZulu-Natal.)

When Biyela started studying at Stellenbosch in 1999, it was "completely white". The other African students were from countries elsewhere in Africa, and very few studied viticulture. An enormous stumbling block was Afrikaans – and people used to challenge her about coming to Stellenbosch if she did not know Afrikaans. "But they didn't think – it was the only place to study viticulture. I would respond by speaking in Zulu." As a student working at Delheim, her manager took her to a workshop. "It was all men, all white. The only woman was the one filling out name tags." She wanted to run away, but was told "this is where you are supposed to be".

Today, ten years later, most people have gone beyond "the colour thing", at least in the circles she moves in. When she feels strange, she just reminds herself: "I'm in the right industry." She would rather people just asked her straight out what they wanted to know about her. Otherwise they stare, and staring is worse. "What I appreciate about the wine industry," she says, "is that they're not just getting black people as displays – they are people who can do the job. It's difficult for blacks to own wine farms, it's a huge investment, and you don't get any returns for the next five years. Black ownership is a long way off." And what about farm workers? "All I can say is that as a student I saw how little they were paid."

Wine is not traditionally the drink of black people. But it has been marketed as a middle-class drink, and the Soweto Wine Festival has done a lot to educate people. "And it's not pretentious. If people don't like the wine, they tell you. And they don't pretend to know when they don't."

As winemaker Biyela has to taste a lot of wines, not only her own, which she does regularly, but other people's as well, to get a sense of what is going on in the field.

"Wine is an acquired taste. When I first tasted wine, it was a red wine, I don't remember which, and it was terrible. And Jabulani, who introduced me to it, was so passionate about it. It's like olives – you learn, by practising, until you finally get it."

She explains that making wine is like cooking: "You learn to do this and this – there's the science side of it, but then there's the artistic side.

You experiment until you know, this is where I want it to be. I love it. Each winemaker's touch is personal, and yes, women have a softer touch," she says. "It's hard to define, but it's there."

Biyela makes red wines for public sale, and a few barrels of white for in-house consumption.

She has had major challenges, but "you face them, and get over them, move on". Not always without stress, however – like the time she had a stuck ferment. "That was nerve-wracking," she recalls. "I couldn't sleep, I couldn't talk, I was working out how many millions of rand I would be losing."

As chief winemaker, it was her responsibility. But she managed to get the fermentation going again, and when it happened again this year, to a lesser extent, she was calm while others did the stressing.

And has her Afrikaans improved? It depends, she says, on whom she is speaking to. And if people insist on speaking Afrikaans, she switches to Zulu. "I don't speak your language, you don't speak mine, let's find a middle ground," is her philosophy.

Research and education – making better wine, and a South African cultivar

"While technical and financial management skills can always be schooled, hard times and the need to make do are the teachers of self-sufficiency and perseverance," writes Spatz Sperling, who did not have the opportunity to study, in his memoirs. Viticulture and oenology training and research, at least in South Africa, is a relatively recent development. One of the pioneers was Abraham Izak Perold, credited with creating Pinotage, the first and only South African wine cultivar.

When science was less rigorous, and possibilities for new wine grape varietals a curiosity, Perold decided to pollinate a Hermitage (Cinsaut) flower with a Pinot Noir. The experiment was done in his garden at the official residence at Stellenbosch University's Welgevallen Experimental Farm in 1925. The generally accepted theory is that Perold was trying to create a cross with the best characteristics of the parents – the classic Pinot taste of Burgundy with the easy-to-grow, disease-resistant quality of Cinsaut. His cultivar came to be known as Pinotage.[167] That is how the story goes and wherever you read it, it seems much the same.

But it may not be true. Wine writer and author Peter May has recently published a book, *Pinotage: Behind the Legends of South Africa's Own Wine*,[168] on why perhaps the Perold story is not exactly true. But not to spoil a good story: Perold's experiment yielded four seeds, and he planted them in the garden rather than at the university where he worked. And then forgot about them. He left no notes about his experiment and he left the university for a position at the KWV two years later. The garden he left behind became overgrown. Enter a young lecturer Charlie Niehaus, who knew about the four seedlings, and was cycling past as the team was about to clear up. He managed to save the seedlings and they were re-established at Elsenburg Agricultural College by Perold's successor, CJ Theron. The first recorded commercial planting of Pinotage was made on the farm Myrtle Grove near Sir Lowry's Pass in 1943.

The designation of the Pinotages of Bellevue and Kanonkop as the champion wines at the Cape Wine Shows of 1959 and 1961 caused a sensation as few people could believe that the classic red cultivars could be beaten in a competition such as this. Stellenbosch Farmers' Winery was the first to use the name Pinotage on a wine label when they marketed the 1959 harvest of Bellevue under the name Lanzerac Pinotage during 1961.

Perold may or may not have created Pinotage, but he was a pioneer in the science of viticulture. Born in 1880, he studied mathematics, physics and chemistry at the Victoria College in Stellenbosch (BA 1901) and obtained a PhD in Halle, Germany (in chemistry, summa cum laude, 1904). He then explored France and toured Europe. In 1906 he accepted the post of temporary professor of chemistry at the University of Cape Town. Soon after he left for Europe again, this time sent by the South African government to explore grape varieties, and brought back 177 varietals which formed the core of a collection which still exists at the Welgevallen Experimental Farm of Stellenbosch University..[169]

In 1910 Perold discovered the table grape cultivar Barlinka, in Algeria. He brought it to South Africa and cultivated it as a valuable grape for export. Under Perold, the Department of Viticulture and Oenology was formed at Stellenbosch University and he became the first professor there. In 1928 he became Dean of the Faculty of Agriculture. He then left and served as chief wine expert for the KWV. He died in 1941.

Academic viticulture dates back to 1898, when the government bought the farm Elsenburg to use as an agricultural school. The Elsenburg College of Agriculture was the foundation for the University of Stellenbosch's agricultural training in 1917. A full Faculty of Agriculture was established at the "new" University of Stellenbosch, which grew out of the Victoria College, in 1918.

The most significant development in winemaking was probably cold fermentation, introduced in the 1950s. Until then, local farmers had struggled to make light, fruity white wines: with high summer temperatures, there was no control of fermentation, which mattered less for red wines, but white wines lost their primary and secondary aromatics. Before the Second World War, white wine from the southern hemisphere was flat and uninteresting.

"Mr Pinotage" – a passion for Pinotage, politics and God

Synonymous with Pinotage's success is Beyers Truter, a colourful character in the Stellenbosch winelands who co-owns Beyerskloof and is known as Mr Pinotage.

After tasting a Pinotage aged by Frans Malan of Simonsig in young oak, which he says was the most amazing wine he had ever tasted, Truter decided to explore Pinotage further. That was in 1982, and he was a young winemaker at Kanonkop.

At that time Pinotage was an easy-drinking fruity table wine, with little status as a wine, other than being popular, he says. "When I started at Kanonkop, Pinotage was the variety which sold the best, at the lowest price, and never got the real treatment."

It had won awards in the late 1951 and 1961, but after some disparaging remarks from visiting wine masters from England in the 1970s, where it was described as tasting like nail varnish and rusty nails, its popularity plummeted and many farmers took out their vines.

"The big co-ops said Pinotage should not be matured in new oak. But Oom Frans (Malan) had hinted that with the right wood-maturation, Pinotage wines could be made with fuller flavours." Maturing in new oak is very, very expensive, says Truter, and he was taking a chance.

"If you're scared about everything in life, you won't get anywhere," he says. "It was the Cabernets that were new-oak matured. We bought three new barrels a year – we almost broke the bank – and I used one for Pinotage every year. At tastings, it was always rated the best wine."

In 1991 his Kanonkop Pinotage won the Robert Mondavi trophy for the best red wine, and he was selected as Winemaker of the Year. International recognition at last.

"In 1993 Pinotage was called Red Gold – the whole attitude of the world changed, helped by Nelson Mandela, and new markets opening up. Here was a home-grown variety and many questions started being asked. From 1992 bottle sales are up 10% a year. Exports have grown from 5,5 million to 9,6 million litres."

Truter is more than just a good winemaker with a passion for Pinotage.

"I have a passion for Pinotage, and politics and God," he says.

Truter's father was a secretary of hospitals, and he grew up in Oudtshoorn, Strand and Cape Town. He is a religious man and attends the local Dutch Reformed Church. "Which is how it should be," he says of his religion. "My mom and dad laid my foundation and I grew up going to church, which charges my batteries, and strengthens me."

Truter was behind the establishment of the Tractor Party, as it came to be known, which contested the first democratic local government elections, in 1995, in the Stellenbosch area. "At our agricultural society, of which I was chairman for 18 years, we decided we needed local government to represent farmers and farm workers on a party basis. So we started our own party. Our slogan was '*stem Trekker en maak plaaswerk lekker*' (vote Tractor and make farm work pleasant). In the first election we beat the National Party and the ANC in the area," he smiles. "And we did stuff. All our children walk to school, the workers walk to the shops – we provided them with reflective bands so they could walk safely along the road. We used subsidies to help farmers provide proper toilets and water and electricity to farm workers. I don't know if we got to everybody, but we reached most farms. We built walkways along the road, we looked at the shebeen problem with the national police. We looked at the concept of agri-villages – we believed if a farm is going to develop, part of that process must be housing, job creation and poverty alleviation for people living on it. But that didn't happen."

After the first five-year term the party disbanded because they were spending more time on politics and less on getting things done, Truter says. In 2000 he became an ANC councillor and served on the local council until a few years ago.

"I always had a good rapport with workers. There are only about 2% of farmers who get it completely wrong, and we could have worked them out," he says. "There will always be farmers and farm workers, and there've been many guys before me who did a lot of good work. Racism is not dead, it will never be dead, until small kids accept each other. We got larney, thinking we are so good we can't mix with workers. But Jesus did."

Local government became political and adversarial and it was a nightmare working in those conditions, he says. “I’m ANC outright, what they stand for is good. But the opposition doesn’t want the ruling party to look good.”

When Truter was looking for a farm to buy, he was told by locals that you could not plant grapes here. “But I learned the worst soils make the best wine, I’m always astounded by that! The trouble with Stellenbosch is that yields aren’t high, income isn’t great.”

Being a winemaker requires passion and experience. “After a few years you’re still learning, after ten you’re getting there – after 30 years you can say you’re done, and you pick up things other people don’t.”

Is Pinotage really Pinotage, or is there some hybridisation at work, as some have suggested?

“It is Pinotage,” says Truter, “DNA tests have shown that it is a cross between the two varieties from Europe. The Pinotage Association has never reacted to allegations of its bastard origins, we knew what it was.”

While our wine industry is more than 350 years old, it is only fairly recently that South Africa began producing consistently good wines. The economics and marketing of wine have always been challenging; a decision on export duties in England could make or break the early farmers. Control of production proved a lifeline at first, but killed initiative and creativity. Today, surplus supplies and a very competitive market make for an ongoing tough trading environment.

CHAPTER 6

Paternalism – an abnormal relationship

Farm work was hard, recalls Petrus van Wyk, a retired farm worker originally from Wellington, with long hours, from before dawn to after dark. "And they worked with the *dop* system. If the farmer wanted to punish you, he hit you, with his hand or a sjambok. It was his farm and his law. He was the law. It was still slavery time," he says.

Van Wyk was speaking at a gathering for retired farm workers organised by Dopstop, an NGO that combats alcohol abuse. As he talks, there is pain, humiliation and anger in his voice. It was 2010, but he was talking about a time, not that long ago, when the worst manifestations of paternalism were still seen as normal.

The early history of farm workers informs the present. It is a history of mobility, of slavery and freedom, dispossession and resistance. Primarily, though, it is a story of paternalism.

Generations of farm workers have seen slavery come and go, wage labour introduced, the beginnings and growth of corporate agriculture and repressive labour laws, both before and during apartheid. In the new era which offered hope, after apartheid, farm workers were for the first time protected by labour laws.

The paternalism of slavery on farms did not end at emancipation in 1838, it just changed form. Workers were seen as "children" who needed and supposedly wanted the guiding hand of their masters.

According to Spatz Sperling, owner of the farm Delheim near Stellenbosch, farmers still administered corporal punishment 20 to 30 years ago.

Punishment, or fear of punishment, was one way in which labour was controlled by farmers. Another was the *dop* system. Housing, and tenancy on farms, was a further form of control.

It would be wonderful to say that that is all in the past, but farm workers in the grape-growing areas are still largely marginalised. And although this is changing slowly, the paternalism and oppression of 350 years of slavery and serfdom has left its legacy of hopelessness, dependency and alcohol abuse that will take time to unravel and heal.

Central to the story of the grape is the story of labour and the relationship between farmers and their workers through the years.

In the case of wine farms, it is a very particular relationship; in the Western Cape the *dop* system has added to the unequal power relations between farmers and labourers, a particularly pernicious form of control. It was not confined to grape farming (the fruit and wheat farms also used it), and it had a particularly disempowering effect on the traditional labour force.

Paternalism has its roots in slavery, where the farmer owned his slaves and saw his role as the *pater familias*, or "father", laying down the law and meting out punishment as he saw fit. Not only did a farmer's slaves live on his property, but more often than not they lived in the house, especially the women, who would sleep in the kitchen.

Joachim Ewert, professor of sociology at Stellenbosch University, speaks of "classic paternalism", where the farmer was lord of the manor, the feudal landlord who controlled all aspects of people's lives. This paternalism and the relationships of dependency it produced have been blamed for many of the social problems which still exist today on farms. It was a power relationship heavily loaded on the side of the farmer. It was up to him to provide decent housing; it was up to him to allow a school to be built on his farm for the children of farm workers; he could say who could come and go on the farm; and when a person could no longer work for whatever reason, he could evict him or her.

There are few first-hand accounts of what life was like on a farm for a labourer; farm workers are largely invisible in history. But a study by JB du Toit on farm workers in the Tulbagh area[170] does give interesting insights into conditions on farms in the 1940s. In Du Toit's 1947 thesis he notes that the farmers no longer have a personal interest in workers; the relationship has become impersonal. The farmers he interviewed knew that better working conditions were necessary, but did nothing about it, he observes. "The practice of holding religious services, or even to come to the farmer's house for this purpose, hardly exists any more. This practice testified to an intimate and personal relationship." Paternalism may have become less personal, but the attitudes to workers did not change much.

Until recently farm workers had no protection from the law against unfair labour practices and eviction, and there was no minimum wage. There was no place for initiative and no prospects for advancement existed. Generation after generation of farm workers had only farm work to look forward to, which was largely menial work with long hours. As farming communities go, South Africa is unusual in having large numbers of labourers living on farms. Perhaps this is because after emancipation in 1838 many freed people had little choice but to stay on farms, or to return there when times became tough economically. Through the next 150 years, paternalism became deeply entrenched.

The old classic paternalism still exists on some farms today. "Although workers have had rights since 1995, there are still some (farmers) who ignore the law and carry on regardless," says Ewert. "But not many. I don't have data, but my guess would be that it's not even 10%."

In the 1980s there were reformist moves in the Stellenbosch area, where the Rural Foundation (a partnership between farmers, the KWV and the government) sought to promote health and social stability amongst families living on the farms and improve working conditions. Farmers were urged to train workers on a more systematic basis and to improve labour relations.[171] The initiatives improved health markers such as infant mortality rates and teenage pregnancies, and significantly contributed to increasing the age at which children on farms left school. "Nevertheless, these changes were not sufficient to change the dominant paternalism that bound employer and employees, " stated a 2006 draft of the Wine Industry Transformation Charter.[172]

This was upliftment rather than empowerment, and while it was a move in the right direction, it was fairly limited in its area of application. For workers in more isolated rural areas, however, little changed.

Today, the new paternalism has largely replaced the old form. Farmers have a personal relationship with workers, will do things by the book, and many invest in workers' social and human development. Social development is also seen as part of commercial success: "It's not 'what I spend on human development I lose', but 'with this investment I will get benefit'," says Ewert.

In many cases the farmer would have grown up having a personal relationship with farm workers. But paternalism remains paternalism, and ideally labour relations should be based on structured relationships, where workers know their rights and obligations, believes Ewert. Examples are big corporate farms such as Boschendal and Vergelegen: they comply with the law, do not avoid unions, negotiate on a regular basis, and there is collective bargaining. To Ewert, this is the most desirable form of labour relations as "paternalism disempowers workers".

Paternalism is of course not uniquely South African, and is still quite common in Latin America.

Life on farms

Living on a farm is an isolated life, especially on those farms beyond the more populated farming areas. Various laws, from as early as the Hottentot Proclamation of 1809, and later apartheid laws, restricted workers' freedom of movement, forcing them to remain on the farms where they lived, or risk arrest for vagrancy if they moved to other areas to search for work.

After emancipation, when slaves were free to leave the farms and the relationship between freed people and the farmer was no longer a captive one, housing on farms was one of the incentives farmers used to keep their labour. Through the years that did not change much, as the shortage of farm labour, and keeping people on farms, remained an ongoing concern. Unlike sharecropping, where a person would grow a crop and share it with the landowner in return for land and housing, farm workers were "given" a house, but only as long as they worked there. And the farmer could justify his low wages by the provision of housing. This meant farm workers could never invest in a house; they had no secure tenure and faced eviction on a farmer's whim.

In the rural areas of the Western Cape dominated by wine and wheat farms, families lived on the farms for generations. They were mostly closed communities with few outsiders and little exposure to other ways of life, especially before the advent of television. The farmer controlled his labourers through low wages, tied housing, corporal punishment and of course the *dop* system.

An account of farm life in the 1930s by Jannie Theron, son of a farmer, which was recorded by the Drakenstein Heemkring in 1987, gives an interesting glimpse into a way of life.[173]

"In the 1930s farmers were a distinctive section of the community," Theron says. "There were wealthy farmers, but for the most, it was a simple life with few luxuries. Farmers were generally less well off than those living in town. Many wore patched clothes, and as a child I remember wearing my father's old jacket to school if it rained. We rarely visited doctors. Castor oil was a remedy for everything. Labourers lived in two-roomed houses with a *misvloer* (dung-smeared floor). Houses sometimes did not have doors, the windows only had wooden shutters. Some families had neat homes and had managed to accumulate some furniture. Others were called *sakdraers* (bag carriers) because all their possessions could be carried in a bag.

"Until WWI farm labourers got cooked food from the farmer's kitchen. Outside the kitchen scoured enamel or tin dishes hung on a wooden pole suspended between two trees. Lunch time each labourer got food – mostly thick bean, lentil or pea soup, a piece of meat and bread. At night, bread and fish. During the day they got a *dop* (of wine) – about four or five times. The farmers and labourers were poor then. The difference between the labourer's wage and the farmer's earnings was quite small then."

By the 1940s industry was being developed in the large towns, and workers had the option to move to town where there was work in the factories, for men and women, which was more attractive than being a labourer. Labour for farmers became scarce, and to add to the acute labour situation, many men joined the army during the Second World War years, leaving women and their children in a precarious situation. "No man, no house" was the farmer's maxim, and many women and children lost a roof over their heads or were forced to live together in cramped conditions.

"No man, no house"

Willie Venneal is an old man, but he is not above still doing some overseeing work on the farm Solms-Delta. "I can't sit at home waiting to die," he says. He is very involved in developing the Dik Delta garden on the farm.

Now in his late seventies, Oom Willie, as he is known, was born in Groot Drakenstein, on the farm Excelcius.

His pa was Daniel, from Simondium, an area between Franschhoek and Paarl, his ma was Hilda, from Pniel. "She worked at the *koshuis* (hostel), where Jannie Smuts visited. He would have breakfast, and go walking and not come back until night. It was *net soos 'n* (just like a) bread and breakfast," he says. His father worked at Boschendal, at Rhodes Fruit Farms, and at Windraai.

"And then my pa went to the army. All the 'war mummies' were then packed into one little house, with all the children. My ma saw it wasn't going to work, so her uncle found us a place at the Pickstones (fruit farmer Harry Pickstone ran a nursery in the area). But a woman couldn't just get a house, one of her sons had to work."

Oom Willie's animated face crumples as he looks down. There is still pain here. As the oldest son, he had to leave school to work. "I was 11 years old, in standard 1. Although I don't want to cry about it, it was very hard . . . today's children don't have it so hard." In winter it was particularly difficult: while friends were warm in bed, he was up early working with the team. "Working in the winter, my hands were *vrek van die koud* (dead because of the cold). But I had to work, otherwise we couldn't have survived. There were eight children, I worked for a roof over our heads and their schooling. I never had a chance to return to school."

One of his jobs was leading the donkeys between the rows of trees. There were no tractors, everything was done by hand. "Only now and then was there a 'Henry Ford'," he says. On his return from the war, where he saw action in North Africa, his father worked as a driver for the Pickstones. "I learned to drive as a 15-year-old, my father hit me a lot learning," he laughs. "I learned on the Franschhoek pass, and it wasn't tarred."

Oom Willie earned nine pennies a day. "Those were good days, people didn't go hungry. We had home gardens, and you could plant what you wanted to." Venneal did whatever work was going, and the farmer hired out his labour. "We went to George, Grabouw, Vyeboom. We'd come home Friday at 10pm, leave again Sunday lunch. Sometimes we'd be away from home for three weeks."

When he was 22 he married his first wife, and had eight children. His wife died, and he married again 25 years ago. His children now all live in the vicinity of Solms-Delta – on Rhodes Fruit Farms, on Allée Bleue (a farm) and in Languedoc and Agter-Simondium. They are all married, and he has 34 grandchildren and 22 great-grandchildren.

Tenuous tenure

There is an underlying and ongoing tension for a farm worker living on a farm: however long he has been living there, the house is not his; he can be asked to leave, his children can be asked to leave. The farmer owns the land where people live. In the past, being tied to housing brought the farm worker under the absolute control of the farmer. Even today, since most farm workers who are given the use of a house are men, when a man can no longer work or is dismissed, the whole family must go. Security of tenure is tenuous, even with the protection of the law.

"Generations upon generations upon generations have lived on farms," says Rose Horne of the Women on Farms Project. Since 1994 farm workers have for the first time been included in legislation that provides for rights to collective bargaining, basic conditions of employment and social security benefits as well as workplace health and safety. In 1997 the Basic Conditions of Employment Act was expanded to include agriculture. Also in 1997, the Extension of the Security of Tenure Act (ESTA) was passed, which promised security of tenure to workers. It stipulates that if a farm worker is disabled, is over 60 or has lived on the farm for ten years, he or she can stay on the farm. If a farmer wants people to leave (which many do), he has to provide equivalent housing elsewhere.

"The legislation has increased evictions on farms," says Horne. Women are particularly vulnerable; they do not have housing contracts even when they are permanent workers and so are dependent for tenure on men. This makes it difficult for a woman to escape an abusive relationship.

"There are gaps in ESTA – while there is now a process to follow and it is better than being thrown out, you can't tell people to *huisskoonmaak* (clear out their houses) and leave the same day, there is no alternative housing available. We've experienced a lot of problems. Farmers get rid of people before they turn 60, they let houses deteriorate and with 2010 (South Africa hosting the FIFA World Cup), we hear about evictions so that the farmer can upgrade the houses for guest houses."

One of the criticisms of ESTA is that it fails to create procedure, through courts or other structures, for farm dwellers to be able to get confirmation of their rights to land. ESTA also focuses on measures to regulate, instead of prevent, evictions.

To compound the issue of housing, around the same time as these laws were passed, the wine and table grape industries were deregulated and many permanent labourers lost their jobs. And with it their houses. Economic rationalisation meant that the safety net of set minimum prices for grapes no longer protected farmers, most of whom were not used to doing business in a businesslike way. According to Ewert, the average farmer was a bad financial manager. At deregulation hard questions had to be asked, such as "do I need 25 people or can I get by with 19", for example. "California farmers run on half the workforce. Unfortunately people lost jobs, and while there are no figures, my gut feeling is that rationalisation reduced jobs by 20 to 25%," says Ewert. "It's difficult to disentangle the effects of rationalisation on housing from the effects of ESTA."

There is an ongoing conflict between the rights of property owners ("I own the farm") and rights of tenure ("I live here"). To get people off farms, some farmers allow houses to fall into disrepair and people who move out are not replaced with new residents. People on these farms are too scared to speak out. One man, who had spent decades working on a particular farm, starting work when he was not yet an adolescent, refused to talk to us in fear of retaliation; he did not want to lose his house, although he is protected by law. He did not trust the papers the farm management had sent him, he said, which he did not understand, as he is illiterate. His family could do nothing to convince him that he was safe. It comes as a shock that even today, in a valley like Franschhoek with its apparent wealth, people on the farm (whose owner is non-resident) still fear for their future.

Maria (not her real name) was born in the Koue Bokkeveld, left school in standard 1 to look after a child, and then came with her family to the Franschhoek area. She is retired now, unable to work because of her health, and at the age of 58 depends on her husband's meagre salary. Her husband will soon reach retirement age. His health is not great, he has breathing problems, perhaps from the pesticide spraying, she says, and should something happen to him, she would have to leave her house, she has been told. No man, no house. Already she has been given notice that her adult children must leave the farm, although one works there.

"How can it be different for us," she asks, "when the owners' children can continue to live on the farm when they are adult? My children are not married: I agree, I've always said when they marry, they must find their own homes. But until then . . . ?"

When the farm changed ownership a few years back, residents were offered R50 000 to buy a house off the farm. But Maria refused. "Show me where I can find a house like this for that amount?" she asks contemptuously. The owners of the farm are "*baie* (very) nice, but they just don't know what's going on here," she says. Her tenure here is uncertain, but her thoughts are for her children's future: "I just hope there's a better future for them."

Housing and evictions, then, are the most visible and enduring sign of the distorted relationship between farmers and workers. Housing on farms is at the behest of a farmer, who decides who can live there. It is, after all, his or her property. And while there are some sterling examples of housing, from the housing development Dennegeur in Franschhoek for workers on the Ruperts' three farms, to Backsberg's housing project where workers own their houses, there are still farms with no running water and pit latrines, where houses are falling down and there is overcrowding. That is happening even in areas like Franschhoek, which have a veneer of prosperity.

Mercia Arendse

Mercia Arendse stands at the door of a now-abandoned house. This, she tells me, is where her family moved to when her father was injured in an accident. The farm where the family lived before in Stellenbosch had a policy of "no man, no house" and although he was expected to recover, the family was still evicted.

Mercia Arendse

Mercia was used to having basics like a toilet and bathroom. Still a young girl when she came here, she was excited, in the way children are, to see her new house, which the farmer at Delta had given them permission to live in, and she ran inside to look. "But where's my bath? Where's my shower? Daddy, where's my toilet?" she called out. The toilet was one of three outside pit toilets, quite a way off; each served three families. There was no place in the small three-roomed house for a bathroom or shower.

Her voice betrays a tension, the sadness of that time, which still lives with her. The family crammed in, sleeping in one room, eating in the kitchen, and made the best of it. Mercia, however, could not get used to it and became sick, as did her brother. They moved to live with their grandparents on the neighbouring farm. She was the only one on the farm who passed matric in 2005. But, in spite of the hardships, she says wistfully, "I have lots of memories. Of my special place I went to be alone . . . of the dances and performances I did on the stoep to make money."

Today Mercia works on the farm Solms-Delta (formerly Delta), which has undergone a startling transformation in a very short time. New houses have been built and old ones renovated. Someone who has witnessed the changes is Aunt Griet, who has lived at Delta for 20 years. Her porcelain cats watch over the lounge, where a television flickers, the sound off. There are two stoves in her kitchen, one to bake in, because the plates do not work, one for stove-top cooking. It beats firing up the *swartstoof* (coal stove) at the end of a long day's work, she says. A heater warms the room, a Jetmaster fireplace sits waiting for a fire to be made. She has warm water on tap, and the house is in good condition. Aunt Griet used to work at the crèche at a nearby farm, and today she still looks after the little ones not yet potty-trained and ready for crèche.

Nearby houses still stand, barely, where people lived less than five years ago. One has a wall which has collapsed completely; the roof has partially caved in at another. Before Delta was bought by Mark Solms in 2002, the houses on the farm had been left to deteriorate while people still lived in them. The owner wanted people to leave; the farm was no longer employing anyone and he had little interest in people's wellbeing.

Housing is a prickly issue for many farmers. Housing means responsibility: under the eviction law, if they want people to move off the farm, they must provide another house of similar condition. An unintended consequence of the Act has been that farmers have let housing stock deteriorate. Most farmers today do not want people living on their farms. Apparently, if you have workers living on your farm, you can knock millions off the selling price. Neighbouring farmers told Mark Solms he was crazy to be improving housing like this, and furthermore, he provided each house with DStv. He would never get people out, he was warned.

Mercia now lives in nearby Pniel with her child and her husband, who owns his house. "I don't ever want to live on a farm again," she says. "Your house is never your own. I'm pleased he has a house, at least if anything goes wrong I have a house for my parents to come to."

"To have a house is to belong"

Louis Conradie is sure about one thing: people need houses, and the system which gives farm workers housing on the farm only as long as they are employed is "criminal" in his view. Conradie is the ANC councillor for the Drakenstein area, and was born on the farm Delta, today a wine farm, then a fruit farm, where he lived with his parents until the age of six before the family moved to George. When his mother Hester died, he returned to Delta to live with his grandmother.

"At the age of 15, I started work. I lived with my *ouma (ma se ma)* (maternal grandmother), who looked after us. If you lived there, you weren't bound to work there; but to keep the house, someone had to work there. I had to leave school – I was at Simondium, then a mission school, and finished standard 5. There were seven children, five sons and two daughters, and one nephew – my *ouma* fed all of us.

"I earned R2.50 a week, and there was a social grant. We lived in a two-bedroomed house, with a lounge and kitchen as one. But in those days a bus cost 2c. Everyone supported each other, everyone gave a bit." Delta was then a farm growing avocado pears and citrus – there were only three months of the year when there was no harvesting.

Conradie left the farm and found a job at Meerlus Bosbou (Meerlus Forestry). "The one thing I can say, we were migrant workers, we didn't have a fixed home. If you didn't have work, you didn't have a house. And you kept on moving on. It was very unfair."

Conradie became involved in politics: "I always understood my rights, I felt it in my heart whether something was right or wrong. And in our country I couldn't just accept that we didn't have the same rights as white people. My feeling in my heart was that in 1652 this land belonged to our people, the indigenous people. It made me sore, that in my own fatherland I was not at home. It was something to fight against.

"The Freedom Charter, which was clear that colour was not a factor, gave me courage that change could come in South Africa. I gave myself heart and soul to the ANC." He remembers exciting meetings of the ANC in Paarl, and later Franschhoek. On Women's Day in 1994 he became the first chairman of the Groot Drakenstein branch, and the ANC was launched. "One thing for sure, the people of Meerlus knew their rights, we educated them."

Louis has traced his surname, Conradie, back to the Dutch – in Namibia it was written as Conradi, he says. "I believe the mother of the nation was the Khoisan. This is a *lieflike vallei* (beautiful valley), here, the first people here were the San. And I am a Nama Khoi. The Khoikhoi aren't hairy," he says, showing me his smooth arms.

Conradie established the Groot Drakenstein Behuisingsforum (housing forum) in 1995. "To have a house is to belong," he says. He wants the land at Meerlus Bosbou to be handed over for a housing village. His mission is to build houses for farm workers. "People have the right to choose where they live. It's the only piece of land that belongs to the government in Groot Drakenstein. Housing is a huge problem. Workers on farms get old. Why not give them houses while they're young, so the farmer is not responsible? Use a housing subsidy, and the farmers can also make a contribution. Unless people (authorities and neighbours) want a squatter camp, they must not stand in our way. We'll fight for our own houses."

Conradie has helped many people with unfair evictions. "We won a successful case in the High Court when 21 people were evicted by Anglo American. The people went to Languedoc.

"I have a big problem with ESTA, you can throw that law into the sea. Eviction is seen as a criminal record. You have to have lived there more than ten years, or be over 60 – what protection is that? It makes a person heartsore. I saw the problem in the old days. It's not nice when the sheriff comes to a house, breaks it open and throws furniture in the street. And they didn't feel a thing."

Conradie, like most farm workers, grew up with religion: his was the New Apostolic faith. "My grandmother wouldn't let us sleep late, it was church on Sunday. She believed God was there for people. On Delta we walked to Sunday school." There was no apartheid in the New Apostolic Church, he says, and politics stayed outside the church doors. "Political life is part of natural life; church is the place you forget politics," he says.

Conradie believes that it is better than it used to be on farms, and that there are exceptions. "But there are farms where it's bad, outside toilets, no respect, people forced to work on holidays. The only way to help people is to get them off farms, to give them a better life."

Strangely enough, Agri SA, which represents farmers' interests, would support Conradie's views: "Ultimately the solution, we believe, lies in off-farm solutions and the provision of adequate housing in rural areas. Housing and land reform remains a government responsibility, not the responsibility of individual private landowners."

Fatima Shabodien of the Women on Farms Project challenges that view: "They ask why they have to provide housing, but under apartheid housing was seen as an economic input cost and the upkeep of housing was subsidised by government. Now, in a leap of logic, they say it's not their responsibility. In the context of a shortage of housing off the farm, bricking up farm houses is losing a public investment."

In a presentation to parliament in 2008, Agri SA[174] said that granting independent rights to the spouses and children of farm workers would "make a mockery of a landowner's right to evict under certain circumstances, as well as of any contractual agreements entered into regarding the right of a farm worker to reside on a farm whilst being employed on that farm". Their concern was that unemployed, adult children of occupiers who live on farms, or move back to live with their parents, often cause problems. In such cases, or when unemployed families stay on farms, the misuse of alcohol and drugs which often leads to criminal and violent behaviour is more prevalent, they believe.

"ESTA has had a negative impact on farm values. Farms with large numbers of occupiers living on them are worth far less than farms with few or no occupiers living there," they maintain. With respect to evictions in the

Western Cape, Agri Western Cape argues that although farmers initially resented ESTA, it has not resulted in large-scale illegal evictions.[175]

However, with no tracking of evictions, says Shabodien, how we can know the scale of it? "We're lobbying for ongoing tracking. People don't move to rural towns from the city – these are evicted farm workers. There are entire informal settlements in places like Keimoes of evicted grape workers. There's a high level of trauma in moving people, it tears families apart."

Lucien Luyt, who farms table grapes near Porterville, is very clear that housing is a separate issue from labour. There are 18 houses on his farm, and the community is regulated by a committee. "There are two legs to my business: the business and the farming community. And they do dovetail," he says. "I employ some people living in the houses, but not everyone. I have a rental contract if I can't employ them. But I employ whom I want to. I prefer to always have someone in the house working on the farm, but people do move around."

Race, prejudice and ideas of "inferiority"

Ideas about race and racial superiority added to the paternalistic attitudes of farmers from early times (long, long before apartheid was formalised). Farmers saw it as their duty to uplift their *volkies* (work folk) to their own so-called "civilised" Christian standards.

The history of the grape in South Africa is inextricably entwined with racism and ideas of inferiority. In reading and speaking to people, time and again attitudes to farm workers come up, not only in the past, but now. How often have we heard "the coloured people . . . " followed by a stereotype, more often than not a prejudice.

Historically, ideas about race have led to a racism which is based on the idea that "the blood" (or the genes) is the primary determinant of human traits and capacities. And so a human being is not determined by his or her individuality, but instead by membership of a racial grouping. Of course there is no racial grouping "coloured", to begin with. In fact, there is only one human race. There is no one characteristic trait or gene that distinguishes all members of one so-called race from members of another. All humans are 99% genetically identical. The concept of race, and racial difference, has, however, been used to justify slavery and the denial of rights and freedoms to people for centuries, as we know well in South Africa.

Race is a social idea that allows people to make sweeping statements about identity and behaviour, usually negative, often derogatory. Once people are lumped together in a category, generalisations can be made, discrimination justified.

People from Europe had long seen themselves as superior to the indigenous people; it was seen as the Christian duty to uplift "primitive" people, teach them morals and educate them. The British idea of cultural superiority is succinctly put in Cecil John Rhodes's statement: "I contend that we are the finest race in the world, and that the more of the world we inhabit, the better it is for the human race. Just fancy, those parts that are inhabited by the most despicable specimens of human beings, what an alteration there would be if they were brought under Anglo-Saxon influence?"[176]

William McDonald's observations along the Orange River, made in the early twentieth century, reflect the prevailing ideas of the time: "Several persons of the older generations of these Bastards [at that stage an accepted term for people of mixed racial origin in this area] are still living on their own land, and are justly respected and admired by their European neighbours, who, however, do not fail to recognise the taint of coloured blood."[177] And: "Stopped at Spannenberg's farm. It is sad to see the commingling of black and white blood in so many parts of this country."[178]

The prevailing idea about race in the nineteenth century was that of pluralism, even though Charles Darwin had already come up with the "radical" idea, for his time, that black and white people were one race, a single species.[179] This ran contrary to the views of the majority of his scientific colleagues who maintained that there were between two and 63 different species of human (depending on whose theory it was), the idea of racial pluralism. A respected scientist of the time, Louis Agassiz, thought there were eight human types which had appeared in different areas as part of God's plan, but they were meant to be separate and unequal. Among those who supported slavery, and perhaps many others, was the common attitude about black people, that they were not far from apes in origin, had no sense of morality and were at a "lower" level of civilisation. This was the prevailing view among people in Europe and America of the time.[180]

Darwin himself was vehemently opposed to slavery. His grandfathers, Erasmus Darwin and Josiah Wedgewood, were very active in the anti-slavery movement. Darwin's first encounter with slavery was during his voyage on the scientific research ship the *Beagle*, when he witnessed slaves landed on the beach in Rio De Janeiro and saw thumbscrews used on women for punishment. He and the captain of the *Beagle*, Robert Fitzroy, had a huge argument about slavery after Fitzroy defended it. Jim Moore, co-author with Adrian Desmond of *Darwin's Sacred Cause*, believes that Darwin was driven to embrace brotherhood science, i.e. that all of life, not just people and animals, but plants and every living thing, is united in a single tree, because he was passionately opposed to slavery.[181] "What we are pointing to . . . is a moral motivation for Darwin's science . . . Darwin did love the truth, but what came before, in his family, in his upbringing, his whole culture . . . was we Darwins despise slavery. Darwin sought a scientific basis for undermining it in his theory of evolution."

In South Africa ideas about race were used to subjugate "coloureds", politically and economically, and justified as "fair" by embracing the idea of coloured "inferiority". The farmer could be like a father to labour because his workers were considered to be childlike and lacking in moral maturity. Farmers referred to workers as "*my volkies*" (a diminutive form of "my people"); it is interesting to reflect on what happens to meaning when people speak of "*Die Volk*" (the Afrikaner Nation) and "*my volkies*". It is sometimes claimed that it is an affectionate term, and often used by workers themselves.

Theories put forward for alcohol abuse and poverty were also underpinned by ideas of "coloured people" (especially farm workers) being "less advanced" than others, at a different "stage of development". This then justified why they did not need better housing, wages or treatment. Farmers in Du Toit's study, conducted during the 1940s, speak of "types". He quotes a farmer saying: "The ordinary type Coloured with whom we deal has the mentality of a child and attempts to try to educate him and improve his living standards wouldn't be crowned with much success."[182] That attitude still prevails among some farmers spoken to in the course of collecting material for this book.

There is little understanding in these narratives of why people are trapped in the cycle of poverty – it is easier to ascribe it to "coloured-ness" rather than to the consequences of years of poverty, powerlessness, the *dop* system, poor education and hopelessness.

"*Stokkiesdraai*" – education for farm work

For many decades it was seen as self-evident that if a family was allowed to live in a house, the man at least would work for that farmer. No houses were given if people worked elsewhere; if the farmer did not need the farm workers' sons and daughters to work for him, they could work elsewhere. At peak times, such as harvest time, however, wives and children were required to work on the farm.

The saying "*stokkiesdraai*", which has come to mean playing truant, originated on grape farms. Children would be required to tie together sticks in the vineyard, and were then not able to attend school. As a young child growing up on a farm, then, schooling was by no means assured.

In Du Toit's study done in the Tulbagh area in the 1940s, which was probably representative of many farms of the time, he found that children attended school irregularly. Reasons given were the long distances children had to walk, especially in the cold, wet winter. Also, they were required to work on the farm during harvest time, whether that fell in the school year or not. Many came to school for food in the morning and because it was a chance to socialise with other children. It was also the only opportunity to experience a world outside of farm life. Most, however, left school after standard 1 or 2; only one a year went to the town school. The education level was poor. One teacher was responsible for many grades, and there was little opportunity for children to do homework: they often had no table to study at, or adequate lighting, at home.

And most parents were illiterate. Du Toit found that the farmers, especially the older ones, were very sceptical about the value of education for the children; they believed the most that could be achieved was teaching them to read and write. Du Toit postulates that the reason for this attitude was that they were scared that if children studied further, they would be lost to farm work. Some farmers, however, did support secondary education, to prepare people for trades and teaching. One attitude was that "the farm coloured is not yet ripe for a sudden elevation of status, and they can't suddenly move from a low to a high status".[183]

But in spite of this, schools were built with the support of farmers, who hoped that through financial support for education they would keep workers on farms. A condition, though, was that children be available for seasonal work. Among farm workers, Du Toit found, there was sometimes a reluctance from parents to encourage their children's education. They saw no future for them other than farm work, so what need was there for education? But there was also an element of shame: often clothing was not clean and whole, and parents did not want children to go to school like this, says Du Toit. Children were also kept out of school to help earn money for the household, and boys started working at the age of 12.

In the late 1990s, on average, levels of schooling among farm workers in the Western Cape were less than six years. Illiteracy, while declining among younger age groups, was at about 20% among adult farm workers, and at more than 50% among elderly women and men in Stellenbosch in 1996.[184]

Research in the 1990s showed that relatively few children of farm workers managed to leave the sector, precisely because of the inadequate educational infrastructure in rural farming areas, and poor social circumstances which manifested in levels of childhood stunting of the order of 30%. "Chronic undernutrition as a child, perhaps coupled with intrauterine insults with alcohol and tobacco . . . will curtail the lifetime potential achievable by young people entering adulthood on farms," wrote public health researcher Dr Leslie London. "As a result, escape from the cycle is extremely difficult."[185]

It would be encouraging to say that things have changed significantly for farm children today. But in 2005, the first report of an ongoing research project at the University of Witwatersrand to explore the state of education for children in South Africa's commercial farming areas painted a grim picture. Its focus was the lived reality of children, parents and educators in South Africa's farm schools, and the social roles played by farm schools in commercial farm labouring communities.[186] Although the study found no direct evidence of a lower standard or quality of education offered in farm schools than in other South African schools, they did find a negative and defeatist attitude on the part of educators regarding the future prospects of the learners. This "must impinge on the prospects of learners, feeding into a negative cycle of dependence on the farm system and an inability to break away to achieve higher education and opportunity,"[187] the report notes.

Pessimism about learners' capacities and prospects was commonly expressed by educators and principals, with one educator blaming learners' poor performance on "low IQs" as a result of "inbreeding" in the (coloured) community, and another referring to his learners as "lazy" and with a "lack of commitment to school".[188]

One educator expressed her views as follows: "Learners don't have the background and support materials at home to really benefit from the system. They should rather be taught the basics – to read, write and do maths. The expectations are too high because they are not going further than the farm – they don't have the opportunity."[189]

Another educator said with reference to OBE (outcomes-based education) in the farm school context: "They can't really do maths, so they won't become entrepreneurs. What is it to tell them about a theatre? They'll only go maybe once in a lifetime, so it would be more important to tell them how to behave than to use special words like ballet, curtain, etc."[190] As disparaging as educators were about learners, their strongest criticism was levelled at parents, who "don't even bother to ask how their children's day was", who show "a lack of commitment to their children's education", and whose involvement in school life is "on the extremely low side".[191] In the words of the most positive educator interviewed: "The biggest problem facing the learners is their home lives, which aren't very stable. There is a lot of alcohol and drug abuse. At 'news time' on Monday mornings, the learners tell me how their parents drink and fight at weekends. I try to instill discipline and pride in the learners but it gets undone every night at home."[192]

It is difficult to separate out the *dop* system, alcohol abuse and poor performance at school. It is likely that alcohol has contributed to the low academic performance at schools. There are no data available on either the dropout rates of farm school learners or the percentages of former farm school learners who make it through secondary or tertiary education. However, interviews with principals and educators suggested that very few of the learners who leave each year completed secondary education, and only about "one in five years makes it to university".[193] According to an educator at one of the few farm schools to teach grade 7, of 37 learners in grade 7, typically about 30 will go to secondary school, but "most will drop out after the first year" as they are "only there for the bus ride". Every year "only about two learners go to high school", but often "both don't make it to matric" and no learner from this educator's school has ever made it to university.[194]

The report states: "The insular and static nature of this poorly paid, but relatively secure, lifestyle militates against alternative modes of life, and contributes to cycles of perpetuation and reproduction of farm labour. The result is a kind of feudal patronage in which the farmer provides housing, electricity and water, as well as employment to family members through the generations, instead of a professional, adequately paid, contractual relationship. Learners at farm schools, living and learning on the farm as they do, are sucked into the vortex."[195]

Although the report painted a bleak picture, there are some pockets of change. Michael Back of Backsberg has followed up on his student activism of the 1970s, when he ran a night school in the township of Kayamandi as a student at Stellenbosch University. "The path to freedom is through education," he says. He now supports young people through tertiary education. "There have been 50 kids so far. It's very simple, the kids they can do what they want to and where they want to, as long as they pass."

Several NGOs have emerged to meet the challenge of supporting children on farms. The Anna Foundation, based in Stellenbosch, works with children on farms in the area, offering them an after-school-care programme with academic and social support, and equipping children with life skills. The programme focuses on the " three Rs" – in this case reading, running and righting (right living – right lifestyle, right choices, right attitude, right behaviour). Children joining the programme are part of running teams that take part in monthly fun runs and cross-country leagues. Cycling has recently been added. In order to qualify to run in the monthly event, each child must read two books a week, complete the literacy worksheets, participate in the sports programmes, and show responsible behaviour and a good attitude. Another NGO is the Pebbles Project, which works with farm worker communities to provide pre-school and after-school-care support.

On farms like Solms-Delta, most of the children now go to the primary school in Franschhoek. And children's aspirations are closer to being reached. Mary Malgas, who was born on the farm Delta, tells me her two children, 19-year-old Gladys and 11-year-old Michaela, want to make something more of their lives. Gladys is now studying at Stellenbosch University. Mary herself has been given opportunities she has never thought possible after working on the farm for 20 years.

She had always wanted to be a nurse or a chef, and told the social worker for the farm trust she would love to work in the restaurant (which was at that stage still just an idea) as she had always helped everyone with baking.

A few years on, and she is the pastry chef at Fyndraai, the restaurant on the farm, after doing two cookery courses. "Mark (Solms) has given us a better outlook on life – I can come out on top. And people drink less," she says.

Not only are there more opportunities for farm children today, but most do not want to work on a farm. The 2005 study asked children about their aspirations: only two learners of a total of 40 in the Western Cape expressed a desire to work on a farm.[196] For the others, farm work was not viewed as desirable because "you work your arse off on a farm", "you earn too little" and "you end up dirty like animals". Children viewed cities positively as places with "big houses", "more excitement" and "lots of jobs".[197] Learners who did not want to work on farms said they would like to become doctors, police officials, nurses and social workers. Educators and principals were, however, sceptical about learners' potential to advance beyond primary school. One educator told researchers: "Only eight have reached matric over the past few years – the vast majority returns to work on the farm."[198]

The wounds of the past, with corporal punishment, *dop*, poor health, limited education and evictions, still linger. But there is a change in labour relations, backed by legislation, and the next generation will hopefully listen to their grandparents' stories with disbelief.

CHAPTER 7

Shadow of the vine – abusing alcohol

"*Another tot, my master.*"[199]
– old custom to praise the tot

"*You can't speak to my grandfather on a Saturday, he's still in the* dop *system. He gets paid, and thinks that the money is for wine for the weekend.*" – August 2009

"*Come Hilda,*" *said Jacob,* "*the sun is getting low and I must be back to help papa with the milking and to give out the men's evening tot of wine.*" – 1826[200]

A "shebeen special", apparently, is a hamper consisting of Easter eggs, a dummy and booties – and wine. That image endures as a potent symbol of the social problems around alcohol. Who would encourage a mother to buy a dummy and a *dop*?

When you talk about farm workers in the Cape, the first thing people say is: "Oh, you mean the *dop* system." Soon after that you will be told about the "coloured people's weakness" for alcohol, and some theories about heavy drinking on farms.

It is an unfortunate stereotype for all those people who do not drink, and do not abuse alcohol. But the fact is that alcohol abuse, and all its concomitant negative effects, remains a major problem on many farms 15 years after the *dop* system was made illegal.

There is no doubt about it: the legacy of the *dop* system, still with us today, is dependency, locking farm dwellers and workers into cycles of dependence on the farm owner. It has many facets: alcoholism, child neglect, absenteeism, low motivation, domestic violence and poor health.

Elbré Jacobs, a fieldworker with the NGO Dopstop, says there is no *dop* system in Stellenbosch. Anyone here using such a system is excluded from competitions and may not export wine. "But there are farmers who offer wine as a perk, for overtime. It's the wine they'd have to throw away," he says. The problem of alcohol abuse has not disappeared: "Now mobile shebeens deliver wines to farms. There's a certain amount you can have – 50 litres – and when police come, you say you're having a party. It's seen by people as an economic opportunity to make money."

And there are still farmers, it is said, who will give people wine at the end of the day, or the week, as a "bonus". Some even have a bottle store on the farm. In 2004, the Human Rights Commission (HRC) was told of incidences of the *dop* system whereby workers are given alcohol as an "incentive" to work harder. The HRC noted in its report on human rights violations in farming communities: "The system rarely appears in its most blatant form, where workers are given alcohol to drink during the day, but more often appears in the guise where workers are given a bottle of wine at the end of each day and the cost is deducted from their wages."[201]

In 1994, 24 farm workers in Worcester were poisoned by pesticides when given wine contaminated with the pesticide aldicarb. Wine had been decanted from a 50ℓ barrel used to store wine for workers. "Despite its illegality, the *dop* system is ongoing. Local health services were reluctant to respond to evidence of *dop* practices, fearing that any attention to the *dop* would antagonise the farmers, and undermine the access that nursing staff had to farms to deliver mobile clinic services," wrote public health researcher Dr Leslie London in a paper in 2003.[202]

It must be said, however, that within the past ten years there have been enormous changes. Dopstop was started in 1997 by a group of nurses running mobile clinics in the Stellenbosch farming region who decided to wage war against the *dop* system because of its health implications. Today Dopstop's approach is that both farm workers and farm owners must be involved in preventing alcohol abuse by providing social alternatives and by raising awareness of the hazards associated with alcohol abuse, says Leonora Safoor, director of Dopstop. "We will only work on a farm where we are invited, it must be a partnership. Ideally someone on the farm is identified to be trained as a community development worker; that person is trained in leadership, first aid, HIV/Aids, health, life skills. A drunk person cannot work properly. Alcohol keeps people dependent, and when they can't work properly, they get evicted."

Health promotion alone cannot address the problem of alcohol abuse; rather a broad developmental approach, placing alcohol abuse within general health and social needs, is required. "We walk a journey with them," Safoor explains. "We ask them to limit their drinking, you can't tell them not to drink. If you do, they say 'what must we do on the farm?' There are no resources and activities on farms. Farm schools are under-resourced, and there are no recreational facilities. Children as young as 12 start drinking. Women take abuse because they still don't own homes under ESTA (the law on security of tenure).

"With the *dop* system, the farmer always kept people drunk. People on farms were submissive, they didn't question, they didn't talk back, they just did as they were told. That wouldn't have happened if farmers didn't give workers wine every day," she says.

Dopstop works in the Stellenbosch, Wellington and the Overberg areas. Safoor believes that they "do make a difference, with ongoing support and counselling. My challenge is, how do we track the changes?"

To this day the legacy of the *dop* system lives on; whether as incentive, reward or part payment, free alcohol to farm workers has created a culture of drinking that has led to serious social problems. We have been told, variously, "without *dop* they won't work" and because of *dop*, "they don't come to work on Monday". Many farmers say that people prefer to work on the farms where wine is given at the end of the day.

"With alcohol dependence it's not to say people are not responsible for the choices they make," says Fatima Shabodien, CEO of the Women On Farms Project, "but rather to understand that the tot system laid the foundation for what we have today – and the industry has never taken responsibility. It is insulting to tell people to pull up their socks – commercial agriculture should be providing rehabilitation services."

History of the *dop* system

In South Africa there is no indigenous grape-bearing vine; the local people are known to have used mood-altering substances, such as dagga, but alcohol was probably unknown to the Khoikhoi and San cultures. There is a vine indigenous to the Cape, *Rhoicissus capensis*, the so-called Wild Vine, a distant relative of *vitis vinifera* from which table grapes and wine come. It is unsuitable for wine production, although the Khoikhoi and San ate its ripe berries.

Wine at the Cape is first mentioned in 1595 when Dutch explorer Cornelis de Houtman landed at Mossel Bay on his way round the Cape. When negotiations for meat with local Khoikhoi were unsuccessful, he is said to have offered them some Spanish wine. They promised to return the next day with cattle.[203] In 1652, then, when the Dutch VOC first established a victualling station at the Cape with 90 of its employees, wine and brandy would probably have been largely unknown to most of the local Khoikhoi and San people inhabiting the area. However, it seems as they took to it readily.

German traveller Peter Kolbe, writing in the early 1700s, said: "They (i.e. the Khoi) love Brandy immoderately, because it presently heats and makes 'em merry . . . they are ever charm'd with a Glass of Brandy, and are your humble Servants a thousand Times over for so agreeable a Present."[204]

The Dutch themselves were not big wine drinkers, as vines did not grow well in Holland, and arak was more commonly drunk. But the vine grew well in the Cape, and while the wine and brandy made here left a lot to be desired, as we have seen, it was plentiful. In early Cape society, taverns played a big role in the social life of the people living here. Keeping a *tappery*, a bar-cum liquor-store, was one of the most profitable businesses at the Cape. There were three kinds:[205] the first were those where wine was sold in a four-pint flask; soldiers, sailors and slaves supported these. The second was frequented by underofficers and similar ranks; pint bottles were served, and sometimes there was music and dance. The third, where more expensive wine was also sold per pint, had good furniture, pipes and tobacco.[206]

The free burghers who produced their own wine offered it to their visitors with meals. In 1665, for example, a visitor to one of the first free burghers described the wine made by the farmer himself, and which he had with a nice meal, as "very drinkable".[207] However, most Cape wine was of very poor quality and only drunk by the labouring classes in the many canteens in Cape Town.

From the beginning of the settlement the drinking of wine at different times of the day was customary. Writing on the drinking habits of early Cape Town, archivist Dr Graham Botha says: "The beverages were tea, chocolate, seltzer water, beer, brandy and wine . . . light wine was always on the table and at 11am everyone partook of a glass of wine and cake . . . Those who indulged in spirits took arrack, Geneva and brandy. There were no coffee houses in Cape Town such as were found in most cities of Europe, but there were more taverns than were necessary for the size and population of the place."[208]

The wine farmers themselves drank large quantities: by the 1730s it was common for wealthier wine farmers to serve wine with all meals. Otto Mentzel, a German who resided at the Cape from 1733-41, wrote: "One sits from three-quarters of an hour to an hour at table, and at none of the three meals is table wine wanting; but well-bred people never drink more than three or at most four glasses between the courses at every meal. After the evening meal one might also drink a few glasses of wine over a pipe of tobacco."[209]

Wine historian Diko van Zyl says he "was astonished to find that farmers drank heavily, at 10am, at lunch, again at 3pm and in the evenings. This habit carried over to the workers. Sailors and soldiers were already heavy drinkers, and it became a habit of workers."

The *dop* system did not originate in South Africa. Wine – or other alcohol – as an incentive to work harder, or as part payment for work, has probably been around as long as there have been wine farms. There was a time when wine was thought to ensure good health and stimulate vigorous work. Some say the French Huguenots brought the *dop* system with them, but since many of them did not know much about farming or winemaking, despite the myth that persists about this, this is unlikely.

In many European countries the *dop* system continues to this day, says Professor Denis Viljoen of the Foundation for Alcohol Related Research, although no one would call it that. "The *dop* system is alive in Europe – as part payment, or bonus. It's not a South African invention. From information we have, the previously communist countries like Romania and Yugoslavia have the *dop* system in wine-growing areas, not as policy, but as practice."

But it was at the Cape where the *dop* system became entrenched. From the early days at the Cape, Khoikhoi would have worked for farmers in return for tobacco, bread and wine. As wine was a common drink for all people, even for morning tea, the slaves would also have been given wine to drink. According to Otto Mentzel, in the 1730s slaves on wine farms received a glass of brandy and a slice of bread before the morning shift (before breakfast).[210] In 1787, the slaves on Groot Constantia were given up to 560 litres of wine monthly (for 60 slaves).[211] That is just under ten litres each.

After emancipation wine was used as an incentive to work. The freed people could move where they wanted to – and wine was one way of attracting labourers, especially during the busy harvesting time. Early farmers, many of whom were poor, paid workers with the wine they made themselves, as it was cheaper than wages.

"By the latter half of the 19th Century the expectation that wine would be given as part of the wage had become a given among labourers on farms of the Western Cape. Wine held a pivotal role in both the economic and social worlds of rural labour," writes historian Pamela Scully.[212] A Jacob Morkel of Tulbagh in 1860 claimed his labour bill included 410 pounds for provisions and wine for labourers. Johannes Brand in 1860 claimed the 1,5 leaguers of wine during harvest cost him 11 pounds 5.[213]

The *dop* system, whether formal or informal, served as a pernicious form of labour control. Apart from wine being an incentive to work, an alcohol-dependent labour force was easier to manage. Reluctant slaves had little to gain by working harder. Whether alcohol actually made people work better is debatable. "Alcohol weakens you," says retired farm worker Petrus van Wyk. "After a day's work, with *dop* at regular intervals, you are exhausted, with no energy for anything else."

Surplus wine, or poor-quality wine, would be given to workers. While providing wine to labourers was an acceptable practice, workers also faced stiff penalties under the Masters and Servants Act if they became intoxicated during working hours. "A servant may be imprisoned with hard labour for a maximum of one month if he becomes intoxicated during working hours or uses abusive language to his master."[214] Whose definition of "intoxicated" is not specified.

The "*strop* and *dop*" party

Alcohol, or rather opposition to high taxes on brandy, played a huge role in politicising Cape farmers. In 1878, to pay for the last Xhosa War of 1877-78 and the war with the Basotho, the Cape government levied an excise tax on brandy.[215] This came just as farmers were pulling themselves out of a recession, when brandy sales to the mines had more than doubled between 1865 and 1875. There was a furious reaction. In June 1879 the Afrikaner Bond, a new political party, was formed,[216] mobilising the wine farmers who emerged as a very significant force in Cape politics, committed to fostering wealthy farmers' interests. The Afrikaner Bond, under the leadership of Jan Hendrik Hofmeyr, formed an alliance with Cecil John Rhodes, who supported the interests of colonial Afrikaners in return for support of his imperialist designs to the north of colony. Both wanted minimal interference from the Imperial government in the affairs of South Africa. In 1890 the Afrikaner Bond attempted to amend the Masters and Servants Act for landowners to win the right to flog their labourers. This infamous "*Strop*" Bill was never passed, but it had Rhodes's support. The Bond became known as the "*strop* and *dop*" party, the party that sought to rule the countryside through the whip and the tot. "It is little wonder that the Bond failed to attract the support of coloured voters," notes Wayne Dooling.[217]

Opposition to the *dop* system came from the Temperance movements of the mid-nineteenth century, and the synod of the Dutch Reformed Church in 1915, with little effect. Until 1928 it was left up to the farm owner to determine how and at what times wine would be supplied to the farm's labourers.

In 1928 the Liquor Act was amended: Section 96(2) of the Act determined how, when and how much wine could be supplied during the day. Notice the wording – it applied to men only, and the assumption was that labour was not white: "In the Province of the Cape of Good Hope any adult bona fide employing in farming operations any native, Asiatic or coloured person, being a male or over the age of twenty-one years, may on any day supply gratis to such native, Asiatic or coloured person one-half pints of unfortified wine or Kaffir beer: Provided that such wine shall be consumed during intervals of not less than two hours and in not less than three equal portions."[218]

Half a pint, about one cup of wine (225 ml), over a day may not seem like a lot. However, that amount was seldom adhered to. In JB du Toit's study in 1947 of 26 farms in the Tulbagh area, only one of them did not supply *dop* to workers, who were "*Wederdopers*" (Anabaptists) who belonged to the evangelical church, and teetotallers. They received coffee instead.[219]

Du Toit found that farmers were aware of the negative effects of the *dop* system, but justified its use by stating that workers were not drunk during the week; if they did not provide *dop*, they would get it elsewhere and there would be more alcohol abuse; furthermore they could not think of anything to be given in its place "that would satisfy coloureds". It was common practice for labourers to move from farm to farm, especially if there had been conflict and they had been punished. Farmers easily resorted to corporal punishment.

Du Toit was repeatedly told that better housing, higher wages or better perks would not attract the farm worker as much as more *dop*s a day. And so farmers would compete and offer more *dop* than the next farmer. Farmers' paternalistic attitudes about the "nature and culture of the coloured people" fed into the practice of the *dop* system; as has been mentioned before, one of the farmers interviewed in this study referred to "the ordinary type coloured with whom we deal" as having "the mentality of a child and attempts to try to educate him and better his life won't be crowned with much success."[220] Increased wages, similarly, were seen as pointless. "As long as coloured men as well as their women remain slaves to drink, a rise in salary will not result in an overall improvement in their standard of living. If we were to control their money, this could happen. But instead they usually demand it all at the end of a week."

Du Toit's study found that workers were given five to seven tots a day – early morning, 8am, 11am, 4pm, and at closing time. In the busy fruit-picking season, when workers were required to start early, they provided two or three tots extra. Imagine the effect of this, accompanied by poor nutrition, day in and day out.

When a young man wanted to be part of the *dop* system, he started wearing long pants to look more adult. Mostly, the *dop* was given at the discretion of the farmer, as it was not always known how old children were. Many farmers saw no problem with the *dop* system, but blamed weekend binge drinking for the workers' problems. Women were not allowed to buy alcohol at bottle stores, and men only three bottles each. A brisk trade, at a profit, was the result, with men buying and reselling it. Although difficult to ascertain, farmers estimated that about 65% of women drank alcohol.

In Du Toit's study, a typical list of household expenses for a worker is illuminating: the most expensive item included 4 bottles of wine, at 5 shillings each, only equalled by the expenditure on 5lbs meat; 4 shillings and sixpence was spent on clothes. This was out of a weekly wage of 1 pound 7 shillings and ninepence.

The *dop* system went hand in hand with poverty. Poor living conditions, poor nutrition and low wages all contributed to high infant mortality rates: Du Toit quotes figures of 51,8 per 1 000 (figures for whites in the area were 18,7). All TB sufferers in Tulbagh were coloured, and there were high incidences of venereal diseases (there were no clinics for VD) and gastro-enteritis.

Almost 30 years later, in 1974, not much had changed. Low wages, chronic malnutrition and poor housing meant that for coloured children coming to Cape Town hospitals, "the norm was for them to be less than 70% of expected height and weight for age", said an unnamed consultant paediatrician quoted by ALJ Venter in his book *Coloured – A Profile of 2 Million South Africans* .[221]

Spatz Sperling, owner of Delheim, writes in his memoirs about the time he arrived on the farm (then called Driesprong) from Germany in 1951: " . . . the local Coloured population, then numbering some 1,5 million, were the biggest wine drinkers, though it was mainly to alleviate the hardships of their impoverished socio-economic situation. This market was gulping down about 170 l of cheap and nasty vaaljapie (an unfiltered, lighter style of dry white wine) per person a year."[222] Vaaljapie was named for its murky or *vaal* (dull) appearance.

Alcohol was also hazardous in the workplace. Sperling recalls that "for years Mondays remained a 'non-technical-appliances day': no tractors, no pumps, no machines were used in an effort to limit alcohol-related accidents.[223] He writes: "The *dop* system was in full swing: a farm worker received a total of seven rusty 200-ml anchovy *visblikkies* (fish tins) during the day, topped up by a bottle at day's end – *uitvaltyd* – when they knocked off. This amounted to a daily intake of over two litres! Multiply this by 250 working days and the end result would be an inconceivable 500 litres per worker per year! By comparison, the French, at the height of their similar system, did not exceed 120 litres."

"How South Africans manoeuvred themselves into such a criminal situation of socioeconomic 'poisoning', can be ascribed to the following," Sperling says. "The *dop* system was an insidious system – like a forced marriage: something neither employer nor employee could get out of – and thus became a habit each new generation simply inherited." He found there was little interest among employers to uplift the living standards of farm workers at the time, and there was also an unbelievably low sense of socioeconomic responsibility. "Maybe if there had been an international market for our wines, farmers would have been forced to improve workers' quality of life and introduce social policies. On Driesprong we gradually cut down the frequency of daily *dop*s by reimbursing good work with a wage increase. Successes were sporadic."

In 1960, as recommended by the Malan Commission of Inquiry, the *dop* system was outlawed.[224] However, that was by no means the end of it in practice. In the mid-1970s the *dop* system was going strong in many districts, as noted by ALJ Venter.[225]

"Very much part of the set-up at Stillerus is the ubiquitous – and invidious – tot system, which operates on more than 80% of the farms in the Western Cape," Venter wrote in 1974.[226] Stillerus in the Clanwilliam district was owned by businessman and financier Charles Ginsberg, who farmed fruit, grapes and rooibos tea. "All male labour is provided with a third of a bottle of rough, young wine in the morning and two-thirds of a bottle in the evening. Those who do not drink receive 10 cents a day extra. The wine, known locally as vaaljapie, is cheap and is bought in barrels at about 45c a gallon. The Ginsbergs defend the system, maintaining that labourers would not work without it, even if offered cash instead." Another farmer said: "Why should I give them cash instead? They do so much more for a glass of wine that they would ever do for a shilling?"

Venter found that on average farmers gave one and a half bottles, some two and a half. Farmers justified the *dop* system by saying it was "a tradition as old as the Cape wine industry itself", and it was the labourers' "due".

"This in spite of the fact that some of the side effects of the system are alcoholism of epidemic proportions, a high assault rate and an abysmally low standard of living," writes Venter. Farmer DD Joubert went on to say: "Coloured labourers have for centuries been the greatest connoisseurs of fine wines" – a strange statement indeed, given the quality of the wine. Farmers interviewed maintained that regular tot handouts "do in fact increase production and are at the same time a form of discipline."[227] They went as far as equating the abolition of the *dop* system with Prohibition.

The *dop* system had scarily crept so deeply into accepted practice that farmers preferred not to see that there was something wrong in rewarding work with alcohol, rather than money and satisfaction. Wages were very low – Venter refers to a survey that found there were many farmers who did not pay enough.

However, there have always been farmers who chose not to use the *dop* system, paying decent wages and offering other incentives, such as better housing. Among them in the period that Venter describes was Doug Ovenstone at High Noon; another was a Mr Houston.[228] Farmer Piet Kriel paid his workers properly, and they had good benefits like free houses, medical aid and an annual bonus. Kriel also formed a rugby team.

Alcohol abuse today

Dina Beukes, who trained as a nurse, worked until recently in the Northern Cape health department. "The *dop* system is still going on," she says. "Workers would tell me they get wine every Friday, but they won't give a statement to that effect. One guy went to rehab, and when he returned the farmer told him to start drinking again, because when he doesn't drink, he complains."

Kakamas is overcrowded, with excessive drinking patterns and low literacy, says Beukes. "People drink to get drunk. But we've had some success stories. I asked one man who kept coming back to hospital why he drank. And he said, as a farm worker, he couldn't provide for his family. 'If I stay drunk I can't hear the cries and complaints of my children,' he told me." And, says Beukes, some women feed their children alcohol to stop them crying.

Lucien Luyt, who farms table grapes at De Tuin in Porterville, said when he took over the farm he decided to end the practice of giving people wine at the end of the day. "Some argue that it's okay to have a bit of wine at the end of the day, so many people do it. But I decided to stop it, and it didn't have any effect on workers. The alcohol problem is a weekend problem." Lucien took it further and decided to switch from farming wine grapes to table grapes as he believes mass production of cheap wine leads to social ills. "Cheap alcohol is bad, bad news. If I can't produce high-quality wine, I don't want to be involved in making cheap wine that ultimately goes into a *papsak* (foil bag) and becomes part of the problem, not the solution."

Lucien is chairman of the local community policing forum, which is made up of farm owners, farm workers and managers in the area. "Alcohol is still the biggest issue, it's a huge problem," he says. One of the forum's goals is to get rid of the illegal sale of alcohol. It's so easily available; owners of bottle stores supply illegal shebeens which are within walking distance of people's houses, and where they can buy on a credit basis. The bottle store even runs a shuttle service from Porterville to the farms. Hermanus Williams, a manager at De Tuin, says people drink excessively on the weekends. "There's nothing else for them to do." He helps out at the Citizens Advice Bureau in Porterville. "I try to help people stop drinking. But it depends if they want to change or not."

André Smith, a table grape producer in Groblershoop, east of Upington in the Northern Cape, says he has a zero tolerance policy on alcohol. "People are fired right away for drinking on the farm." Now people do not want to live on his farm. Gerrit Boer, a supervisor on the farm, lives in the nearby community of Wegdraai. He is active in community work, and also believes that the availability of alcohol at shebeens is the biggest problem. "I tried setting up sport programmes, but half of them arrive drunk to play soccer." He shakes his head: "You have to improve yourself; if you don't want to drink, no one can force you. If you drink, no one is to blame."

This view is echoed by Mr Venn, now retired, who worked in Devon Valley near Stellenbosch. Now 70, he did not go to school and started work when he was 14. "No one forces the alcohol down your throat, you can say no," he says.

That may not be as easy for everyone. Petrus van Wyk, a retired farm worker, says: "It is so that some people wanted the *dop* system. One white woman said she was going to stop it, and three of us agreed; the fourth one said he refused to work without wine, he was so used to the wine. I'm not saying it's so, but it is possible that because our grandfathers and fathers were part of the *dop* system, it comes through to us – through the generations."

Are genes to blame?

Van Wyk echoes an oft-repeated belief: excessive alcohol use is in the genes, drunkenness is somehow inherited, whether it is a genetic defect or a change in the genes due to generations of abuse. The idea that drunkenness is "in the blood", caused by genetic information, has some basis in science. Whether it applies to people who call themselves coloured, which is by no means a homogenous genetic group, is not known.

How different groups react to alcohol has been the subject of much speculation. History tells how indigenous people at the Cape were very keen for the arak and brandy the European settlers brought with them. Along with Jared Diamond's "guns, germs and steel" we should perhaps add alcohol, the fire spirit, as one more factor that led to the destruction of indigenous cultures. Local people's so-called propensity for alcohol abuse has been blamed for the dire circumstances their once strong cultures deteriorated into. There are sad tales told of the loss of land by Basters (people of racially mixed parentage) along the Gariep River, and elsewhere in the country no doubt, to unscrupulous white traders, who plied people with alcohol before they signed documents, not knowing what they were signing.[229]

As noted earlier in this chapter, as far as we know the San and the Khoikhoi did not know strong alcohol before the arrival of Europeans, although there is mention of the honey beer of the Namaqua. To the local people, brandy and arak would have been a novel experience. Many are the accounts of how indigenous people enjoyed the fruits of the fermentation process – and how quickly they became inebriated. Chronicler Nieuhof wrote that they were "wonderfully avid for brandy and Spanish wine, although a little suffices to make them drunk".[230] They shared this "instant drunkenness" with other indigenous people, such as Native Americans in America and Aboriginals in Australia.

Was it just that they were unused to this new substance? Those who drink regularly become habituated to alcohol, and need more and more to get inebriated. To the uninitiated, it takes little to get drunk. Or was something else at play? Among certain populations in the world are those who metabolise alcohol differently because of differences in genetic information for one of the two main enzymes.

Were the Khoikhoi and San among these people? We cannot know for sure in South Africa, as no studies have been done on genetically pure San or Khoikhoi (there are now no pure Khoikhoi left, and few San), says Professor Denis Viljoen of the Foundation for Alcohol Related Research (FARR). Eugène Marais, Afrikaans poet, writer and scientist, writing in the 1920s, noted the destructive nature of alcohol among the Khoisan, Griquas and Korannas, whom he referred to as the "yellow races". He wrote: "There was the same utter want of restraint in consuming the fiery liquids they purchased so recklessly and paid for so dearly . . . The race has almost disappeared . . . and I do not think that any South African historian of the future will hesitate to ascribe this rapid decline not so much to hostile invasions and conquests of white and black foes as to the destructive effects of alcohol."[231]

Alcohol, when broken down in the body to acetaldehyde, is highly toxic and the body must get rid of it through the bloodstream. This is done via a complex pathway using enzymes, which converts the alcohol into acetaldehyde, then acetate and then CO_2 and water.[232] There are two main enzymes needed to process alcohol, each of which has many forms, encoded by different genes. The enzymes also have different kinetic properties which account for the variation among individuals in how quickly alcohol is eliminated from the body.

Among ethnic groups there are genetic differences in these enzymes. In some groups there is a facial flush reaction, nausea and rapid heartbeat, making drinking unpleasant. One, for example, is common in Chinese, Japanese and Koreans and rare in Europeans and Africans; another is found in 15 to 25 % of Afro-Americans. These are both protective, as the alcohol is metabolised very fast and drinking is unpleasant. There are also some groups with a gene that results in a slow metabolising enzyme.

The various effects of alcohol relate to the concentration of ethanol, or its metabolic products, in the tissue. Acetaldehyde quickly forms free radical structures which are highly toxic if not quenched by antioxidants such as Vitamin C and Vitamin B1. These toxins probably cause some of the ill effects of hangovers; the free radicals can result in damage to the embryo in the case of pregnant women and can lead to severe birth defects.

Heavy drinking clearly has serious effects on the body; but what role genes play in causing someone to drink heavily is the question. Some researchers say that because of metabolic differences and differences in sensitivity, some populations have a genetic predisposition to alcohol abuse and alcoholism. However, addiction is clearly not linked in a straightforward way with genetics, but is a result of a complex interplay of many factors.

A question, says Professor Denis Viljoen, is why human beings have genetic information for enzymes to metabolise alcohol. "Why do humans have the ALDH gene there at all? Is it to process the 3g of ethanol the gut produces a day through fermentation of its contents?" If the body had no mechanism for catabolising the alcohols, they would build up in the body and become toxic. "Alcohol has been around for along time, it developed in primitive forms. There's even an ALDH gene in the worm," he says.

Factors other than genetic in alcohol tolerance also come into play, one being body size and mass. The indigenous Khoikhoi and San were very small people, unused to alcohol, and therefore they had no tolerance. And we do not know their nutritional status, says Viljoen. "Nutritional deficiencies of minerals may play a part in catalytic enzymes."

Sensitivity to alcohol, heavy drinking, alcohol abuse and alcoholism are different things. Why does one population that lacks the enzyme drink less, and another that lacks the same enzyme, drink more? According to Viljoen, "slow metabolisers are found mostly in Asian populations – 25% of people in Japan and Korea. They flush, sweat or vomit when they drink, and that tempers how much they drink. We don't have the Eastern groups' genetic intolerance here, our population is so mixed."

While metabolic differences and variations in sensitivity to alcohol have been found among ethnic and cultural groups, these group differences have not been found to predict alcohol misuse. Psychologist Stanton Peele, who has done extensive work in the field of alcohol addiction, writes:

> The most striking case of divergent cultural patterns of drinking in the face of prominent racial reactions to alcohol is the pattern established by the Chinese and Japanese Americans on the one hand, and the Eskimo and American Indian groups on the other. Drinking in these groups is marked by a distinctive facial reddening and accelerated heart beat, blood pressure and other circulatory system measures, as well as by acetaldehyde and other alcohol metabolism abnormalities. However, the Chinese and Japanese Americans have the lowest alcoholism rates of all American cultural groups, and the Eskimos and American Indians have the highest such rates.[233]

Additionally, despite the fact that more Native American people die of alcohol-related causes than do any other ethnic group in the United States, research shows that there are no differences in the rates of alcohol metabolism and enzyme patterns between Native Americans and whites.[234]

Perceptions of drunkenness and alcoholism

Through the years drunkenness has been viewed in different ways, often with a strong ideological and cultural bias. A former editor of the *SA Medical Journal*, AP Blignaut, writing in 1968, said:

> . . . there are radical differences in the cultural drinking practices of people and nations in regard to the degree of their pathological drinking. In general . . . the Swedes, the Finns, Irish Americans (though not the Irish in Ireland), the Northern French, Swiss, Poles and North Russians and the Cape Coloured people fall into the high-risk category. In these groups excessive drinking and even intoxication in public are socially acceptable. It does not matter what the man's social position is – to drink to excess is regarded as a sign of virility and drunkenness tolerated as being entertaining, amusing and even dashing. On the other hand there is the so-called low risk group – Italians, Greeks, Chinese, Southern French, Southern Spaniards, South Russians . . . and, let's hope . . .

> White South Africans. Amongst these people intoxication is not socially acceptable. Drunkenness is traditionally frowned upon as being something which one is ashamed of – a boorish, brutish and disgusting state . . .[235]

Quite astounding, really, and one wonders on what the doctor based his findings.

Historian Tracey Randle, who as part of her research into wine tourism went through back copies of *Wynboer*, a magazine for farmers,[236] says that in 1948 drunkenness was seen as a psychological disorder, most prevalent amongst those people "of nervous inheritance or temperament". There were another three "classes" into which the causes of drunkenness could be divided: ignorance, economic conditions and fashion. "Only certain sections of the 'Cape Coloured Population' were seen to be the 'drunkards' of society," she writes. Furthermore, "it was especially those 'Skolly Types' consisting of the habitual loafers, drunkards, dagga-smokers, and ex-convicts . . . who were 'so apt unduly to colour European opinion regarding the whole coloured population'."

Alcoholism as a disease, separate from drunkenness, appeared on the social stage by 1952. The alcoholic was not merely confined to the "lower social strata", but rather had a disease that could affect the "inner maladjustment" of the upper classes as well.

Today alcoholism is seen more as a disorder of behaviour – while genetics may influence a person's reaction to alcohol, it does not cause him or her to drink without control. The social and individual controls which keep people from drinking to excess are now considered the most important factors. Values, expectations and social setting have a strong influence in encouraging or discouraging excessive drinking.

Over centuries alcohol became established as a way of life on farms in South Africa; it was offered as an incentive to work, and was the only form of socialising for many a labourer. Today, when Dopstop comes with its message of "drink less", people say "then what must we do?" "Drinking is what you do, during the week while you work, and at weekends. It's drinking to get drunk, for whatever reason; it's the only form of socialising, to forget. It's what you do," says Leonora Safoor.

Research has shown that social categories are important predictors of drinking problems and alcoholism. For example, in one study of Boston ethnics, Irish Americans were found to be seven times as likely to become alcoholics over a 40-year period as Italian Americans living in the same neighborhoods. "Research uniformly finds alcoholism to be 3 to 10 times as prevalent among men as among women. Even researchers with a biological orientation acknowledge that group differences of such magnitude cannot be explained by genetic factors; certainly no such genes have been identified," says psychologist and researcher Stanton Peele.[237]

No doubt alcohol played only a small part in what happened to the Khoisan – loss of land, superior weapons and diseases, smallpox in particular, coupled with assimilation and starvation, contributed to the destruction of the Khoikhoi and San cultures. But whatever might have caused their propensity for drunkenness, the consequences were dire for them.

The missionaries tried their best to keep alcohol away from people: Pniel and most mission stations were "dry" for many years. In the Northern Cape, the assistant magistrate for the Northern Border, John H Scott, warned of dire consequences should the liquor trade be allowed: "The Bastards at present are a very sober race but if once liquor should obtain a hold on them, the result will be that a very worthy class of people will be utterly ruined . . ."[238] British Bechuanaland Proclamation 113 of 1891 extended a ban on the sale of alcohol to "natives" to include "persons of mixed race in Gordonia" with the specific intent, as the magistrate wrote, of preventing them from being "relieved of their farms". But despite their best attempts, alcohol could not be kept away. A hotel was opened in Upington itself in March 1892, and was soon alleged to be illegally selling liquor to "natives and bastards". By 1893 there were two liquor stores. In 1910 the magistrate at Upington reported that, while "several persons of the older generations" of Basters were "still living on their own land, the younger generation have not followed in the footsteps of their fathers and have much degenerated. The main cause has been probably the introduction of liquor. The great majority of farms formerly held by them has passed as the price for their downfall into the hands of Europeans."[239]

Foetal Alcohol Syndrome – "migrating poverty into the future"

One of the most debilitating effects of alcohol abuse is on the unborn child. Foetal Alcohol Syndrome (FAS) can cause severe defects in a child whose mother drinks during pregnancy. New findings show that damage may go further than the gross physical and intellectual disabilities, and Foetal Alcohol Spectrum Disorder describes lesser, but still alcohol-related, birth defects that affect mostly the brain and nervous system.

Denis Viljoen is the former head of Paediatrics and Genetics at Wits

University, and now head of Genred – the Centre for Human Genetics Research and Education at the University of Stellenbosch. He is also a founder member as well as chairperson and CEO of the Foundation for Alcohol Related Research (FARR).

While it seems obvious to link the *dop* system and FAS, the research shows a weak link, says Viljoen, with only 3% of women having children with FAS exposed to the *dop* system.

"The *dop* system may have led to the legacy of social drinking, with the concomitant binge drinking, where women learned to drink, and drink more frequently," says Viljoen. "So while there's no absolute direct link, it's not to say there's no connection."

"Unfortunately, FAS is a coloured problem, only because the risk factors for FAS (such as smoking and low body weight) are found in the coloured population. Add rural conditions, and concomitant poverty, and you'll find the highest incidence in the Northern Cape, in an area where there are no wine farms."

"It's linked to socioeconomic conditions," explains Leana Olivier, national manager of FARR. "These women are poorer, and they typically drink with a group of four to five women in a party on the weekend in a '*gooi*'. They put their money together and buy as much as they can afford, usually beer (70%) in the cheapest and most concentrated form, for example Black Label in a quart bottle. One bottle gets passed around. That's the more rural scenario."

It does not take much to be a heavy drinker in pregnancy: heavy binge drinking during pregnancy means two drinks a day. (In general, heavy drinking is considered to be five to six drinks per occasion). "One drink in our terms is 15 ml alcohol, about 150 ml wine."

However, according to Olivier, "even heavy-drinking women can produce a child which functions normally; it depends on genetic make-up. There are rapid metabolisers of alcohol, and slow metabolisers. We did a study in the Western Cape and rapid metabolisers were more protected from having a FAS kid than those with slower metabolism."

Alcohol consumption is just one risk factor for FAS: others are nutritional status, smoking, other drug abuse, education levels and the size of the woman. Alcohol will have a different effect when you weigh 40 kg than when you weigh 80 kg. "The Native Americans drink twice as much alcohol in volume in a month, and have two to ten times less FAS," says Viljoen. The second most important person, after the mother, in FAS is the woman's mother or partner who drinks.

"In the main, 60% of women who are drinking put their children at risk," says Olivier.

One area of concern for Viljoen and Olivier is that there are many children being diagnosed with FAS that are in fact not FAS. "FAS is a subtle diagnosis and it must be diagnosed clinically. The danger of misdiagnosis is stigmatisation – and when teachers and nurses are not trained to do so, there are high levels of overdiagnosis. Children with Khoisan or Asian features are often misdiagnosed, which leads to stigmatisation. There are many charlatans in the industry; scientifically, the rates of FAS in South Africa are between 40 and 120 in 1 000." These are the highest in the world.

Viljoen was instrumental in getting a large-scale FAS study done in Wellington in 1996, the first in South Africa. "I went to the United States in 1996 to try to raise funding for research here," says Viljoen. "When doing clinics at Red Cross Children's Hospital I was seeing one in ten children with FAS; one in four children in children's homes had FAS."

To make a diagnosis of FAS one needs a detailed history. "The first factor is binge drinking. It is poverty related. In De Aar there are 100 shebeens for 29 500 people and unemployment is at 80%. But that doesn't mean it's not as bad in many other towns."

Binge drinking is also linked to the "Allpay grant" (social grant), paid each month to unemployed mothers.

The best age to diagnose FAS is from three to ten years – by three the face is properly formed. Clinical observation must be confirmed by maternal history and a neurodevelopmental assessment. "It's easier to label than diagnose; we must make sure there's proper diagnosis. We need a prevalence study to be done in the country." To date that has been done in only three provinces, the Northern Cape, Western Cape and Gauteng.

"Without figures we don't know how to plan health services," says Olivier. "The second thing is identifying risk factors, and whether they are the same in all centres, so we can tailor our programmes."

Research now also needs to focus on the countrywide prevalence of FASD – Foetal Alcohol Spectrum Disorder. Then there is Alcohol-related Neurodevelopmental Disorder, which has few physical signs, but children have behaviour problems and a poor concentration span, poor maths abilities and poor grammar skills. Research using a Functional MRI shows that these children's brain circuits are not wired the same way as in a normal child. "Apoptosis, programmed cell death, is speeded up with exposure to alcohol and whole areas of the brain are denuded. Ninety percent of problems are in the central nervous system," says Viljoen. "The problems depend on when the mother drank: organs are affected in the first trimester; the rest of pregnancy is for maturation, for brain cells."

Basic research now being done is on alcohol-genetic studies. "We understand that some groupings are more at risk than others. The wheel of misfortune is working here. The risk for some alcohol disorders is the same as the risk for HIV, TB, nutritional deficiencies and compromised immunity. They speed each other up. But if we can influence one, we can slow the wheel."

"Importantly, we can prevent the next baby from being FAS," says Olivier. "So many mothers say, 'I didn't know'."

In the United States, the average age for a woman to have a child with FAS is 33 years; in South Africa it is 27 years, and it is usually the third child. Why is this? Firstly, younger women are generally drinking in a healthy body, and drinking less.

"You habituate to alcohol as you go on; as you drink for longer, nutrition falls off; rands are contributed to alcohol rather than food, and it reaches a critical point," says Olivier.

Like those of Dopstop, FARR's programmes are aimed at uplifting people. "FAS occurs mostly in very poor communities, where people are poorly educated and living on social grants; mothers are depressed, they live in awful circumstances and there's no recreation other than to drink."

There are still *papsakke*, and very cheap wine is made available illicitly.

"Our problem is that there is little research money," says Viljoen. "R500 million will be spent on sports sponsorship, R1,5 million on research. Something is out of balance. But of course those who sell the alcohol do not want to be part of the solution – it would be admitting they're part of the problem."

Taking responsibility for the effects of the products you sell is an area of debate, complicated by the fact that more tax rands are earned through alcohol sales than from the mining sector. Sobering.

The *dop* system, paying wine in lieu of wages, is not confined to South Africa, neither is heavy drinking unique to farm workers. Social problems caused by alcohol abuse are widespread throughout society. There is no available research on the social impact of the demise of the *dop* system, although in 1998 the Medical Research Council estimated alcohol dependence at 31% in the Western Cape region, 10% higher than the national average.[240] A Human Sciences Research Council household survey in 2005 reported higher levels of hazardous and harmful alcohol use in rural areas of the Western Cape (21%) relative to urban informal areas (17%) and urban formal areas (12%). A similar pattern emerged when binge drinking was examined. Rural formal areas had higher levels of binge drinking (20%) relative to urban informal areas (16%) and urban formal areas (15%).[241]

The legacy of the *dop* system, alcohol abuse and its social problems, continues.

CHAPTER 8

The consumer is queen – the story of table grapes

It is often the small things that make the difference for farm workers. At "7de Laan", a small community between Kakamas and Keimoes in the Northern Cape, lives a group of women who prefer not to give their names. The farmer they work for lives in De Doorns, and they do seasonal work. It is August and the pruning has just been done.

"This farmer is very strict, you have to have a doctor's certificate for staying away one day. If your children are sick, it breaks your heart; you can't afford to go to the doctor, and you can't stay at home with your child."

One woman tells how she and her sick child were dropped in Kakamas, but there was no transport home. On wages of R65 a day, paying for transport is difficult. Eleven people, mostly women and children, live in the two-roomed house, made of corrugated iron.

The problem, says one woman, is the older people: "No one cares when you get old – there's no work, no pension. And there are no clinics here."

7de Laan is one of many small settlements that house the people who have been evicted from farms. These are the invisible people, who have difficulty accessing the rights they have in law.

With casualisation of labour, there are more women in agriculture than ever before, says Fatima Shabodien, CEO of Women on Farms. Women are the primary breadwinners, and while that may be celebrated from a feminist point of view, it does not mean their domestic and reproductive functions become less. "If you're sick, or your child is sick, you choose between a day's wage and the cost to get there, or going to clinic," says Shabodien.

The women tell us about the wine they drink, and show an empty bottle marked *"Baie Sterk"* ("Very strong"). It is made by the Orange River Cellars, in a 750-ml plastic bottle, and costs about R12. This is *"salie halie"*, the highly sedimented wine left behind after winemaking. The name is a contraction of *"jy sal nie by die huis kom, jy sal nie die huis haal nie"* (you won't make it to the house after you drink it). As they are talking about their health concerns, the proximity of the houses to the vineyards becomes apparent. What happens at pesticide-spraying time?

Undue burden – pesticide poisons

If you live anywhere near vineyards, the smell of pesticides lies heavy in the air around spraying time. Travelling through towns like Riebeek-Kasteel, you will need to close your window. Often vineyards are sprayed by a person without protective clothing, pesticide billowing out behind him.

Pesticides, however, do not only go where they are needed, and pesticide drift is one of the hazards of vine spraying. Those living close by vineyards are no doubt affected, says Professor Leslie London of the School of Public Health and Primary Health Care at the University of Cape Town. "It is particularly problematic for children, who spend a lot of time on the ground where pesticide residues might collect," he says.

It is also an issue of great concern to Women on Farms. "Pesticides have a cyclical use, so we know they're linked to complaints of respiratory and skin problems. Big unknowns are the effects on reproduction and children, and their role in contributing to Foetal Alcohol Syndrome," says Shabodien. "Houses are next to vineyards, there are few protective measures and we see a pesticide layer on windowsills."

She explains that the problems are often around storage. "And women can't tell us the name of pesticides as it's decanted into containers. Even literate workers can't access instructions."

"Pesticide drift" takes place over many kilometres. But, as London points out, exposure to such toxins may not have an acute or immediate effect; the effects can accumulate over many years.

Pesticide exposure is a significant hazard for South African farm workers, particularly in the fruit industry. Grapes require high doses of pesticides, one of the highest sectors, second only to pears and apples. While it is easier to keep track of accidental poisonings due to poor handling of pesticides (thought to be under-reported), tracking the long-term effects of pesticide exposure is more difficult. Workers are also exposed to chemical residues on leaves and fruit, and people most at risk are those who mix and apply pesticides. There is also domestic contamination of drinking water, with contaminated containers being reused.

Use of protective equipment is low, as is the level of training in using pesticides. "The Department of Labour is responsible for occupational health and safety," says London, "but usually doesn't get to farms because of distance, dispersion, etc., until there is a fatality. Many farms are part of fair trade or export-linked labour standards, which helps, but does not substitute for proper oversight."

Widespread alcohol dependence and abuse has resulted in myriad poor health indicators among farm workers.[242] Add pesticide exposure to alcohol use, and there is potentially a serious effect on health. London writes in a 2003 paper that high levels of alcohol consumption may predispose workers to occupational injury and increase the risks of the acute and chronic effects of pesticide poisoning. "Physiological impacts on the liver and on metabolic processes may potentially increase toxicity of pesticides and their breakdown products," he says.

London describes pesticide poisoning as a spider's web – a complex of intertwined actors, interests and agencies, at the centre of which is located the event of pesticide poisoning.[243] Workers are often blamed for accidents, but what needs to happen is to shift the responsibility from the end-user – the worker – to employers, public officers and health professionals.

Research done in 1998 in the Western Cape by London and others shows that workers are well aware of the effects of pesticides.[244] In interviews with farm workers, researchers were told by one worker: "(It) makes you so terribly nauseous, immediately you have heartburn." But it is difficult to challenge a farmer: "A lot of things are not right, which I do not like, but a person cannot really talk – if you talk then all hell breaks loose," said a worker. Another said: "Your contract states . . . that you may not refuse . . . any work."

Researchers were told: "We feel that we also want to provide insight into the spray or in the farming . . . the problem that we sit with is that if we come with an alternative, a better suggestion, it is not accepted."

The law stipulates that protective clothing must be available and that clothing must be washed by the employer, says Shabodien. "But people come home with it and it's all washed together. If you're a permanent worker, you will be given clothing; if a casual, you have to buy it. Once more, if it's a choice between food for your children or protective clothing, there's not much choice. People also say, our mothers and fathers were okay. But pesticides have become more poisonous over the years."

When pesticides were first introduced 50 years ago, it was in small quantities and sprayed by hand. Today aerial spraying and tractor-driven sprayers spread pesticides over a large area.

And the chemicals have changed. The organophosphate pesticides now being used are derived from nerve poisons that were developed originally as nerve gases for use in chemical warfare.[245]

Another issue raised by London is that toxicity of pesticides considered safe in northern Europe do not take into account factors that may increase toxicity here. "The current legislative framework in South Africa is poorly geared to ensuring safety of end-users – namely farmers, farm workers and their families. Chemical companies can continue to do good business in SA without having to worry about impacts on end-users. Not surprisingly, a large number of pesticides banned or severely restricted in developed countries, such as paraquat, adicarb, methyl parathion continue to be registered for agricultural use in South Africa." [246]

The fruit industry has been at the forefront of Integrated Pest Management (IPM) development in South Africa. "However, given an IPM focus driven by market preferences, this has led to a focus on environmental impacts without necessarily placing worker health at the forefront of its agenda."

Shabodien says the system needs to change: "We don't want to see land reform reproducing the existing agricultural system. We don't want to get land back if it's dead land. Our women's co-ops' crops focus on organic crops. It's not a case of replacing white farmers with black farmers – race should not be the end point. We're focusing on convincing farmers about alternatives. There is a spectrum of pesticides to use, some are less harmful."

Health impacts on vineyard workers

A study published in 2001 suggests that those exposed to pesticides in grape production suffer a higher incidence of allergic rhinitis, respiratory problems, cancers, and chromosomal and nuclear abnormalities, as well as lower neurological capacities. The study was done by psychologists on 528 vineyard workers employed in Bordeaux in France.[247]

Compounding the problem of pesticide exposure is that of pesticide residue. Grapes are among the most contaminated food products on sale in the European Union (EU), a study found, and receive a higher dose of synthetic pesticides than almost any other crop.[248] Pesticide Action Network Europe analysed 40 different wines purchased inside the EU and found that 100% of conventional wines (34) sampled contained pesticides, with one bottle containing ten different pesticides. On average, each wine sample contained over four pesticides. The 24 different pesticide contaminants included five classified by the EU as being carcinogenic, mutagenic, reprotoxic or endocrine-disrupting.

The health of farm workers is a serious concern. Farm workers are vulnerable to an undue burden of health problems, says London, and TB incidence in rural farming areas is two to three times higher than urban rates. Childhood stunting among farming communities is 30%, twice as high as the national averages for urban children.[249] (These figures are from the mid-1990s).

"And HIV/Aids is a time-bomb about to explode," says Shabodien. "An MRC (Medical Research Council) study a few years ago showed it was lower in the Western Cape than the national average, but this was among relatively settled communities. The reality is that casualisation has opened that up."

Table grape farming

Table grapes are a completely different story to that of wine, with a much more recent history. The consumer is queen in a globalised world where choice is wide. And with table grapes, an increasingly educated and informed consumer not only knows what she wants in a grape, but is also concerned about the conditions under which it is grown. Because of the small local market in South Africa, 90% of table grapes are exported.

Table grape farming is a scientific business: the product that ripens on the vine must be perfect in appearance, and it must taste good. That requires careful preparation long before the harvest, as well as careful harvesting and packaging. Labour requirements are huge.

It can take up to five years for vines to become fully productive, so choosing the cultivar to plant for the market he or she is serving is one of the most difficult decisions for a table grape producer. New cultivars are the lifeblood of the table grape industry, says Pieter Raath, a table grape expert at the University of Stellenbosch. "We have to keep up with locally developed and foreign cultivars that are seedless, resistant to berry crack, have low labour inputs, good cold storage capabilities and characteristics like good Muscat flavour, colour and taste. Seeded varieties shouldn't still be in the ground, word out there is that people are not interested. But they are hardier," he says.

There are five different groups into which table grape cultivars are divided: white, red and black seedless, and white and black seeded. As consumer taste shifts, producers must adjust accordingly. Facilitating this choice is the large number of cultivars available to farmers, or producers, as they apparently prefer to be called. No longer can the guy who grew up on a farm just grow grapes, emphasises Raath: "It has become a scientific, professional business to produce table grapes economically. A producer must be scientist, businessman, manager, know labour law, and so on."

Grapes must look good and taste good. Seedless is fashionable in the United Kingdom (UK); in Europe consumers do not mind seeded grapes, neither do they in the East, where they prefer large black grapes. The challenge is for exporters to have grapes on the table all year round. Exporters must provide white, red, black grapes over as many days a year as they can, and at expected volumes. Grapes are non-climateric fruit – they do not ripen further once picked, and so cannot be stored for too long.

"Exporters have three weeks from the picking to the vessel; one to two weeks on the water, and one week to the destination, for example a supermarket, and then they (the grapes) must last another two weeks," says Raath. If they are the right variety and quality of table grape, they can be stored for 12 to 14 weeks.

De Tuin – exporting quality, empowering people

Labour on table grape farms is intensive – a bunch of table grapes is handled 28 times before it gets to the consumer, and at every stage great care must be taken. Table grapes require 30 to 40 times more labour than wine grapes, and so quality labour is critical. With labour costs high, productivity and skills are essential.

From the moment the grapes are picked off the vine, they start deteriorating. Unlike wine grapes, where it does not matter what they look like, table grapes will sell on appearance first. And of course taste. But South African grapes, because of growing conditions, naturally have a good taste.

The real work with table grapes starts months before the harvest. Each bunch is trimmed and cosseted through its various stages as it is prepared for the largely international market. It must be the right size, the right shape; the berries must be spaced so as to be neither too close nor too far apart. This work is done mostly by the women who watch over the grapes from when the berries set to the harvest. This is far from unskilled work.

Sylvia Erasmus is a supervisor on the farm De Tuin near Porterville, which is today owned by Lucien Luyt.

For 15 years she has worked in the vineyards and packing houses on the farm as a contract worker. When she first came here in 1970 to marry her husband, who lived on De Tuin, she did housework.

When Louis Luyt and Jan Boland Coetzee bought the farm in 1994, she was identified as possibly being a good supervisor, and she agreed to move into the vineyards. Since then she has had extensive training, and believes she works very well with people.

Sylvia prefers to work on a contract basis, which works out at about six months of work a year, as she is now 53 and has been a diabetic for 10 years. "My children say ma, you must retire now and stay at home. But I love the work," she tells me.

One appreciates just how physically challenging it is when taken around the vineyards. Hermanus Williams is the production manager, and has seven teams working for him, six made up of women, one of men. In late November and at 8am the temperature is already 29 °C. The season is late, with late rains in winter, which means a late harvest. Teams of women patiently cut out the small grapes from each bunch, and remove leaves, so that the grapes can have air, light and warmth. Stray branches are tied back; each bunch is trimmed to size. Each vine must have a certain number of bunches, depending on the cultivar.

One team of men chops the long branches off. It is tiring work, constantly reaching upwards. The pressure is on the team leader to get his or her team to work; the team works on incentives, a bonus to keep people on track.

From 7am to 6pm the women attend to the vines. From now until harvest it is a stressful time, as the weather changes daily. First the black seedless grapes will come in.

Being a supervisor, says Sylvia, requires having the right attitude to your team, and it helps that as supervisor you choose new people when a vacancy arises. The rest of the team remains constant from year to year. "You must understand your people," says Sylvia. "The new ones must also be given a chance to fit in, to learn to work as fast as the others, and the rest of the team must help them at first. We have goals for the day – 26 vines must be cut. But it's all about the team, not the individual."

Sylvia has her daughter Georgina Isaacs and granddaughter Sunet Isaacs in her team, which is a challenge for her. "They say, 'you always make an example of us'. But I can't show them any favours."

It is physically demanding work, and whatever can be done to make the work easier, is done. Little benches to stand on mean the women do not have to reach up all the time; water is on hand to cool them down – with summer temperatures in the high 30s and early 40s, a day in the vineyard is a long, hot one.

Sylvia left school in Standard 4 to look after a child on a farm; "*Ek was so spyt*" (I regretted that so much), she says. But hers is not an unusual story for children on farms in the past, who seldom finished primary school, let alone high school. Their labour was needed in the vineyards, and their income was needed by the family to survive.

"There are lots of advantages at this farm. They help with burials; there's a savings scheme, which they take off your wages every week; there's a lorry that takes workers to Paarl to do Christmas shopping. And we have every Friday afternoon off, unless there's a crisis. There's transport to the doctor if needed, they don't charge for that, and every Tuesday the truck takes some people to town to collect government grants, the 'Allpay'. And once work on the De Tuin vineyards is finished, workers have the option to help out on other farms."

Lucien Luyt's farm has an enviable reputation: there is a less than 5% casual-labour turnover. Not that he does not have Monday absenteeism at peak labour time – harvesting – when it is so crucial. But there is a reason so many workers return year after year. It may seem self-evident that if you treat your workers well, you will see the returns in production, but it is not obvious to all: some farmers claim it is a waste of time training labourers, as they are not "worth it".

Lucien is not from farming stock; in fact, he grew up in Johannesburg and studied marketing at Wits. When he came to De Tuin in the 1990s after deregulation of the table grape industry, it was to see what could be done with the farm which belonged to his family. He brought his "modern" ideas with him.

There is a weekly production meeting, for planning and feedback. There is also a workers' forum, which is democratically elected. Every person gets to plot their career path.

Leon Nel is manager of the farm, and has worked 11 years in table grapes. This is his third production year here. "This is a hard industry," he says. "There are no shortcuts with table grapes. Production is six times more expensive than wine grapes, and there's not a lot of room for error."

"We go out of our way for our people"

Hermanus Williams did not start out doing farm work – for seven years he worked as a painter and construction worker. He started working at De Tuin, and when the senior manager on the farm retired, he was sent on some courses. Training is important at De Tuin. "I don't think I'll move away. In this valley you'll see that on courses that cost R5 000, there will be three from this farm, one from the other," he says.

"Every day we must go to every block and we must pick the leaves off. This wind affects the vineyards, and we must refasten the vines when it blows them loose," Hermanus tells me. Occupational hazards are snakes, which come looking for water, and birds. The target for the day, working between two posts, is five vines, 80 bunches on one side, 80 on another. At harvest time another 20 people are required. The women move into the pack shed; the men harvest the grapes.

"People like our culture here. We provide services, we go out of our way for our people. People know there is an opportunity here to become permanent," says Hermanus.

"The most important aspect of my job is that I can work with people. I know my people, most of them like me, and it takes a while to get to this point. I am strict, but only when needed." The labour complement on De Tuin is 40 permanent workers, 150 seasonal. People vary in age from 22 to 59. At 55 they get softer jobs.

Martiens Janse is the new vines manager at De Tuin.

"I was born on this farm, grew up here and have lived here for 27 years. I finished school in 1999, but there was no money for college and university, so I came to work on the farm for pocket money. Mr Luyt called me to the office and said there was an opportunity to be a tractor operator, would I take the job? I was then head of the chemical store, and last year became a manager.

"I'm responsible for all new vines, and have three men working for me. It takes three days to spray 30 ha. We do plant preparation, and give them attention as they grow up. You can lose a year if you don't give a young vine attention."

Martiens studied 15 modules at Elsenburg, three a month, including how to grow vines, manipulate them, and manage weeds.

Farm work was not his first choice: "Every child has a dream, mine was to be an electrician, an auto electrician, but I didn't have that opportunity. I had to choose a road – I could have stayed at home and done nothing with my life, or taken what was offered. My mother worked on the farm, my father left us when I was seven years old. It broke my heart," he says.

"I grew up on a farm and saw things being done which I didn't understand. Now I know why they're done, and I love it. My love for this farm is that I have the opportunity to make something of my life. I can also be the farm manager here."

His mentor when he needs advice is Oom Paul van Wyk, now retired.

"He's very wise," says Martiens. Oom Paul, now 64, grew up in Grassy Park in Cape Town. "I worked for the *'Slams* (Muslims), but they didn't give me Sunday off. So I came to the farm." He looks around at the packing shed, and the new Vizier production system: "I built this *stoor* (shed)," he says. He is not that impressed with the new machine: "Machines are fine, but there must still be people around. I've trained men and women to harvest, to pack. When I came here, there were no vineyards, just *groente* (vegetables). Later, the vineyards were changed from wine grapes to table grapes.

"*In daai tyd kry ek R15* (those days I got R15)," he chuckles. But food was not expensive then, he says. He retired when he was 55. "*Dit was lekker gewees*," he says of his life, "*ek kan nie kla nie*." (It has been nice, I can't complain.) All his children were born on the farm and still work on the farm.

Raising literacy levels

Elmien Swartz, 35, is De Tuin's office administrator, and her enthusiasm and energy spill over when you chat to her. Elmien was born in Porterville, grew up there and still lives there.

"I finished Standard 8, fell pregnant, and after I had the baby came to work here, at 18, as a seasonal worker."

But Elmien had plans for her life, and in 2000 she finished matric. In 2004 she bought a computer, which she taught herself to use, so she could teach her children. For 15 years she worked as a supervisor on De Tuin. "I was the first to become a female supervisor. Before, it was always men."

In 2005 she did a two-year Adult Basic Education Training (ABET) course at a technikon in Cape Town, and has a diploma to train people in basic literacy. In 2008 she was offered the administration job. Now she does the administration, keeps records, service controls, payslips. While she enjoys it, she says, "I miss the people. When I was the supervisor, I bonded with people. Now I'm inside.

"The choice here (at De Tuin) is whether you want to grow with the farm, or not. At this stage I will stay here. But I'm keen to study, I want to be an advocate," she laughs.

Basic literacy on farms is low, with more than 40% of workers on grape farms reaching only Grade 4 or less.[250] Elmien's willingness to give of her time has made a huge difference in Sara Esau's life. Sara, a worker in her 60s, could not read or write before she started the ABET course. "I wanted to learn very much – at the shop you don't know if you're getting the right change. You send money along, you don't know if you're being cheated. And I want to see my payslip, I want to see the slip at the supermarket," she says.

Humanity, respect and opportunity

The farm needs to compete on a competitive international market. To do that it needs everyone to participate in making it a success. "We may not be the best paying, but we must be productive, and people are very positive about goal setting," says Lucien Luyt. "It's a privilege, and enjoyable, to see what's being achieved. Once you get into a positive cycle, it becomes a positive snowball."

His approach is not upliftment, but empowerment.

"People are mentored; they're appraised, but also knocked down. We won't carry people too long. As an organisation and as individuals we know where we want to go. There are clear lines of communication and responsibility. Everyone understands what's expected. Everyone has a proper contract and job description, and an evaluation four times a year. For those who want to advance, there must be opportunity.

"An independent company is involved in development of staff. That's so important to me. You have to develop human capital. In-house mentorship is also important.

"From 23 ha to 43 ha in three years – that's intense expansion. We will now stop expansion on table grapes, and look at the cattle leg."

Lucien, who was trained in the vibrant world of commerce, says he never wanted to farm. He was used to, and loved, the fast-paced commercial world of Johannesburg, and still does. "I didn't think I'd be here long, my wife worked with hearing-impaired kids and needed to be close to a city." But he built a house, they had children and they enjoyed it so much, they stayed. "It took a while to get used to the Boland and its stone-age attitudes. I wanted to change everything," he says. But he has realised that it takes generations to change entrenched thinking and ways of being. The table grape industry has progressed somewhat, believes Lucien, but racism is still a huge factor, undermining people on a daily basis.

"So this is where I am, and I will try to have a positive effect on people around me." His work philosophy has three basics: connect with people's humanity; show respect and give opportunity.

Lucien is not "*baas*" (boss) to anyone. When he first arrived, people warned him he would not be shown respect for this. That has not happened. "I'm disciplined, and no one has shown me disrespect."

Lucien says he has done nothing major at De Tuin, except create opportunity. "And not everyone can take it. Some have bought in, others not. The practical implication of this is that people started trusting me. I was consistent. We have very few disciplinary hearings."

Harvest

It is February 2009, and nearing the end of harvest time at De Tuin. The crates of just-picked grapes come into the packing shed through the pre-cooling section, which is water cooled. The grapes stand here until they reach 22 to 25 °C before going into the packing area.

It is a long day at packing time – people work from 7am to 6pm in season.

This is Lucien's first season using the Vizier, a machine whose main advantage is to reduce the number of times the grapes are handled. The grapes are packed out bunch by bunch by the women first in the production line, who do a spot check of the bunches, snipping out any bruised or broken ones. The pack shed is noisy with the sound of the machines and loud music.

Bunches of grapes move along the conveyor belt to be weighed, and a computer assigns each to a certain packer. Lights flash on if that bunch is for her box – in this way each box will have the exact weight of grapes required. Once a box is full, the quality controllers check that the grapes meet the specifications. At the end of the line a sheet saturated with sulphur dioxide is placed on top of the full box of grapes, to kill bacteria, and it is closed and loaded onto a pallet.

An inspector from the Perishable Products Export Control Board visits three times a day to check on quality. The pallets are then loaded onto a cold truck and sent to a cooling facility in Paarl. Here they stay in cold storage for 72 hours, where their temperature is reduced to minus 0,5 degrees, and then they are shipped off in containers.

The speed with which grapes move through the pack house is important, and can make or break a season. Packing is hands-on, skilled work. One squashed piece of fruit, and the box will spoil.

Most producers say they have huge problems with getting labour: people cannot or do not want to work. How do producers meet the challenge? Lucien, although he has more success than many with seasonal labour, still faces Monday morning absenteeism. "Twenty percent don't arrive on a Monday," he says, "10% on a Tuesday. But 20% of people are new, we don't have control over them, they're only here for payday. People living day to day work as they want to.

"The work ethic is lacking – generally – in South Africa and the message is not coming down from leadership. Unions fight for rights, and that's great, but people are bad employees. In the long term the cultural work ethic has to come from home and school." He brightens up and, ever the optimist, he says: "But remember, 80% do pitch up."

The demographics of farm labour are changing, and will continue to change.

"We brought a black team in this year to supplement our labour. We fetch people from Khayelitsha or Wellington and we'll build up the team over time. This is the first time we've used the hostel on the farm," he says.

Changing demographics

Many grape producers today are looking beyond the traditional workforce, who were mostly coloured, for new sources of labour. Over the past 15 years, the establishment of table grape vineyards for export production has created thousands of new jobs on farms in the Piketberg region.

Most of these jobs are seasonal, and the majority of seasonal workers are female. Initially, workers were recruited from the surrounding areas. Over time, however, the local labour supply has dwindled. Seasonal workers have come from as far as Namaqualand and the Northern Cape. There has also been a large influx from the Eastern Cape, and more recently, seasonal workers are now also sourced from townships in the greater Cape Metropole.

The past few years have seen a dramatic increase in non-Afrikaans-speaking – mostly Xhosa-speaking – workers on farms in the area.

Added to this has been an influx of people from beyond our borders, Zimbabweans in particular. In De Doorns in the Hex River Valley in late 2009, Zimbabweans were forced by other residents to flee their homes. Although xenophobia was blamed for the attacks, and this no doubt played a part, labour issues also contribute to the story. Although Zimbabweans were allegedly willing to work for less, this might not have been the only reason. Labour brokers, who recruit workers for farmers in exchange for a fee, were also blamed. Some say the farmers had bypassed the labour brokers, who then fuelled the violence.

Over the past five years De Doorns's population numbers have swelled as migrants from other parts of the country have come here looking for work, and stayed. Although not well paid – in 2009 an average wage was R60 a day – seasonal workers could earn enough to live on for the time they worked. Squatter camps have sprung up here, as in many small towns, and there is competition for jobs. With this influx, and the perception that foreigners work harder and are prepared to work on public holidays and weekends, tension built up.

Seasonal and temporary workers are at the bottom of the pile when it comes to fair treatment. Labour brokers are here to stay and you cannot ban them or they will go underground, says Professor Nick Vink of Stellenbosch University. It is up to the Department of Labour to police them properly, he believes.

Studies in 1994 and 1996 found that the permanent labour force was almost exclusively coloured and Afrikaans speaking, with very few African workers employed on a permanent basis, while some 75% of cellar workers were African, and both male and female Africans feature much more prominently in the seasonal labour force. That has changed in some areas, though. The percentage of African workers, both permanent and casual, is increasing. "But I don't think black people have exceeded 10% of the workforce, and it's mostly casual work," says sociology professor Joachim Ewert.

Changing demographics have presented farm management with difficult challenges, according to research done by Jacobus Odendaal for an MBA degree at the University of Stellenbosch Business School (USB). He looked at labour conflict experienced on five export table grape farms in the Piketberg area. [251]

Whereas farm workers have in the past been coloured and Afrikaans-speaking, the workforce on Western Cape farms now often consists of a majority of African, mainly Xhosa-speaking workers. Ground-level managers and production team leaders lack the ability to communicate effectively with all workers. Instructions are misunderstood, and the situation frequently leads to serious conflict.

Odendaal found that most of the conflict on the farms he studied could be explained in terms of the practical working conditions on the farms, differences between the workers' ethnic backgrounds, and the lack of any formalised strategies to address these issues. "It is clear that farm managers have not prepared themselves for the practical implications of such changes in the racial, cultural and linguistic composition of the workforce. It seems as if the senior management of certain farms believe that the problems will sort themselves out with time, and adopt a wait-and-see attitude."

In recent seasons there had also been a shortage of labour, with farms having to compete among each other to get workers. Workers easily migrate from farm to farm in search of better conditions, or a few rand more. The result is that the labour turnover may be as high as 85%, he established. In the case of a particular farm in the area, it was reported that to maintain a labour force of 440 people, 800 appointments had to be made during the season.

The ongoing need to teach skills to new workers implies costs and also puts team leaders under tremendous pressure to maintain the required production quality. But the most worrying manifestation is the high levels of conflict, usually between team leaders and seasonal workers. This poses a serious threat to productivity, says Odendaal.

Salaries and wages alone make up 40% of other escalating input costs, a trend which is outpacing the income from exports and putting profit margins under pressure. Lost time because of conflict cannot be afforded much longer.

Besides open forms of conflict, workers also protest in the form of staying away, or moving to the next farm. This is often the result when disciplinary action is taken against workers.

Odendaal's study found that on farms where team leaders had been trained in management skills, they were better equipped to handle conflict situations. However, the language barriers almost nullify these advantages in dealing with non-Afrikaans-speaking workers. The inability to convey instructions clearly to new and inexperienced workers causes frustration, and even stress and anxiety, among team leaders.

Cork dust, sawdust and paper shavings – early export attempts

The local market for table grapes has always been small, and the isolated Hex River Valley at first produced mostly wine grapes and other deciduous fruit. Today it is the biggest and oldest table-grape-producing area.

The isolated nature of the Hex River Valley began to change in 1875 when the Hex River railway pass was surveyed by Wells Hood. In the late 1870s the first railway tunnel was built – the expanding Kimberley diamond boom in the 1870s made it essential for the government to secure a suitable rail route through the mountains. The mountains were very steep and could only be scaled by a narrow-gauge railway. Built at a cost of R1 million, the route opened in 1879, and with it the local market for selling fruit from the valley. Fresh produce could now get to markets inland and be taken to Cape Town –

and the harbour. Seven years after the opening of this railway pass, the first tentative export of table grapes was made to Britain. [252]

In 1886 the grapes were privately dispatched to a Dr Smuts in London. Owing to Hanepoot being a fragile grape, they did not arrive in very good condition.[253] This is the reason it is used as a wine grape, not a table grape. Later, in 1888, a small experimental consignment of Muscat d'Alexandrie grapes from Robertson was shipped to London on the steamship the *Pembroke Castle*. Not a single berry was edible when it arrived. At the time it was thought unlikely that "grapes would under the best care travel so far under such conditions". That same season, however, Hanepoot grapes were exported, and these arrived in excellent condition. The next year another trial 15 tons of grapes were sent in a steamer fitted with a cool room. This consignment also failed because of the poor shelf life of the variety, Muscat de Frontignan (Cape Muscadel).

The first successful export of a large quantity of fresh fruit was in January 1892, when the *Drummond Castle* sailed to Plymouth with 14 cartons of peaches.

Encouraged by its success, Percy Alport Molteno and his brother decided to establish an export company, the Cape Fruit Syndicate, and by June 1892 they had exported 1 900 cases of grapes and other fruit.

In the same year Leicester Dicey, Fred Struben and Percy Malleson established the Cape Orchard Company in the Hex River Valley, buying fruit from growers for export.

In the early years of export, little was known about the right kind of cultivars, suitable packaging and the best temperature to ship them at, three essentials of the export industry, but soon Molteno started publishing advice on which cultivars were preferred by buyers.

Producers today would shudder at early attempts at exporting table grapes, which met with varying results. Packaging material was a challenge: cork dust proved disastrous, it was expensive and it stuck to the grapes and covered the bloom of the grape; sawdust imparted a flavour to the fruit; bran heated up; wadding and paper shavings were not up to the mark. Finally, wood wool was used.[254] Cooling facilities on ships were unreliable, and different materials were tried for packaging. In the days before pre-cooling, every batch was a gamble, and endless trials went on to determine the best methods of avoiding waste.

"It would amuse a fruit grower of today to see the way in which we went from farm to farm packing fruit, " said Rodbard Malleson, who worked for the Cape Orchard Company. "We took boxes in shooks and were accompanied by a box maker, who made them up as we found the crops. As to the packing, I had to do that entirely myself, until I trained an intelligent coloured man to help me."[255]

Most varieties at the time were unsuitable for export and new ones had to be developed. In 1892 Harry Pickstone, a nurseryman, arrived fresh from studying in South California, and because of his expertise he received 100 pounds to start a nursery at Nooitgedacht farm, where vine cultivars were grafted.

By 1899 table grape export volumes had grown to 12 000 cartons – mainly of Waltham Cross and Almeria cultivars. The good returns that were received encouraged the development of new grape varieties grown especially for the table, with the emphasis on appearance and shelf life. In 1910 the first Barlinka grape cuttings from Algeria were imported, smuggled in by Dr Izak Perold, hidden in his cane. This grape was much tougher and grew to its full glory in the Hex River Valley.

The world is watching – Money back to the farm gate

As with the wine industry, the deciduous fruit industry was also regulated by a single-channel marketing system. The Deciduous Fruit Board (DFB) appointed Unifruco in 1989 as the sole marketing and exporting agents for grapes for all producers under the "Cape" brand. All the grapes were pooled and everyone received the same price for their grapes. While the DFB provided a good service, there was little incentive for individual farmers to produce quality produce. These were the years of sanctions.

"Table grapes traded on world markets through difficult times. It was hard to be good, as products were discounted because of who we were," says Fred Meintjies, who worked for Unifruco for many years.

In 1994 Capespan was formed, an amalgamation of Unifruco and Outspan. It held the export monopoly until deregulation of the deciduous fruit industry in 1997. When the Capespan monopoly was broken up as a result of deregulation, one of three export permits issued by then minister of agriculture Derek Hanekom saw The Grape Company being formed. Hanno Scholtz is the director. "Deregulation has brought huge opportunities," he says. "We didn't intend to take on the big boys, just give table grapes a different spin, but we're now one of the bigger exporters in South Africa." In 2007 Capespan exported 12 million boxes, The Grape Company five million, and the rest three to five million each, with a total of 50 million boxes exported by 25 exporters.

The Grape Company has chosen top quality as its selling point. "Our base is quality," says Scholtz, "we work with forward-looking farmers. We've said, let's select the top 30% quality, and we've stuck to that. We've had hits and misses – we're dealing with a live product – and we have to manage that. It's emotional."

The Grape Company works with farmers from all areas: "We export five million boxes over 20 weeks, mainly to Europe and the Far East, and pool grapes according to variety, size, destination, packaging. Pooling ensures like-mindedness, the same quality coming from each farm. We can't turn a blind eye on quality – at the end of the day, no matter what, it's about money back to the farm gate. As exporters we fight on the part of growers. We want extra bucks for them. Farmers don't know where they're going to be next year. European farmers have more security than we do. In South Africa government doesn't support growers."

China as a producer is getting bigger and bigger, with around one billion boxes, but their quality is still very bad. India is growing, but it is counter-seasonal to South Africa, although there is no infrastructure for exports yet. South Africa's main competitors are Chile, Brazil, Peru and Argentina, and their focus is the US market. "We don't do the US and Canada because of protocol, it's not worth it," says Scholtz. "South Africa still has barriers to trade: the protocol for table grapes signed in 2007 with the United States, Israel and China demands cold sterilisation for pests, but it's about red tape, not the product. Fruit fly here is not an issue. Historically we didn't threaten them, now we do. Australia exports to the Far East. With the Australian drought, they came to us."

Despite recent expansion into new global markets, northern Europe remains the primary export market for South African grapes. The port of Rotterdam receives in excess of 25 million cartons of South African grapes annually (2008), much of which is moved through Holland to Belgium, France and central Europe. Other exporters to Europe are Argentina, Chile, Brazil and Peru, and lately Egypt and India.

Fair trade and "food miles"

Producers today, especially with a product like table grapes, cannot ignore the outside world. Adverse publicity is bad news for the industry. Fair trade, which encompasses social conditions on farms where grapes are grown as well as ethical trade practices, is important to savvy consumers.

Exporters and producers now have up to six audits to comply with, at their own expense. These include Sedex, the Suppliers Ethical Data Exchange, which uses the latest technology to enable companies to maintain and share data on labour practices in the supply chain. Among others are Fair Trade, Global Gap, Field to Fork (Marks & Spencer) and Tesco's Nature's Choice. Some of these include strict food hygiene standards and European supermarkets that sell South Africa's grapes have recently introduced a system of more stringent food safety measures. It is called the EurepGAP system, and producers are altering their farming practices in order to follow these standards.

Climate change is also indirectly having an impact on the agricultural industry through consumer behaviour and purchasing patterns which currently favour environmentally "friendly" products.[256] Suppliers now need to report on greenhouse gases, social conditions on farms and "food miles".

There is a debate about "food miles", a measure attached to food reflecting the distance travelled from where it is produced to where it is consumed, and hence its carbon footprint. It is an important issue with table grapes, says table grape expert Pieter Raath, as their carbon footprint is high because our table grapes are transported to Europe. "Today's consumers are educated and informed. But there are other dynamics behind carbon footprint. If you calculate the CO_2 in a production system in the way crops are produced in Europe, they may use more CO_2 than us, even factoring in transport, because we have a better climate here. Some suggest that carbon miles may be a smokescreen for a market access issue."

Another issue for European and British consumers to consider would be the impact of a choice not to buy food from the developing South. A recent study by the International Institute for Environment and Development estimated that over one million livelihoods in Africa are supported by the United Kingdom's consumption of imported fruit and vegetables alone. In general in developing countries manual labour still forms the backbone of agriculture and production, while in developed countries much of those processes are mechanised.

"This means that although an apple from Grabouw has to travel much farther to get to the UK retailer, the skills development, job creation and local economic growth that result from that imported good, need all be considered as part of the product choice and price equation," point out James MacGregor and Bill Vorley in a 2006 paper.[257]

What about the local market?

The table grape industry would not be here if it had to survive on the local market, which cannot support the price asked for top-quality grapes.

However, building the local market is incredibly important, with a huge market in Africa. Most agree that not enough has been done to develop the local market, which is provided with substandard produce. African markets are picking up for all varieties, but they are a high risk for credit, says The Grape Company's Hanno Scholtz.

The grapes that do not make the export grade are sold to the local municipal markets and to hawkers. The offcuts and spoilt grapes are delivered to the local KWV winery, where they are distilled to make spirits. Table grape varieties cannot be used for wine, as their selections are based on appearance, shelf life and flavour, in that order, whereas wine grapes have thin skins and are grown purely for the quality of their juice.

Exporting grapes has opened up local farming practices to the scrutiny of the public. An informed public, especially in the UK and Europe, wants excellent quality grapes grown in an ethical way, where people are treated well and adverse environmental effects are taken into consideration. This has given impetus to change: those who export table grapes (and to a lesser extent wines) have changed their labour and farming practices. Pest control is still a major challenge, but many producers are moving towards more judicious use of pesticides.

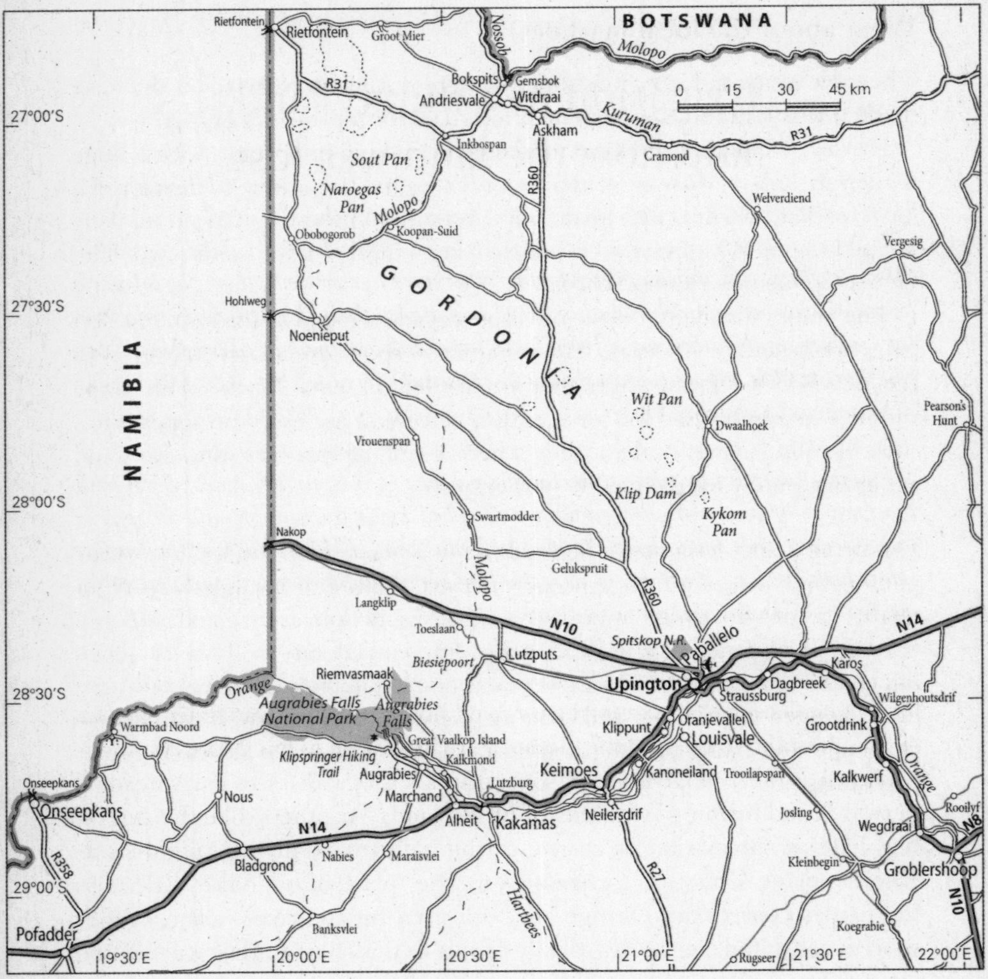

Grape-producing areas in the Northern Cape

CHAPTER 9

Irrigation in a thirsty land, and how the land was lost

"Where whites trek into a country formerly occupied by coloureds, there the coloureds go backwards very quickly. Most of them do not keep their fixed property safe, they take money, make debts, are offered large sums and lose their fixed property. Some trek northwards, others roam around, or must take service."[258] – Rev. Christiaan Schroeder, Upington, 1893

"How few can tell any more than the mere name of this mighty river! How little the farmer dreams that her verdant valley-bed holds the richest land in Africa! How strange that no railroad builder forestalls that chainless rush of the human tide which ere long must sweep westward by her splendid, shortest pathway to the sea."[259] – William McDonald, 1913

The Gariep is an extraordinary river, flowing from its catchment area in Lesotho to the Atlantic Ocean, a distance of 2 340 km. More commonly known as the Orange River, at some places it is as wide as 10 km, spreading outwards and forming hundreds of little islands. At others, like the Augrabies Falls, it narrows into a chasm, crashing down and giving Augrabies its Khoisan name *!oukurubes* (or *Aukoerebis*), the "place of big noise". (Because the names Gariep and Orange are both used for the river in the various sources consulted and stories told by people in this chapter, they will be used interchangeably.)

As you approach it from the south, through a hot and thirsty desert, the sparsely grassed plains become a little denser, the bushes greener and slightly bigger. You know you are approaching water. Somewhere in the arid expanse ahead lies the Gariep River. Water is the most precious commodity in Bushmanland; there is so little of it.

The Gariep's abundance is the bounty which has made farming possible in the desert.

Even if you are expecting it, it is still a surprise to come across block after block of vineyards as you drive from the semi-arid desert of Bushmanland towards the river. About 90% of South Africa's Sultanina vineyards, used for raisins and wine production, are situated along the Lower Orange River in the Northern Cape. It is also the second biggest table-grape-exporting area in South Africa, the Northern Cape's amazing agricultural success story. This was the fastest growing farming area in the world in the late 1980s, early 1990s.

Raisins have been grown in this region for as long as crop agriculture has been here, mostly as part of mixed farming. Raisins are forgiving of the heat, and Sultanina grapes offer up their sweetness in this climate. Grapes for wine were grown on a large scale in the late 1960s when farmers here were given a wine quota by the KWV. Today the traditional mixed farming has been sidelined to make way for the very lucrative table grape, but sultanas and wine grapes are still a profitable venture.

While grapes grow best along the Lower Orange River, from Groblershoop east of Upington to Blouputs in the west, the stretch between Upington to Kakamas and then on to Augrabies is the most verdant. The climate is good – hot and dry – and water is plentiful. The heat is not a problem, but rain is because this is a summer rainfall area, and grapes do not like rain once their berries are formed. Fortunately rainfall is low, but hail poses a major threat, as does black frost.

The earliest grapes were probably planted in this area in 1883 by a Canadian, Robert Frier, one of the first white men to farm north of the Orange. He had married a Baster woman (we do not know her name), which allowed him to be granted land in "Basterland" (as Gordonia, the district with Upington as principal town, was then known), "Bastaards" (later to become known as Basters) was the name given to children born from relationships between frontier farmers and Khoikhoi women; they were often baptised as Christians, spoke Dutch and had their fathers' Dutch names. Initially they had the same rights as burghers, but in time the frontier community began to see them as "other", separate and inferior. Many left for the untamed frontier and better opportunities at the Orange River and beyond.

On his ox wagon Frier had brought vines – probably Hanepoot and "*Kristaldruiwe*" (crystal grapes), along with citrus, from the Boland.[260] *Kristal* is an old, white seeded variety, used for eating, still found in some home gardens. Hanepoot and *Kristal* were well suited to the climate and grown on a limited scale, mostly for distilling. Frier soon became known for his potent *witblits* (home-distilled raw spirit), which he traded in Bechuanaland for cattle, although it was illegal.

The story is told that in 1886 a Jan de Wet travelled from Goudini with a load of alcohol to sell in Basterland. De Wet tasted the sweet Hanepoot grapes, which were much sweeter than those in the Boland, and returned three years later and bought a piece of Friersdale.

De Wet, it seems, knew viticulture, no doubt one of the earliest farmers to do so in the area, and was soon making wine. Each householder was allowed to distil 30 gallons of wine, and many made a reasonable income out of "Keimoes *blits*", even though it was illegal.

Later, in 1918, a Mr AS Brink brought Sultana cuttings from Robertson, and had them planted at the poor-white labour colony at Kakamas. In January 1922, he sold 70 bags of sultanas, of 200 lbs each, to the Wellington Co-op.

It is often remarked upon how sweet and flavourful the grapes grown along the Gariep are – and that is why they are in such demand on the overseas market.

Narratives of the Gariep area revolve around landownership and irrigation, the lifeblood of the area. Land is an emotional issue in the Northern Cape; this is not the "old country" of the Cape Winelands, where land was settled in the 1600s and 1700s, long before the cut-off date for land claims. Land issues are still an open wound here. It was a little over 100 years ago when land was parcelled out and assigned, north of the Gariep to Basters, south of the river to trekboers, and feelings run high here about land alienation through underhand "deals".

"In 1880 the country wherein the Bastards were invited to settle was regarded as a worthless desert, and no one envied the people to whom it had been allotted. But all this is now changed . . . there are persons who now regard the Bastard settlers with jealousy, and look with envy upon the land their industry has made so rich," wrote a Cape official in 1887.[261]

In 1913 the area around the Gariep, or Orange River as it was called, was underdeveloped, prompting William McDonald, with his colonial outlook, to write: "The Conquest of the Desert opens up a vast country eminently suited to colonisation, while it offers to the youth of the Empire a healthful, profitable and fascinating life in a 'Land of Eternal Sunshine'."[262] The desert was the Kalahari; McDonald was an exponent of "dry farming".

That was less than 100 years ago: already the land was inhabited and farmed by a mixed group of people, mostly Basters and trekboers, along with those Korannas who had not trekked further north. A wave of emigration from Europe at the end of the nineteenth century century had also brought new people to the area; many farmers, impoverished by the Anglo-Boer war, drought and the rinderpest also made their way here to seek their fortune. The north became more and more attractive.

Today farming in this area has many faces – huge established commercial table grape producers farm alongside small-scale raisin farmers working in co-ops; empowerment deals mean workers on some farms own part of the farms they work on; on other land, emerging farmers are just starting out. The Blocuso Trust has been formed at the former Congregational Lands to farm grapes commercially. There are uplifting stories of workers being treated well; there are communities of seasonal workers living in dire poverty.

Irrigation is the subject of many of the heroic stories of the area – harnessing the waters of the Gariep by building canals to get the water to where it was needed was no easy task, and required much sweat and hard labour. Irrigation is at the heart of white Afrikaner folklore in some areas – the Boegoeberg Dam, one of the first in the area, was part of the Smuts government's solution to the "poor white" problem. The dam and water channels created jobs for hundreds of impoverished white people. Those who lost their jobs on mines and elsewhere flocked to the construction sites and worked very hard for meagre wages and an opportunity to rent some land.

All along the Gariep, local histories go into detail about who built which canal, and when. The Groblershoop area east of Upington today exports table grapes and sultanas. The local wine cellars have an annual intake of 12 000 tons of grapes. But the canal system is old and ailing, and new walls need to be built, to manage the flow. André Smith, a table grape farmer in the area, is in the process of setting up a community-based project to rebuild the canal system, which he says is at the end of its lifetime: "We need R500 million to rebuild the system, and have drawn up a feasibility study."

The Gariep today is still a mighty river, but it has been tamed. Hoewever, floods are by no means a thing of the past, and the devastating floods of early 2011 caused extensive damage.

Land

Just outside Upington, north of the Gariep, lies Ouap. Here Abraham September was granted a farm in 1882, one of 81 people, mainly Basters, to receive land. Another 58 farms were granted from Kheis (opposite the present-day Groblershoop) to the Augrabies Falls and 23 in the interior. In 1887 the population of the Gordonia district was estimated as 1 200, mostly Basters. In 1891 the first census counted 735 whites, 1 429 "aboriginal natives" and 3 121 "other coloured persons". [263]

In the course of our research in Upington, Aubrey Beukes, a former Uniting Reformed Church minister and now a social activist in Upington, takes Jeanne to visit what is said to be the house at Ouap that September, a former slave, lived in. The building is just after *Dominee* Nico Jansen's church, where the road turns to dust, but we miss it, and stop along the way to ask where it is. We have overshot it considerably, and so we turn round.

It is a simple structure made of stones and mortar, with a curious handwritten sign attached. We stop to read it: *"Geen Toegang, Privaat Eiendom. Betree op eie Risiko. Oppas Jakkals kanale gestel"*. (No Entry, Private Property. Enter at own risk. Beware Jackal traps set). We venture a little closer – there are vineyards here, and a canal runs past . . . this must be it.

A white bakkie draws up, fast. Something in the stopping, something in the way a small grey-haired woman strides out, tells me "here comes trouble". I say hello, introduce myself, mention Abraham September, and because I realise that good Afrikaans may be an advantage here, I turn to Aubrey for help. "I can speak English," she hisses at me, and tells me in no uncertain terms that this is NOT where Abraham lived; yes, his wife lived here towards the end of her life, with PERMISSION from the family of her husband (a portly Mr Fourie, who remains sitting in the passenger seat. At 80, perhaps he is not so mobile). And Abraham September did NOT build this canal, she continues, and she hears that name and she wants to spit. She's had quite enough of this story, she continues, she's ready to bulldoze the house, and people can come and take the bricks away, brick by brick if they want. But this is her husband's farm, and has been his family's for three generations, and she's had to spend thousands upon thousands of rands on lawyers, money which they can ill afford at this stage of their lives. It's got nothing to do with white or coloured, this is THEIR land, and the Kimberley people came here and they wrote nonsense about this, and she's had enough, and how dare we trespass, and take pictures. (I had not had a chance yet).

Admittedly, we had taken a few steps onto her land, so we apologise. But she is on a roll, her face now matching her postbox-red shirt. I am ready to get huffy and say I will take pictures if I want to; but Aubrey listens, eyes downward. And then asks her about farming. There is a vineyard behind us; but they do mixed farming, she tells us, and slowly, slowly her anger eases. They make raisins from the grapes. We part. I still have not taken pictures.[264]

This is my initiation into the emotional question of land along the Gariep River's abundant banks.

As Aubrey says, land is an existential, not a developmental issue; people are fierce about wanting to live on the land they believe belongs to them. Few want to be compensated with money.

(Abraham September's descendants have questioned the sale of the land in violation of the terms of his will. The matter is still unresolved.)

Irrigation

Along the Gariep from Upington to Augrabies, the name of Christiaan Schroeder is a familiar one. A Dutch Reformed Church pastor, he started one of the first mission stations in the north in 1871 at Olijvenhoutsdrift, now called Upington, when the Koranna chief Klaas Lukas requested that a mission station be established in the area to bring stability there. (The Koranna were a nomadic Khoi group that had settled north of the Gariep.) Schroeder's followers were mainly Basters and he believed that fertile land should be used for agriculture, not grazing, to create a fixed and economically strong community. Land transactions were forbidden, and no strong drink was allowed to be sold.

Schroeder is usually credited with the building of the first irrigation canals in Upington, but it seems the idea was inspired by Abraham "*Holbors*" (Hollow Chest) September, mentioned above. September's story, as told by the historian Martin Legassick,[265] is closely tied to the complex land issues around the Gariep at the end of the nineteenth century. September, as his name indicates, was a former slave, born in Calvinia probably before 1818, the son of a slave and a woman named Matjie van Wyk. His wife Elizabeth was also born around 1818, to Abraham and Lena Goeiman. Abraham and Elizabeth were married in Carnarvon, at that time known as Schietfontein, a Baster and Xhosa settlement established by the Cape government in 1830, and with a missionary presence from the end of 1847.

At Ouap, "this old man (September) discovered that there was the possibility of leading out the water of a lateral branch of the river on to some alluvial soil on his farm. He set to work and succeeded in getting a small stream on to a low-lying portion of his ground". This quotation, from Percy Nightingale, in Cape Parliamentary Papers of 1887,[266] prefaces the following: "Mr Scott and Mr Schroeder hearing of this [Abraham September's irrigation], inspected the place, and as it seemed to them practicable to lead the water from this point on to the alluvial soil lining the river bank for many miles, even beyond the village of Upington, a meeting was called, and steps were taken to begin irrigation works on a scale of considerable magnitude. Many difficulties had to be faced, but they were all eventually overcome."

The Upington canal was the largest work of its kind in South Africa at that time. In organising its construction, Schroeder – and John H. Scott, then special magistrate for the Northern Border stationed at Upington – took their lead from Abraham September, who had first led water from the Orange River, notes Legassick. "Indeed, they began the canal from the very place that he had selected."

While history credits Christiaan Schroeder with the idea of irrigating the land around the Orange, writes Legassick, "such historiography takes for granted that white drive, innovation, and 'know-how', assisted at most by black labour, developed and 'modernized' South Africa. But, so far as irrigation of the Orange River is concerned, the above quotation sets matters straight."

The wild frontier

As you drive from Upington to Kakamas along the N14 it is difficult to spot the Gariep because it is largely hidden from view, unless you cross it. The indigenous people, the pastoral Khoikhoi and the hunter-gatherer San people, inhabited this region long before recorded history. It was also home to wild animals such as elephants and hippo, and was a fertile hunting ground for the San, and later the settlers who ventured into this "wild" land, first to hunt, then to settle.

A map of the societies living here in 1779 is surprising in the number and diversity of groups it shows. From Pella in the west to Prieska in the east, historian Nigel Penn names 20 different Khoikhoi or San societies.[267] These San and Khoikhoi groups were linked through various alliances and allegiances; some San groups were allies or clients of some Khoikhoi groups; others were not. Among the many groups along the river, there was low-level livestock raiding. Some San groups here also owned cattle.

Although the islands formed by the river were covered with luxuriant grasses and wild cucumbers, and the soil was very fertile, the only crop to be grown, by the Namnykoa (Khoikhoi) was dagga. Fishing and hunting along the river were plentiful. The Anoe Eis (San), for example, who lived at the Augrabies Falls, lived by catching fish, hunting, and digging pits to trap hippo, elephants and rhino. They were friendly with the Einiqua but enemies of the Namaqua. They had cattle, as did the Nannigai (San, meaning "mountain climbers"). The Gyzikoa, living about seven and a half hours upstream from the Aukokoa, were a mixture of people of Tswana and Khoikhoi heritage, mostly Einiqua. Some understood Xhosa.

These were the people whose way of life was to be severely disrupted, first by hunters in search of ivory, and then by a motley crew of trekboers, displaced Khoikhoi and San, *drosters* (deserters) and Bastaard-Hottentots (as they were known), Oorlams groups (more organised bands, with military and other skills), deserting soldiers and *knechten* (overseers on farms), runaway slaves and anyone else in search of a better life. As Penn writes: "Namaqualand and the Orange River were thus not just a crucible where different races were mixed; they were a haven, an opportunity, a destination for people of mixed race or lowly social status from other parts of the colony."[268]

But Penn observes that "(t)his was a mixed blessing – for every runaway slave or deserting soldier who wanted nothing more than a chance to lead an independent existence, there was another who saw the freedom of the frontier as a licence to violence. For those Bastaard-Hottentots and Bastaards who sought the opportunity to become successful pastoralists, free from the increasing racial discrimination of the Southern Cape, there were others who perceived their best career opportunities to lie in hunting and robbing and raiding."

Company control on the northern frontier was always weak, and the trekboers (farmers who had left the colony and trekked northwards to graze their cattle) were hardy, fearless and often cruel as they established themselves in Khoisan territory. In 1786 the VOC did try to investigate complaints of unbridled violence against Khoikhoi, to little avail.

During the 1800s, the Orange River area became increasingly lawless. Trekboers launched themselves over the river in the Great Trek of the 1830s and there was constant movement in the area as people looked for better pastures and water; there were frequent clashes, raids and counter-raids. Bands of outlaws formed powerful groupings, and the Koranna fought fiercely to protect their grazing grounds.

In 1847 the Cape Parliament declared the Orange River the northern border of the Cape Colony; the region south of it was called Bushmanland. This was now deemed Crown Land. The trekboers who had established themselves along the border were allowed to graze their livestock north of the river, with permission, as were the Basters. Bushmanland was declared a communal grazing area in which white, Khoikhoi and Baster farmers had equal rights (the rights of the San were not considered). More magistracies were set up in Calvinia, Namaqualand and Fraserburg in the 1850s.

In 1865 many Basters moved to Groot and Klein Mier, northwest of Upington, under *Kaptein* (Captain) Dirk Vilander. Others moved to mission stations, which were being established in many parts of the northern colony.

The missionaries' attempts to convert the indigenous people met with little success initially; they had more success with the Baster people.

To combat the lawlessness in the area, the Cape Parliament established a special magistrate in Kenhardt, south of the Orange, in 1895. Shortly afterwards the area around it was cut up into farms and sold to the highest bidder. The more prosperous, mostly white, farmers could afford to buy; the less well-off could not and moved to areas where farms were not measured out.[269] Some crossed the river, moving northwards.

Elize Beukes – the Sultana Queen of Eksteenkuil

Finding Elize Beukes's farm on Skaapeiland (Sheep Island) is a long and difficult process.

The road that turns off between Keimoes and Kenhardt meanders, twists and turns, the bumpy dirt road crossing canals and bridges, passing houses and small farms. It takes a long time to find her.

Beukes is a small-scale farmer in the Northern Cape, supplying sultanas to the local South African Dried Fruit Co-operative (SAD) for export. In 2008 she was honoured as the Top Producer for Export Markets in the Female Farmer of the Year competition. These small farms are a far cry from the huge manicured commercial farms along the Orange River. There are 113 farmers here on the maze of 16 small islands that make up Eksteenkuil. Skaapeiland is one of them. About 80 of the farmers on Eksteenkuil have vineyards of between half a hectare and 15 ha. Some do not farm at all.

Beukes was born on another of the islands, Langklaaseiland, in 1958. Her mother Johanna Elizabeth Mostert was a white woman, she tells me, and her father Willem Wells, a "*bruinmens*" (coloured person). Both were born and grew up in Vaalhoek, 15 km from Keimoes. They were removed from Vaalhoek to make way for white farmers in 1934, when the "*bruinboere*" (coloured farmers) were given plots of 4 to5 ha, for which they had to pay an annual rental. They cleared the land themselves of trees, rocks and bush. White farmers, struggling to make it here, were removed in the 1930s and given better farms in the Western Transvaal and Grootdrink, she says.

Beukes's father and four other farmers petitioned the government to build bridges – at that stage they had to carry their goods to market strapped on their back, wading through the water. In 1955 a white farmer, a Mr Burger, was contracted to build the first bridges, says Beukes.

In 1946 the farmers at Eksteenkuil were given the option of buying or renting the land, but since only three, her father included, wanted to buy, they remained tenant farmers.

Her great-grandfather, Willie Wells, was from England. Her husband Gert's father was Christiaan Beukes, his mother Jacoba. Gert's one *ouma* (grandmother) was Katrina Mostert, also a white woman. Skin colour is often mentioned in these parts – divisions from apartheid times and before still run deep.

The piece of land Elize Beukes now farms so successfully belonged to her husband Gert's father; she moved to this farm in 1994 and bought it in 2000, at R1 500 per ha. "They should have given it to us, we have farmed it so long, *maar toe maar* (but never mind)," she says. She now owns 8 826 ha. She would like to expand and is looking for a further 25 ha to buy. "Then I can live *lekker gerieflik* (comfortably)" she says.

From tenant farmer to owner is a huge advantage. "It feels good to own the land. And it opens doors for me, I can go to the bank and get loans."

Beukes has been farming since she was seven, helping her father plant maize, beans, lucerne, "*kafferboontjies*" (black-eyed beans) and lentils. She recalls burning a sheep's horn "to bring the wind to blow the lentil husks away" once they had been harvested.

A white man, Coppel Siepker "*van die buiteland*" (from overseas), owned a pont on Graseiland, which they used to cross the river. "But not to Sononder," she chuckles, "where people say a big river snake lived."

As a youngster she used to lead, with a rope, the donkeys and mules carrying the harvest. "When I was seven I planted my first vine. In those years you ploughed, and then with a wooden scraper measured the rows with a fish line. For every one stride of my father's, I took four, and I would plant the cane, two eyes in the ground, two above; a handful of manure, water."

"My great love is farming," Beukes says. She was the youngest of 11 children. "I stayed at home the longest, as a result I had the most knowledge of farming."

Her mother played a significant role in her life: she was a white Afrikaans woman, and had learned the secret of bottling fruit from the Voortrekkers. Beukes is keen to expand her bottled-fruit industry: all of it is grown on her farm. She is adamant that she will continue to farm organically – it is the way she learned.

"Look at my earthworms," she says, pointing to the worm castings.

"That's what shows the soil is healthy." There is no problem farming organically, she says, it is nature's way. Her secret is to plant fruit trees with fragrant flowers – the insects would rather go there than to the vines.

With her R50 000 cash prize for winning the Top Producer award, she bought drying racks for her sultanas and peaches as well as bottles for her fruit, and built a new sheep kraal. Her aim is to increase production, expand and obtain more land. Beukes has done a course with the SA Agri Academy (SAAA), an article 21 company based in Stellenbosch, which focuses on training support for exporters. She was funded by the Northern Cape Department of Agriculture, and the course gave her confidence, she says. On a visit to Safmarine, she saw for the first time how her fruit was exported; she also learned about costing and drawing up a business plan. It confirmed for her that she was indeed an organic farmer, and taught her how to increase her yield. "And it gave me the papers I needed."

Beukes produces 17 tons of sultanas, which she sells to the SAD. Even though they are organically grown, she does not personally get a premium, as the quantity is too small to market separately. She dries them herself on her new wooden drying racks. Now she produces golden sultanas, made possible with her new equipment, and has increased her income. Raisins and sultanas are different products from the same grape – one is dried in the sun, the other is soaked in potash, covered with a cloth and smoked with sulphur for six to eight hours. "There's no sleeping then for me," she laughs. She harvests her grapes from mid-February to the end of February, five blocks in three weeks; she employs 17 seasonal workers and four temporary workers, who keep the vineyards watered and clear of weeds.

Her idea is to teach small farmers, especially women, that land is money, and that you can get everything you need from farming. She loves her small farm: peach trees and quince trees line each side of the vineyards of H5 Sultanina grapes (grown on Ramsay rootstock). To encourage healthy root growth, she loosens the ground between every second row.

Beukes also keeps a few pigs – "that pays for my labour" – and some sheep and chickens. Her father taught her that a farm must be diverse. Everything from the vineyards is composted, and everything stays on the land. She also cultivates half a hectare of peaches, mostly Oom Sarel, some Pink Lady apples, as well as white and brown figs.

Farming along the Gariep/Orange River means floods are inevitable. Beukes recalls stories told to her of the 1934 flood, which followed a drought. "Police came on horseback to warn people, but they didn't believe them. Many drowned." The 1965 flood did not reach them, but in 1974 the water rose 7,4 m. Beukes, her mother and two sisters were rescued by a helicopter: Her father decided to stay behind. For two weeks, living in tents in Keimoes, the family waited for news of him. "It was a terribly long wait," she says. Only then were people able to swim over the subsiding waters and tell them he was safe.

Farming on Eksteenkuil

The fertile land along the Gariep was owned and farmed mostly by white farmers, with a few exceptions; during the apartheid years they were supported by the policies and practices of the government.

Eksteenkuil is the place where many coloured farmers were settled in the 1950s as a "reward" for fighting in the Second World War. The islands have seen much movement of people – they are not easy to farm. Around 1913 Rooikopeiland was leased to 30 "poor whites". In 1928, after a flood, they moved to Kanoneiland. The irony, says Nelie Kok, chairman of the Eksteenkuil Agricultural Co-op, is that coloured farmers were resettled on farms where white farmers could not make it. On Sandeiland, for example, an area of 30,09 ha, 17 coloured farmers were expected to be successful where one white farmer was not.

And while the farmers here have made a success of it with sheer hard work, increasing arable land by chopping out trees, they did it alone, with no help from government. "They weren't even given a spade," he says. In the 1970s the farms were enlarged by consolidating some plots, and the 200 plots became 147. "But it was a struggle to make ends meet," says Kok. Hardships meant most of the children were taken out of school at an early age, and there is still a low literacy rate among the farmers.

Landownership is still a vexed issue here. Until recently Eksteenkuil was state land, an "Act 9" area, held in trust by the minister of agriculture.

The Transformation of Certain Rural Areas Act (Trancraa), the first comprehensive legislation to reform communal land tenure in South Africa, was passed to fast-track the transfer of land in 23 former "coloured rural areas". However, by 2009 only 30 to 40% of farmers were in possession of a title deed, says Kok. The process has been hampered by the Department of Land Affairs which has dragged its feet, by the politics of party affiliation, and,

Kok believes, by his outspokenness. "Ownership is of great concern for the development of the area," he tells me, "farmers can't progress without collateral, which they can't get if they don't own the land."

Eksteenkuil farmers have done what farmers do when they need muscle: they have formed a co-op, now a legal entity, which lobbies on behalf of its members. Accessing funding is a difficult process: "Our members will never access funds on their own," says Kok.

The Eksteenkuil Agricultural Co-Op has had a business relationship since 1995 with TraidCraft in the United Kingdom (UK), a joint trading company and development charity which practices trade that helps poor people in developing countries transform their lives. Raisins are sold to the organisation at a premium, bringing in an annual income of R300 000 to R400 000 a year to Eksteenkuil.

They also work with the European Fair Trade Association (EFTA), an association of 11 Fair Trade importers in nine European countries, which works mainly with marginalised small-scale farmers. "Fair Trade" is a concept to which many organisations subscribe. The Fairtrade Foundation in the UK defines it as "working with businesses, community groups and individuals to improve the trading position of producer organisations in the South and to deliver sustainable livelihoods for farmers, workers and their communities".[270]

The premium is used to buy water pumps, fund the office, and supply children with schoolbags. The Co-op also extends loans: "People have no reserves and no overdraft facilities," says Kok. "They also can't afford to purchase implements; the Co-op has bought slashers and tractors for each of three groups of islands."

Kok says commercial farmers now also want to benefit by being aligned with the Fair Trade Association, a move he challenges. "Raisins are earmarked for small-scale producers. White farmers were fortunate in the apartheid years, they were subsidised to a large extent; it will take us another generation to get there."

The Co-op has 106 members. The SAD, once the only marketing channel, processes the raisins from Eksteenkuil. Kok is disillusioned with government support for small-scale farmers. There has been little local funding for development, and the Co-op has had to look overseas.

"With European Union funding we have identified people who don't have vineyards. We've been helped with building capacity. Another project is to survey people who want to grow wine grapes. Even today, although we have excelled, we get no help with exports."

Deteriorating roads and water canals are of great concern.

"Up until 1994 Eksteenkuil was governed by a Management Committee," Kok explains, "which tended to water and roads. Ever since the 2002 demarcation there is a vacuum in the Ka!Gariep municipality – when we ask about service delivery, they shrug their shoulders. Roads and water are going backwards. We are now doing a feasibility study, funded by the Development Bank of SA, to rehabilitate water distribution. The river is channelled into dams; the dams silt up. That water is needed for irrigation and domestic use."

Irrigation comes from the mostly grass or soil trench canals, and a lot of water is lost on the way. The soil is also brackish. Cement canals were only built on the islands in the 1970s – before that they were clay and had to be dug and maintained with a spade. Some canals are still clay.

Danie van Schalkwyk of the Agricultural Research Council (ARC), who has been doing hands-on training with the Eksteenkuil farmers, says the biggest problems with raisins in the area is the rootstock. Phylloxera is not a problem up here, but the old rootstocks mean low production. "We've now established grafted vines on better rootstock," says Van Schalkwyk. But even this, at a cost of R20 000 per hectare, is expensive. "But at least there's stable production. With old rootstock, the yield could vary from 30 tons a hectare to nine tons . . . with no way of predicting from year to year."

Says Kok: "Farmers established vineyards here with a very inferior method. People assisted commercial farmers with pruning, and then took cuttings from them. We're still catching up. We are changing the mindset of farmers with Farmers' Days, but still, to establish new vineyards costs R100 000 to R120 000 a hectare; a 25- to 30-year investment. We have to go abroad for funding."

The Co-Op has started to do its own exporting to increase income. There is also an opportunity for small-scale farmers in grape juice, with a juice-processing plant near Keimoes. The Villard Blanc cultivar is a very resistant one, but so far only four farmers are making use of it, says Van Schalkwyk.

While Eksteenkuil seems like a good model for emerging farmers, the farmers operate in a false economy, says Professor Mohammed Karaan, Dean of the Faculty of AgriSciences at Stellenbosch University. "The cost of the land is externalised, the cost of infrastructure is externalised. Dams, roads, irrigation and planting are subsidised."

Cillié

Cillié is a small community near Kakamas. Oom Willie Coetzee, now 84, raises his arms in an open gesture, and says in the days when he was young, people here were free. The area close by was called Bassonsdrift, and the land belonged to the Bassons, a Baster family.

Cillié was an *NG dominee*, a minister of the Dutch Reformed Church (DRC). There are many settlements along the road between Keimoes and Kakamas named after *dominees* – Alheit, Marchand, Cillié – attesting to the prominence of the Dutch Reformed Mission Church in the area.

Oom Willie recalls that the vineyards here were small, and they made raisins from them. He spent most of his life working for white farmers. His wife Katrina, 80, came from Noudap, and they married here.

Money didn't stretch that far, she says. "We lived badly, there was no childcare. But, 'no work, no pay'. So when I went to work, my baby came with me. There were times when there was no milk, and I had to give her water. I was plucking cotton one day, and my child was left in care of an older one, who fell asleep. She was two years old, and she bent over to the water. Her cap got stuck on a branch, and I heard her crying – that branch saved her life."

She shows me a large portrait of the child who survived, as a young woman. "That's how we lived; the child could have drowned. For nappies I washed out 200-lb flour sacks. If I hear young people complaining, I say: be quiet, my child, you have not drunk from the cup I have, those were very hard times. You can't live without God, God provides for you."

Things were better when there was mixed farming in the area, she says, people could at least eat from the land. But with grapes only being grown, there is no food, and young people must go to the towns.

Parts of the farm known as Bassonsdrift, on which many people in Cillié lived, are subject to a land claim, lodged in September 1998. The committee of elders, which heads the group, arrives at the Coetzees' home: they are Jan Henning, 64; Jakob Afrikaaner, 53, and Jan Filander, 62.

They tell of how the vineyards now grow over the graves of their people. "Our history is under the ground," they say. Worse, they are not allowed to visit the more recent graves. The story goes that a white farmer moved to the farm when the land was supposedly ceded to the DRC for a debt. The claim is for the Witrand piece of Bassonsdrift.

The committee of elders: Jan Henning, Jakob Afrikaander and Jan Filander.

This land was granted to Jacobus Basson in 1894, who fought against the Koranna. They have the title deed to prove it.

Dirk Pienaar, deputy principal of Cillié Primary, takes up the story: "Basson allowed the Khoi and San to live there," he explains. "People here used water from the river, but when the poor whites wanted to build a canal here, our people agreed and helped, so they too could benefit. But when it was finished, they started charging a *heffing* (levy), and month by month debt built up. Because of this people were removed from the land. Later it was claimed that our people had sold the land to the church, but no one here knew about that, and no one had any papers. You know, people trusted their *dominees*, they were seen as close to God, and no one questioned them. If they said sign something, people would. Until recently, most *dominees* were white. Even today the old people will not question their actions."

"They knew everything about us, and we trusted them," says Oom Willie Coetzee.

Later, in the 1970s, the man who farmed the land refused to allow people to visit the graves of their forebears. He threatened them with guns, and there was a quarrel because he said he rented the property, said Coetzee. He became more aggressive, saying he had invested a lot in the property, and if they did not sell to him, there would be trouble.

"People couldn't go to the law, this was the 1970s, and you couldn't say a farmer was lying. Families near him were terrified, and one of the Bassons sold him a piece of land. Which makes you ask, how could he have, if it supposedly belonged to the church?"

However, says Coetzee, two-thirds of the original land still belongs to the Bassons, and a community property association was formed in June 1998 to lay claim to it. The final date for land claims was 28 September 1998; they got their claim in on 20 September.

"For years, no one came here," says Filander, who describes the slow land claim process that has now taken almost ten years, during which five people have been on the case. Documents have been lost. With each new person, they have to start again. The perception among them is that in the Northern Cape the claims of "*bruinmense*" take longer – the Tswana people have their claims settled quickly, they claim.

Aubrey Beukes and Jeanne travel to Augrabies to find Jacobus Basson, grandson of Jacobus, the original owner of the land, to find out more. He is around 100 years old, his sight is weak and his voice faint, but his mind is sharp. For many years he levelled fields for farmers, and he was a builder. The original Basson was a corporal in the war (against the Koranna), he says, and Queen Victoria gave him land. "There was an irrigation canal at Bassonsdrift," he recounts, "but we got water from the river." The original Basson stipulated that there was to be no land alienation: if a son did not want to stay, someone bought him out for £25.

How did the land get alienated then? "*Dit was 'n stelery*. (It was stolen.) My *oupa* (grandfather) had debt, the white man took the land," he says.

Debt and land alienation

The story of debt and land alienation along the Gariep is often told, still strong in people's memories, and it is a sad one.

Both Abraham September and Jacobus Basson were part of the original group of Baster families who were granted land in Korannaland, north of the Orange, after the two Koranna wars as reward for fighting on the sides of the colonists. Their presence was intended to act as a buffer between the farmers on the south side of the river and the Koranna, then a largely weakened group.

Briefly known as Basterland, it became Gordonia and in 1889, when the area north of the Orange was annexed, the Gordonia district became part of British Bechuanaland. Until 1889 the land was largely reserved for Basters, but then the administration freed the market in land.

The inhabitants of Gordonia were mainly Basters, with a few whites, at first largely related to them by marriage, as well as remnants of Kora, San, and some Xhosa. The congregation of the Dutch Reformed mission ranged in this period, in the words, of Rev. Schroeder, "from wholly white to wholly black".[271]

The village of Upington was resurveyed in 1892 and a village laid out in Keimoes in 1893.

As early as 1887 there were land transactions between Basters and whites. Keimoes businessman Heinrich Lutz was one of these, and the first map of the town in 1896 shows that he owned a water erf, bought from an original Baster owner.[272] Wilhelm Frank, an emigrant from Germany, came to South Africa in 1878 and started as a *smous* (itinerant trader). He then opened the first shop in Keimoes, made money and brought agricultural land from Basters, often to then make it available to white farmers at a profit.

It is difficult to unravel the stories of losing land: land is taken away for small amounts of debt; new systems of tax and charging for water are introduced, and debt piles up. It was of great concern to the Reverend Schroeder that whites were settling in the area to the detriment of the Basters. Unscrupulous whites were using the illegal sale of alcohol and hastening the decline of the Basters, he observed. The Basters easily, too easily, lost their farms to debt piled up at shopowners and white neighbours; they had no idea about the price of their goods and were taken for a ride by whites. "They get into debt . . . in this way they lose their huge properties. Some move northwards . . . others hang around or must work for others," Schroeder wrote in the early nineteenth century. "The whites are beginning to push the coloureds out. At Keimoes most erfs are already in the possession of the white man."[273]

Compared to the first census in 1891 referred to earlier, when 735 whites, 1 429 "aboriginal natives" and 3 121 "other coloured persons" were counted in the Gordonia district, in 1904 Gordonia (by now including Mier) had 1 712 "European" inhabitants, 2 374 "Hottentot", 9 "Fingo", 1 245 "Kafir and Bechuana", and 3 888 "Mixed and other".[274]

In 1898 the Dutch Reformed Church established a labour colony for "poor whites" left destitute after the drought of 1895-97 and the outbreak of rinderpest among local cattle in 1896, on land reserved for this purpose by the government on the south side of the Orange, at Kakamas.

"Although claimed to be the cause of the poor white problem by many intelligentsia of the time, the rinderpest of 1896/97 and the Anglo-Boer War should rather be thought of as events that increased the pace at which white poverty became evident", writes economist Johann Fourie.[275] The rinderpest was devastating to cattle farmers, killing close to a third of cattle in the Cape, but unsustainable farming methods made the impact of the droughts more severe. According to Fourie, "the cultural tradition of the farmers was not conducive to successful commercial farming. The Roman Dutch law of inheritance entitled every child to a portion of his father's estate, even if these portions were insufficient for supporting a family. Consequently many successful farms, once divided, ended up overused and unsustainable as the source of a livelihood. The severe impact of the droughts was one consequence of the unsustainable farming methods used on many of these divided farms."[276]

The population of Kakamas grew from 806 in 1903 to 3 000 by 1915. The colony was headed by the same Reverend Schroeder that had started in Upington, and it was run along strict rules. The first settlers arrived in Neus, near Kakamas, in 1898. After the South African War (also known as the Anglo-Boer War, 1899-1902) there was another large influx of farming families, brought to the northern Cape by drought and poor economic conditions. Many started as *bywoners* (tenants) on farms owned by whites or coloureds.

Land Grab at Kanoneiland

Downstream from Upington, before Keimoes, is Kanoneiland. In the late 1700s, before the colonists had made their way up here in any significant numbers, the Aukokoa, a Khoikhoi group, lived and prospered on the island and its adjacent islets. The grazing was fine and there was good protection from the forests of the river bank. Around 100 men women and children lived in about 23 huts.[277] The Aukokoa were just one of many Khoikhoi and San societies living along the Gariep/Orange River at the time. Kanoneiland is formed where the river splits in two near Keimoes.

The island was named after the abortive cannon built by the Koranna who had sought refuge there during the Second Koranna War. It was made from a hollowed-out aloe stem, loaded with stones and gunpowder, and pointed at the colonial troops. It was fired, exploded, and killed many of the Koranna.

But there is another interesting story here: this was where a group of white farmers in the 1920s did a "land grab", as we would call it today. In 1925 a group of indigent whites applied for grazing licences on Kanoneiland and 29 families, led by a Mr PJ Strydom, moved here and began digging an irrigation system. Only 32 licences were granted, but the group had grown to 52 families. The magistrate ordered the last 20 to leave, and that all irrigation must stop. The group steadfastly refused, and the authorities relented and gave them permission to stay for a year. They lived under trees, with not enough food, and worked on building canals. Strydom later wrote: "If I look back, I see a group of poor people without help, without income, with a strong urge and desire to own a piece of ground . . . "[278]

The Karstens

Today Kanoneiland is home to the biggest table grape exporter in the country, Karsten Boerdery (known in English as Karsten Farms). Piet and Babsie Karsten started with 5 ha in 1968, growing crops like beans and lucerne. In 1982, when nobody planted grapes on the islands or along the river itself, the Karstens decided to grow table grapes for export. Today they have 240 ha here.

"When I met them in 1986/7, they lived in a caravan, with four children, and a flat at the end of the pack house, with an office at the back. But the workers all had houses," says Joa Bekker, human resources manager. "Karsten made it clear from the beginning that the table grape business was a people business – you can't grow table grapes if you don't value people. They also believed that you must develop people socially and religiously and let them share in the business."

Religious instruction, a share scheme, and the only grassed soccer field along the Gariep make this farm special. Karsten Boerdery has under its umbrella four farms as well as an export company, New Vision Fruit, and a farm in Egypt. It is certified with EurepGap, a pre-farm-gate-standard that covers the process of the certified product from before the seed is planted until it leaves the farm; Tesco's (a supermarket chain in the UK) Nature's Choice, which is a standard fresh produce growers must meet to ensure that the produce comes from growers who use good agricultural practices, operate in an environmentally responsible way and with proper regard for the health and wellbeing of their staff; and the British Retail Consortium (BRC), a trade association representing a wide range of British retailers.

Bekker came to the farm in 1993, having met Piet Karsten through the Rural Foundation in which he was involved.

"When I arrived, in charge of 713 seasonal workers and four farms, I wondered why he had appointed an HR manager. I started looking around to see how I could grade jobs. Piet came into the office, handed me a pair of black scissors, and said to take them and go into the vineyards for six months. These people are your clients, he told me."

And so he learned the work of a table grape farm. "The workers taught me skills, and the customs of the Tswana people. Afterwards, when I had problems, the team leaders would help me solve them."

Various empowerment schemes have been tried here, with varying success: as early as 1994 shares were sold to 34 people; in 1998, 330 workers bought preferential shares with the help of a Land Affairs programme.

"Experience taught that shares were not necessarily the best way," Bekker says. For most people, whoever you are, shares are the last thing you do with your money, after you've bought a house, paid for your children's education, etc. – and then wait 35 years for them to do well. So, Piet thought, give people a vested interest in what they do all their lives. "People want cash, education, and to build houses in the villages where they come from." Some workers come from the former Bophutatswana and Vryburg, 120 km away.

In 1997 Keboes Fruit Farms, the management company of Raap en Skraap, a 350-ha farm 140 km west of Kakamas, was formed. It is a separate entity from Karsten Farms and is 23% owned by workers, 27% by Black Management Forum Investments and 50% by Karsten Boerdery. The 23% ownership was acquired with the assistance of the IDC (Industrial Development Corporation). Company profits will pay for the shares. Grapes and dates are grown here; new projects being planned are citrus, sheep and goats, with an emphasis on empowering women. "Our aim with adding citrus," says Bekker, "is that if we can employ people for nine months, we will be satisfied."

Keimoes

The town of Keimoes is a sleepy one. Two bottle stores, a Spar, a few banks and a pharmacy, plus a furniture shop. Until Saturday, that is, when it comes alive with people from the farms around who come to town to shop. Early braais are set up and *roosterbrood* is being prepared outside one of the bottle stores for the hungry who come to shop.

Between Keimoes and Kakamas are many small communities.

The community of 7de Laan is one such, 4 km outside Keimoes, in Friersdale. Opposite it is Marvin's bottle store. The area is named after the Canadian Robert Frier, mentioned earlier in this chapter, who came to the area in 1882. Frier was one of the first people to grow grapes here, and built irrigation canals over 6 km, perhaps the first in the Keimoes area, with simple tools and the help of the Vlakplaas Basters.

A short way along is Loxtonvale, the home of one of the original Baster families. In 1886 Frederick William Loxton acquired two farms – Eenduin and Loxtonvale. Eenduin was probably bought or exchanged from a Coetzee or a Diergaardt. Frederick came to the area with his Baster wife Anna, who was much younger than him. When he died, she carried on and developed the land for her surviving children, Frikkie and Anna.[279]

Trevor Loxton is the son of Gert Loxton, and together they still farm here. His grandfather was Frederick William Christopher Loxton, born in the early 1900s; he had five children. Today Loxtonvale has five owners – three brothers and two sisters, and it is one huge farm. Grapes are grown for wine, they have won awards for their grapes, and 60% go to raisin production.

"We all take rain chances here," says Trevor. "The only grape that can take rain is Daturra, which has about seven skins, and can take 20 mm water."

Land and water along the Gariep will no doubt always be contested; they are not only valuable resources, but also hold the memories of generations. Slowly things may be changing for some farmers and some farm workers. But many still live in poverty. As one old man told me: "The coloured people developed the Gariep, played a major role here. Somewhere, something went wrong . . . "

The Gariep/Orange has always provided the lifeblood for the people who have lived here, but it has been a struggle: farming on the edge of the desert, with frequent flooding and extreme weather conditions is not easy. However, the success story of table grape farming here over the past two decades is a remarkable one. The years ahead will show whether the pressing issues of land and poverty can be met with the same success.

CHAPTER 10

Adapting to change

Climate change is the buzzword of our times, and grape farmers are taking notice. There are already changes in weather patterns, they say, and some have started to change the way they farm, moving towards more earth-friendly methods.

There is also a growing awareness of fair trade and "going green" among consumers. Agriculture contributes significantly to greenhouse gas (GHG) emissions. One South African farmer has become carbon neutral to offset his carbon footprint, others are farming organically. Integrated pest management is now being used as a way to lessen pesticide use. In the Western Cape there is an initiative to conserve biodiversity on farms.

Many efforts, small but significant changes.

The impulse to change may come from producers themselves, or from pressure from consumers and an industry which competes on a global market.

Science and technology has some answers for the challenges of farming in difficult conditions, such as new cultivars and ways of growing grapes. Delving into history and going back to basics, such as maintaining healthy soils, may provide other answers. Creative responses to daunting problems stretch all our imaginations.

Growing grapes in the desert is one story of pioneering innovation. Meeting the challenge of climate change is another.

Grapes from the desert

Grapes have been grown along the Gariep River in the arid Northern Cape for a long time. But there is a world of difference between raisins, the area's traditional product, and plump, juicy table grapes for export.

As we have seen earlier, a metamorphosis has taken place in the table grape in the past 20 years, and it has resulted in the Northern Cape becoming a major exporter of table grapes. Huge commercial table grape farms have been established along the river, replacing stock farms and mixed farming.

Human manipulation is responsible for changing the way grapes are cultivated to meet different demands, whether it be stimulating the natural growth process or adapting to adverse weather conditions. Dormancy can be broken, ripening can be manipulated, and cultivars that can adapt to harsh conditions have been bred.

Initially it took a degree of risk-taking on the part of producers as they experimented with table grapes. Vines follow the rhythm of the seasons. In winter they rest, needing a dormancy period before they bud in spring, and for this reason they thrive in places with cold winters. When soils get warmer in spring, the sap rises and moves up through the plant and the vine buds, flower clusters form and the berries set. Come summer, the berries ripen. In autumn the leaves change colour, and fall off as winter sets in.

Grapes like a Mediterranean climate, and until the 1970s, table grapes were grown mostly in the Hex River Valley where environmental conditions are favourable for them.

While grapes are not new to the semidesert areas of the Northern Cape along the Gariep River, the hot conditions made them good only for raisins. Table grapes only began to be a viable export in the 1980s.

"It's all about being willing to take risks," says Pieter Raath, who specialises in table grape production at the University of Stellenbosch's Faculty of Agri-Sciences. "Ironically, the warmer and drier the area, the better the vines. Table grape vines want good vegetative growth, warm, dry weather and enough water." The Gariep/Orange River area has plenty of water as well as hot and dry summers, and if the right cultivar is chosen, grapes will thrive in the alluvial soils along the river. Because of the low rainfall, the rain does not affect the grapes – they are fungus free and a stronger product, which travels well, he says. The grapes here ripen much earlier – and herein is the key to the Northern Cape success story – they can be on the table before Christmas. For the farmers, that means high premiums on northern hemisphere markets.

In the 1980s and 1990s producers were getting unprecedented prices for their grapes. And, as has been mentioned, the Orange River region was the fastest-growing farming area in the world.

The Nels

The *Rooipad* (red road) runs from the N14, between Pofadder and Kakamas, to the Augrabies Falls. Just beyond Augrabies is Rooipad Boerdery, today a highly successful table grape farm.

Abie Nel was one of the pioneers of the table grape industry along the Gariep. He was a stock farmer, a descendant of Abraham Pieter

Nel, one of the first livestock families to settle here in 1866. He bought the land in 1893 from the state on auction; on the title deed is marked "Great Waterfall" – the Augrabies. The waterfall was sold back to the state in 1964.

His sons Izak and Hannes Nel, who run the farm, are the fourth generation of Nels to farm on the Rooipad. It was only in 1972, with the Gariep Dam (then known as the Hendrik Verwoerd Dam), and 1977 with the Vanderkloof Dam, that thousands of hectares of agricultural land could be converted to productive irrigated land. But even then, getting water to the land needed power.

"What sparked grapes here was electricity – which only came here in 1979," says Izak Nel. "With electricity came new possibilities. We could now pump water. Before, it was all flood irrigation from a canal which is still there." Electricity also meant cooling facilities were possible – an essential requirement for exporting table grapes.

Apart from some vines for raisins, grapes were a small part of the farm, which has always been a stock farm. Livestock included karakul, but that industry came to an end in the 1980s.

"My dad started experimenting with raisins on the *buitegronde* (the land further from the river) in 1980, and planted the first vines then. He began experimenting with Thompson (grapes), making them larger, and selling first on the local market and then exporting them," says Izak.

The first trial was one hectare. The soil here was very different from the *binnegronde* (the land next to the river), which were clay and alluvial soils deposited as the river comes down.

Others were also trying to manipulate grapes. Initially raisins were the end product.

"But three years later we changed to table grapes, because with input costs and capital outlay, raisins wouldn't pay. Pipelines 3 km to the river required a huge capital outlay. It developed from there, and we exported through Unifruco." At that stage producers had no choice – there was a single-channel marketing system.

It was an unsophisticated business when people started growing table grapes, and it only gained momentum in the early 1990s. "It was extremely tough, there were strict rules. It was a big learning curve, with no technical people to tell you how to do it." There were no holidays for the brothers Izak and Hannes while growing up. "Every vacation I worked on the farm, pruning in the September holidays, and in December it was just grapes, grapes, grapes," Izak recounts.

In 1991 the brothers took over the farming from their father. "In his heart he was a livestock farmer," says Izak. Hannes had studied for a BCom degree at Stellenbosch, and Izak is an engineer. The Nels also have two other farms – a neighbouring one, and one at Onseepkans.

The brothers converted Rooipad Boerdery from a family farm to a business, employing 70 to 80 permanent labourers; they have 120 ha of table grapes, 25 ha for raisins, and employ 500 to 600 seasonal workers. "We must provide housing for everyone, there is no other place for them to live. One of the managers runs the local shop, and all basic food items are sold at cost," Izak explains.

"We're in the top 10 table grape producers. Our focus is on premium quality. Selection is very, very strict in the packing house."

The Nels export through The Grape Company, which they have done for 12 years. "Our big customer is Marks & Spencer (in the United Kingdom). And the local market has improved."

Izak tells me that this area produces the best table grapes in the world, in taste and quality. "Climate and soils and the attention to detail of South African farmers are unparalleled. The Chileans come close. But British retailers will tell you the Orange River grapes are the best."

And then there was Gibberellic Acid . . . giant firm berries

Growing grapes in the desert has its challenges. Vines need to go into dormancy and some of the newer grape-growing areas do not have cold-enough winters for this. As a result, bunches break unevenly, making it difficult to produce and manage a good crop. Two discoveries have revolutionised the table grape industry, says Pieter Raath.

Both are plant hormones, or plant growth regulators.

The first discovery, in the 1950s, was that of Gibberellic Acid (GA) by Japanese scientists who were investigating the causes of the "bakanae (foolish seedling) disease" which seriously lowered the yield of rice crops in Japan, Taiwan and throughout the Asian continent. Their findings were then developed by scientists in the United States. GA is one of five classical plant hormones, and gibberellins occur naturally in immature seeds, shoots, root tips and young leaves. GA has been used on table grapes on farms along the Orange River from the early 1980s, mostly for its effects on fruit formation.

In seedless grapes like Sultana Seedless (Thompson), still the most widely used cultivar, it improves bunch size and berry development and causes bunches to be looser. Very few seedless grapes are produced in South Africa without the use of GA, says Raath. "GA meant we could now have seedless Sultana grapes, the most popular grapes, with a good taste. The challenge was that it made the vines infertile. It also requires more labour as the grape bunches have to be dipped into the GA by hand."

The second discovery was that of the synthetic cytokine CPPU (common name forchlorfenuron), which stimulates cell division. This was also discovered by Japanese researchers, in the mid-1970s, and tested on a variety of plants in the late 1970s, including tobacco, citrus, pears, apples and grapes. Initial work on Sultana Seedless showed berry size could be increased 100% or more. The Japanese did not register the product and the agency was bought by a German corporation. In the mid-1990s the compound was registered for use on table grapes in South Africa. This was a huge revolution, according to Raath: "Sultana was already the most popular table grape. The challenge was to breed other seedless grapes that were less labour intensive, both red and black."

Cytokinins play an important role in the stimulation of both cell division and cell enlargement, as well as tissue maturation and fruit ripening. CPPU's primary effects on grapes are the regulation of fruit set, berry growth and berry development; it can, however, retard colour development in sensitive cultivars like Flame Seedless and Red Globe; it can also affect the taste and texture of berries and change the berry shape, especially in elliptical or cylindrical berries such as Thompson Seedless or Crimson Seedless. CPPU can be used to delay the ripening of a cultivar by two weeks or more if this is a market advantage.[280]

A much earlier discovery, in the 1940s, was the development of a synthetic ethylene compound known as Ethephon. When fruit ripens, it releases ethylene, a volatile compound which stimulates the surrounding fruit to ripen. Ethephon has been used in grapes in South Africa since the 1960s to improve the colour, hasten ripening and control vegetative growth. The problems associated with too high doses are a decrease in post-harvest quality, because it increases loose berries, berry crack and soft berries spoilage, and decreases acid content, which can cause an insipid taste.

Other modifications

Apart from chemicals, there are many other ways to manipulate the bunch of grapes you get. One intervention is to cut off a number of bunches in order to increase the berry size on the remaining bunches. "You also don't want the bunch to overshatter, which results in too many berries and a loose bunch. To prevent this you cut shoots, remove leaves and trim bunches before flowering, and girdle the vines. You can do all this, but there are still other growth conditions that affect the grapes. They can overset, with tight bunches, and you then have to cut out the berries.

"This is the time of year that's most stressful for producers," says Raath.

When the industry first developed along the Gariep River, all the grapes were white seedless from ungrafted Thompson Seedless vines; over the years, grafted vines of white seedless varieties such as Sugraone, Regal Seedless and Prime Seedless have also been planted. More recently the area has seen the introduction of red seedless varieties such as Prime Seedless and Flame Seedless.[281]

Producers have also experimented with climate modification. To regulate temperature, overhead irrigation is used to cool the temperature, but it is not always practical as it causes fungal disease. Evaporative cooling and cooling the vines from underneath – water sprayed a few times for short periods – are also used but can cause too much humidity and wet soil. In frost areas, overhead irrigation is used on cold nights. Smaller producers burn oil in cans throughout the vineyard, the idea being that the layer of smoke formed keeps the air below warm. For hail, nets and directional trellising are used, and plastic covering is used in Limpopo Province. Trellising is also used for wind protection.

Dormancy breaking

Throughout the world dormancy-breaking substances are used, particularly in warm areas such as the Northern Cape, when buds reach the "green tip" stage. In areas with a moderate winter, there can be an uneven budburst, or a low percentage of budburst, which results in fewer bunches on the vine. Uneven budburst leads to uneven shoot growth and bunch development, which makes it difficult for a producer to use hormone treatments, or spray for disease control, and makes them less effective.

Dormancy breaking optimises grapevine budding. Plant growth regulators, such as hydrogen cyanamide, are applied with backpack sprays or directed tractor sprays, leading to early, strong vegetative growth. However, hydrogen cyanamide is toxic, and spraying has implications for the safety of workers; it also has disadvantages for the plant. Other ways to stimulate budburst are hydro-cooling, shoot treatments with warm water, shoot bending and shoot wounding. Partial dehydration of buds and anaerobic conditions also break dormancy.

The research field for table grapes is wide open, and part of Pieter Raath's job is to generate postgraduate students to do research in the area; and of course to educate producers to be better equipped for the table grape industry.

"In South Africa we are committed to changes and development to meet the expectations of people who buy the grapes in Europe. Table grape cultivation is an underexposed area in South Africa, and few students are drawn to it, being more attracted to wine because it's seen as a funkier business, and a more flashy job," says Raath.

Peu Bezuidenhout – in the field

Peu Bezuidenhout, fresh out of the army as a young man, rented 34 ha of his father's farm. He planted 3 ha of Sultana Seedless for raisins and a little wine. On the other land he rotated crops like lucerne and cotton.

Bezuidenhout, who was born in Keimoes, about 15 km away from where he now lives at Naftali Estate at Dyasonsklip, is one of the Northern Cape's largest producers of export grapes.

In 1983 he started experimenting with table grapes, one of the first farmers to do so in the area. They were not a huge success, he says. He packed 16 pallets, of which seven were rejected at cold storage. For the first five or six years he was not very successful. Why did he persevere?

"It was a niche market, new and something to go for as a young farmer. But we didn't tell our bank managers," he laughs. His expertise grew and exports picked up. Today he has 250 ha cultivated, 80% table grapes, all export, 10% raisins and 10% wine. He bought another farm eight years ago in Summerdown, near Upington.

In November 1987, 6 ha of table grapes were wiped out by hail; and then in January, after the harvest, there was a one-in-100-years' flood. All his grapes were gone. "I had to start all over again." It may have been tough, but it presented him with an opportunity, he says, as a lot of land became available and he doubled his landholdings.

Bezuidenhout remembers the early days. "Initially, we tried to copy what the Western Cape grape area was doing – but it didn't work. The Deciduous Fruit Board ran a programme to help farmers, and there were a lot of mishaps in the beginning. You have to learn the cultivars to learn the tricks."

Today he farms many varieties. "The market wants, all year round, a red, white and black grape, seedless. Previously there were no seedless black grapes. But I also have to plan planting with the harvesting season in mind – we have three weeks to harvest each cultivar – and we plan according to the volumes of vines and infrastructure."

Bezuidenhout's father was a sheep farmer, and in 1954 bought the land at the Orange River for lucerne for his sheep. His land includes a railway siding, and a few years ago he began to rail table grapes to Cape Town harbour. "Within the next ten years we will be back to rail," he says. "The road to Cape Town is so busy in December and January, with a truck every ten minutes, and it's damaging the road."

Bezuidenhout employs six production managers and an IT manager – necessary in today's business world. He has 87 permanent workers who live on the farm, and between 600 to 700 contract workers, depending on the season. "A table grape is handled 28 times before we pack it," he tells me.

The Orange River is a summer rainfall area, so heavy rains are expected in February. "We just hope there are no rains in November and December," says Bezuidenhout. "In fact, we never want rain from November to February – and of course the sheep farmers do want it. Hailstorms at the beginning of the season can be disastrous – hail runs in zones, and you can see it approaching. It wiped out 75% of the Flame Seedless in December (2008)."

Some people use hail nets, but it changes the microclimate and it becomes necessary to spray more pesticides for diseases. Later varieties can also get frost bitten. "In September the vines start to bud – and we had frost on 28 October one year." A black frost is a dry frost with an easterly wind: it can kill a vineyard. Bezuidenhout recollects making fires from old tyres to warm up the vines to counter the black frost. "I don't do that any more. I realised I was just doing it for my own comfort, but it doesn't work."

Harvesting table grapes along the river takes place according to elevation, longitude (earlier in the west) and cultivar.

"On my land an elevation of 153 metres can make a difference of two weeks in terms of time of harvest," says Bezuidenhout. "And if you put more yield on the vines (through various practices), you get grapes later."

Interestingly, Blouputs, west of Augrabies, used to be the earliest harvest, but not any more. Since the valley has been farmed, its microclimate has changed.

Phyllis Burger – rescuing embryos in the laboratory

The black grape Phyllis Burger gives to me to taste instantly takes me back to my childhood and popping sweet, juicy Catawba grapes into my mouth. They are known as "*glippertjies*" in Gauteng where I grew up, and they have a distinct and delicious taste.

But these grapes are not Catawba – they are bigger and do not have the same tough skins, and you will not find them on the supermarket shelves. They are one of Burger's "babies". Burger is a plant breeder at the Agricultural Research Council (ARC), a job she loves. Nothing stuffy and restrained about this scientist – she is keen to talk about her grapes and share the excitement she feels as each embryo she has carefully nurtured grows up and she can evaluate and taste the new variety she has created.

I taste another black grape, which is truly sublime – a taste I think will surely be a winner on supermarket shelves. Sadly, it will not make it there – at least not in this particular cross. Burger points out to me the cracks appearing in the berry – it may be a taste winner, but it does not respond well to cold storage. But she is using it in other crosses.

Burger's speciality is embryo rescue, which has made possible the breeding of seedless cultivars, either with each other or with seeded varieties.

In 1985, says Burger, no seedless grapes were exported. Today very few seeded cultivars are exported, as consumer demand is for seedless grapes.

Seedless grapes have been around for a long time – Sultana (also known as Sultanina or Thompson) is a naturally seedless variety. Its only problem is that it has small berries and was suitable only for raisins, not table grapes.

"We can go far back in the parentage of seedless grapes, but we're not sure where Sultanina comes from," Burger says. "We assume it was a bud mutation, appearing before there were breeding programmes. It would have been naturally selected: if something is strong, special and different, the farmer takes a shoot and grows it. Sultanina probably originated in Anatolia, but we're not sure when it came to South Africa."

Most grapes belonging to *vitis vinifera*, the Old World species, originated in the area around the Caspian and Black Seas and Turkey. There are also wild species in other parts of Europe. French settlers in America took their vines with them, but America already had indigenous grape species, one of them *vitis labrusca*, my favourite Catawba.

The only *vitis* indigenous to South Africa is in the Knysna area, known as the *bobbejaantou* (literally "baboon rope") – and it is nothing like the grape. The *vitis* family is diverse and even includes a succulent.

When the phylloxera outbreak devastated the local vines here in the 1880s, it was found that rootstock cultivars from the United States were resistant or tolerant to the louse, and so it was used to graft Old World cultivars on. This still happens today. But along with it came powdery and downy mildew from America, major problems in viticulture.

Burger studied agriculture at the University of Stellenbosch and worked for a year in the Herbarium there. She started work at the ARC in 1992. "When I started off there was no tissue culture lab, and I was employed to sort out the embryo rescue programme." For this she received her MSc degree.

Today her work starts in the lab and ends in the vineyards, and – ultimately – with the release of a new cultivar. She emphasises that it is always a team effort.

Why an embryo rescue programme?

The grape is a flowering plant (although the flowers may not seem obvious), Burger explains, and most viniferous plants are hermaphrodite (female and male on same plant), pollinated by wind or bees, although insects play a small role.

"If I think two plants' children will be interesting, before they flower I emasculate them by removing the anthers. This is done one by one, by hand – you can't damage them, and every one has to be taken off." The pollen from the other parent plant is placed in a plastic bag and tied around the emasculated flower. Pollination takes place, followed by fertilisation and the development of an embryo.

Seedless-grape breeding is not that easy or successful. Most seedless grape cultivars are in fact not truly seedless. Although a hard seed does not develop, soft green rudimentary seeds do, which may not appear to the consumer as a seed. The only part of the new grape's DNA is inside the seed. In so-called seedless varieties, the rudimentary seed stays soft and green, and cannot be germinated. At some stage the embryo aborts. Tissue cultures are used to literally rescue these embryos before they abort, and make it possible to develop hybrids from seedless grapes. Embryos are then cultured on a growth medium under aseptic conditions.

Seedlessness is not one gene, explains Burger. There are three recessive genes – seedlessness is called a complex trait, and there is a continuum of seed size from seedless to seeded. Once the embryos germinate, they are carefully looked after until they are seedlings. The crosses made now will be seedlings the next year and by spring of the following year they will be planted out in vineyards. Once the seedlings are 30 to 40 cm high, they will be grown further if they look promising.

Once the vine is producing, an evaluation phase follows. Burger will look at how labour intensive it is, and its fertility. "It's no use having a fantastic grape if it only produces two bunches on a vine," she says. And then there is the cold storage test: how does the cultivar hold up to storage?

It is a long process from embryo rescue to new cultivar release: it can take 12 to 15 years to release a variety. After five to six years on the experimental farm, the new cultivars are grown in field trials, with the assistance of co-operative producers in various areas.

Before a cultivar can be commercialised, it must be registered for plant breeders' rights by the Department of Agriculture, which will look at all the collected data on that cultivar. This takes around two years.

When a cultivar is finally chosen for release, it needs to be grown in large quantities. SAPO (the South African Plant Improvement Organisation) is responsible for the production of certifiable propagation plant material, and is the main supplier of this plant material to deciduous fruit nurseries.

Burger is in the process of taking two new cultivars to Spain to be evaluated and for a decision to be made on their release for commercialisation in Spain.

Plant breeders' priorities now are to breed disease-resistant varieties. Less spraying of fungicides, or any other manipulation, is desirable. Even Gibberellic Acid, which is natural, requires extra labour and the cost of diesel, and it has other effects on the vine. Breeding for a naturally large berry size is also on the programme.

The breeding focus in South Africa is on cultivars, not rootstocks. While rootstocks affect the quality of the fruit, so too do soil, propagation material and viruses such as leafroll and fan leaf, which have devastating effects on berry size and fertility of the vine.

Being a scientist does not mean that Phyllis Burger is confined to a laboratory. She spends a lot of time in the field, evaluating her "babies". And she is constantly meeting people visiting from overseas to evaluate the ARC's varieties. That includes building good relationships with importers. "They're excited by our varieties, and can tell us what is happening in the market," she says.

In the world of exact science, there is a lot of scope for creativity.

"I cross things I think could be interesting. It's sort of creative. For me the most exciting is the seedling phase, when they live up to expectations. There's always something new I'd like to try."

Here today, gone tomorrow

Things move fast in the breeding of new cultivars. There is constant improvement, and a lot of competition. So, unless a new variety is really special, it will not go anywhere.

According to Burger, "what's important now is a crunchy berry texture – consumers don't want a soggy grape; the skin mustn't be tough, and increasingly flavour is important, not just sweetness."

The Eastern markets like colours – red is important, but it must be a pinkish red. "We've been breeding towards naturally big berries; but interestingly the Muscat varieties are popular, and while size is important, it's no longer that important."

In France they are focusing on traditional, pure varieties of grapes. In Germany they are breeding varieties that are disease resistant. They will use that as a lever: the wine industry is suffering because of quality competition. They can use a low carbon footprint as a marketing tool.

While China has the biggest table grape industry, India and now Egypt are also growing. Brazil has an interesting industry, as they grow grapes in a tropical area on a rotation basis. They do not have winter, so there is no dormancy. Dormancy has to be forced, and they can plan exactly when they will harvest.

The ARC did embark on a programme for genetically modified (GM) grapes years ago, and at the time had a five-year project with the Volcani Institute in Israel (with USAid funding). Their aim was to breed a grape genetically resistant to Botyris rot. "We made a decision to not pursue this avenue any further as we had requests from table grape exporters for statements that we are not using GM grapes in our breeding programme," says Burger. "The University of Stellenbosch was also concentrating more and more on GMs, and we've decided that it should be their mandate."

Going east – new areas

The Gariep/Orange River success story now extends beyond the traditional grape area between Upington and Kakamas. Over the past years vines have been cultivated in limited quantities in the Gauteng, North West, Mpumalanga, Limpopo and Free State provinces. In some areas harvesting takes place as early as November, almost two months earlier than the traditional harvest time.

André Smith

André Smith grew up in Groblershoop, east of Upington, on a farm which grew raisins and cash crops like wheat, maize, lucerne. "Today our best product is pecan nuts; but we also grow table grapes, wine grapes and raisins," he says. Smith entered the table grape business when it was booming. "Table grapes are a money-spinner. I worked at Sasol (he had studied chemistry), but then came back here with expectations of making bags of money, the boom in 1996 was so good." Working as a partner with his father did not work out, so he hired a vineyard and a tractor and made enough money to buy his present farm, an 80 ha piece of land.

At some stages of the table grape boom years, people could pay off their farms in two years, he says. The boom is now over.

"It's a sifting process – if you're not the best, you won't survive. People made the mistake of growing too fast. The thing here is that you can easily invest in production costs which are more than what the farm is worth. In my very first year, 6 ha of table grapes were lost to hail."

And then, with deregulation of the export industry, the game changed. "You were linked to the market, and you paid for your own mistakes." The newer farmers at the Gariep, like André, learned from the more established. "We'd jump in our bakkies and go and look at what was being done at Kakamas," he says.

The early ripening of table grapes along the Gariep River is the marketing advantage farmers have here. "At that stage, if you packed at week 1 (January), you were early. Now we start at week 48 (the beginning of December). For every kilometre you farm away from the river, harvesting is a week later. But there's also the risk of frost closer along the river. Hail is another threat, all along the river. There's less rain in the west, which is good."

Climate change

Everyone is talking climate change. Late rains, a hot summer, floods and frequent fires – people nod knowingly, attributing it all to climate change.

The effects of climate change are already being felt in the traditional grape-growing areas of the Western Cape. Research shows significant trends in rainfall and air temperature, and climate change is projected to lead to warmer and (mostly) drier conditions. Also predicted is a higher incidence of extreme events, such as severe storms.

In a 2010 paper on climate change and the future of the wine industry in South Africa,[282] Prof. Nick Vink and his fellow authors cite a 2005 study of 12 weather stations over the 1967-2000 period[283] which found that very warm days have become warmer and have occurred more frequently during the last decade, particularly during January, April and August. Studies on future expected climate conditions for South Africa show that temperatures can be expected to rise everywhere in the southwestern Cape, with the smallest increases in areas adjoining the coast. Typical increases range from around 1,5 °C at the coast to some 2-3 °C inland of the coastal mountains by 2050. In the Northern Cape, temperatures are expected to rise by between 2,5 to 4,5 °C.

How will this affect viticulture? The vine is a hardy plant which produces better fruit when made to struggle. But how much struggle can it take? Wine grapes may tolerate, and even like stress; table grapes do not.

There is no doubt that a change in climatic patterns will affect fruit and wine production and such impacts are already being felt within the South African fruit and wine industry, according to a report released in 2009.[284] These include direct impacts, such as physical changes in climate, and indirect ones, such as the growing environmental awareness amongst consumers and the corresponding demand for carbon-efficient business processes.

Historically, the South African wine industry has been characterised by its diversity, writes Vink et al., but this diversity is threatened by climate change. "When a warm region, for example, becomes a hot region, diversity in the type and style of wine that can be produced is limited. On the other hand, the industry is situated in an area where there is still potential for further expansion into temperate and cool areas, for changes in viticultural and oenological practices, and for changes in wine styles."[285]

Suzanne Carter, an environmental and geographical scientist at the University of Cape Town (UCT) who drew up an interim report in 2006[286] on the influence of climate change on the South African wine industry, has made some projections of what might be in store. There is a complex system of interactions between the many factors contributing to climate change, and projections are just ideas of what could happen. The four main changes predicted are changes in precipitation (rainfall), extreme events, temperature and carbon dioxide levels, as explained in more detail in the box below.

Possible effects of climate change[287]

Rainfall

There is some consensus that rainfall will decrease in the Western Cape, but by how much is not known. Conservative estimates indicate only a slight decrease in annual rainfall. Most vineyards use irrigation – either overhead sprinklers or drip irrigation systems – which are more water efficient and cost effective. Currently most farmers do not use their full quota of irrigation water, writes Carter, and therefore they could possibly draw more water as temperatures rise. This would come at a cost and as demand for water increases, wine growers and producers will pay more per unit of water.

The winemaking process is estimated to use between two and eight litres of water for the production (excluding irrigation) of every litre of wine. Of concern is the distribution of rainfall events. In the last 50 years there has been an increase in the number of dry days between rainfall. If dry-spell duration increases, the period of increased evaporation also increases. In the last 50 years there has already been an increase in dry-spell duration of roughly two days on average in the Western Cape.

Extreme events

Climate change is also expected to increase the occurrence of extreme events.

Heavier rains less frequently are not always desirable, as a lot of water is lost to runoff. Floods are also capable of ruining agricultural crops, although vines are usually cultivated on well-drained soils. Increased drought (which is more likely, given the longer dry spells already observed) is of great concern. Irrigation can be used to offset any deficit; however, if there are water restrictions or an increased demand for water, it will become increasingly difficult to provide supplemental irrigation, writes Carter.

Temperature

In the Western Cape, models suggest the region should expect an increase of around 1,5 °C at the coast and 2 to3 °C inland. So far the trend of warming has increased the quality of wines, with higher ratings for recent vintages. However, in some areas where the warming has been more pronounced, there seems to be a threshold over which quality can be sacrificed if ripening occurs too early, according to Carter. Each cultivar and style of wine and table grape will have different susceptibilities and coping ranges.

There is some speculation as to the resilience of vines to adapt to climatic stress, she writes. Greater resilience may make the vine more water efficient; however, it is unclear whether this may also affect the quality of the wine. Vines produce better-quality fruit when they are made to struggle – the yield is smaller but of better quality. There is a threshold of viability between better quality and lower yield, however. If the yields become too small, the capital invested in the vines is not recouped in sales of the wine.

Carbon dioxide

Carter writes that increased levels of CO_2 encourage greater biomass accumulation (larger fruit/yields) in plants and increased water efficiency. Experiments have shown that the grapevine will react similarly. That may, however, not be beneficial as higher sugars would change the flavours (and therefore potentially the quality) of the grapes. This could have serious implications for vines, as wine is so heavily reliant on grape quality in determining its price and profitability.

Peter Johnston, who is part of the Climate Systems Analysis Group at UCT, says: "Grape people don't want rain, especially summer rain. They want dams and rivers full, but not rain." But he notes that apple farms have become risky. "Temperatures are too hot, and there's no competitive advantage because apples can be stored year round, grapes can't."

Table grape producer Lucien Luyt, from De Tuin near Porterville, collects weather data at his farm and feeds it back to Peter. "We work together," explains Luyt. "They've been spot-on in their forecasting, they've got good models, even though it's not an exact science."

Luyt believes climate change is an issue for everyone. "We're big wasters of water, generally. Farmers, however, are not such big wasters," he says. They, more than most, know the value of water. His farm has plentiful water, fed by the melting snow from the nearby mountains. "My dam is full 365 days a year. I'm pretty frugal, though. The problem for people is expanding capacity."

As the effects of climate change become more evident, farmers will no doubt make changes. Luyt uses the services of Chris Barnard, who runs an irrigation academy. "He's a specialist and genius on how to use the right amount of everything, simple usable technologies. Already there's a trend to biological farming, and we're incorporating that," says Luyt.

Table grape expert Pieter Raath believes we must exercise caution in ascribing every fluctuation in weather to global warming. "Climatic conditions may seem more dramatic to us now, such as hailstones and untimely rains," says Raath, "but can that be ascribed to climate change? This season (2008) we had a late winter – my colleague reports two such seasons in the 1970s. We should beware of using climate change as a scapegoat for all issues".

"Nobody can ignore climate change any more," says researcher Phyllis Burger. "Climate change is happening too fast." Producers are not really talking about it at this stage. "But in California they are breeding rootstock for drought tolerance." Table grape vines have short lifespans, unlike wine grape vines, and producers work on a 10-to-15-year plan. The choice of rootstocks and cultivars will increasingly become important. "We've seen in the Hex River Valley in 2005 and 2006 (when there was less rain) how the quality of the berries was softer and smaller, with more damage. Producers may have to restrict the size of crops (if there are water shortages) so as not to stress crops," she says.

Izak Nel, who farms table grapes near Augrabies, says producers are talking about climate change, and everyone has an opinion. "It's not affecting business now. But yes, we may have to have more netting structures, although some grapes don't like netting, such as Thompsons. Each variety has its own recipe. The storms are more erratic; and five of the hottest years in the last 100 have been in the last ten years. People say it hasn't been cold enough."

Producer Peu Bezuidenhout is well aware of climate change: "Something else is happening now, it's raining more and more every year – the last drought we had was 20 years ago. In January and February it's hotter than normal – 48 to 50 °C. Luckily it's dry at that time. Above 35 °C, nothing happens in the vine – late sugars don't form in the berries, and it delays ripening and affects quality. We do use hydro-cooling, using water and a light breeze, which can lower the temperature by about 5 °C."

Producer André Smith has been involved in the crop insurance industry, and says storms are definitely becoming more severe. There is more rain and more wind. Ten percent of farming costs go on insurance, he estimates. "As a farmer, it's your job to manage risk," believes Smith.

Su Birch, CEO of Wines of South Africa (WOSA), says South Africa has not been as hard hit as other countries. "But we're talking about it, thinking about it. In Australia the drought caused wine people to go bankrupt . . . "

The changes, then, are definitely making themselves felt.

Going greener

People in the wine and grape industries are looking at ways to change farming practices to adapt to the changes mentioned above, or to mitigate some of agriculture's negative effects. The agricultural sector contributes significantly to greenhouse gas (GHG) emissions through the use of agrochemicals and liquid fuels such as petrol and diesel, as well as land-use change, and there is an increasing focus on the "GHG footprint" of agriculture produce. A newer concept is "virtual water", which assesses trade in terms of the amount of water used in producing a commodity.

Sustainability, biological farming, organic farming, biodiversity and carbon neutral are terms you will increasingly see in wine and grape agriculture.

Biodiversity is an offshoot of organic agriculture, as many beneficial insects and microbes return to the soil, but many wine farms have gone further and joined the Biodiversity and Wine Initiative (BWI), a partnership between the South African wine industry and the conservation sector. Its goals are to minimise the further loss of threatened natural habitat, and to contribute to sustainable wine production through the adoption of biodiversity guidelines. Some measures are removing aliens, planting carbon sink plants such as spekboom, and better cellar and farm management processes. A BWI Champion farm must set aside 10% of land for conservation. The BWI already has 15 Champions and 142 members. These members must have at least 2 ha of natural or restored natural area on the farm that can be conserved.

The BWI includes the Integrated Production of Wine (IPW), a voluntary environmental sustainability scheme established by the South African wine industry in 1998. It consists of a set of guidelines specifying good agricultural practices related to grape production as well as a set of guidelines specifying good manufacturing practices for cellars to produce wines that are "healthy, clean and environmentally friendly".[288] One of its most important principles is that production should proceed in harmony with nature.

Registered IPW members represent 97% of harvested grapes in the country. "However, the proportion of actually audited farms and cellars is much smaller – the system is still mainly regulated via self-monitoring. Compliance can be achieved by scoring a minimum 50% of the total score, a fairly low threshold by international standards. To our knowledge, however, the IPW scheme is unique of its kind in the wine-producing world," writes Vink et al.[289]

According to Vink and his fellow authors, the concept of precision viticulture and precision irrigation is important, as water has to be saved within the concept of sustainable viticulture.[290]

One example of a farm conserving water is the on-site closed-system water treatment plant used on the wine estate Spier near Stellenbosch. It recycles all the estate's water, using a natural process which results in high-quality water that is used for irrigation.

The water is grey and black water (sewage), which comes from the whole estate, including the cellar, Spier's three restaurants and the hotel. The problem with cellar wastewater is that it has a low pH, is low in nutrients and has a high or variable organic load and is generally only suitable for watering kikuyu grass. Pollutants in this water only partially biodegrade and eventually end up in the riverine catchment area, harming the water source for everyone.[291]

"We see water as more than a resource – it is a fundamental element in the complex web of life, and our focus was to create a holistic solution," says Spier CEO Andrew Milne. "Our core value that we are committed to is financial sustainability," explains Milne. "We don't see the environment as separate, as part of our corporate social responsibility programme. It's a value that we base our business on, we think about the future" He says: "Inherently, we are a wine farm, an agricultural entity with a high water demand. We see changes in the physical world, through the seasons, the impact of heat and drought and rain on our business. As a business, there's a strategic reason to look at the environment we are working within." It is good for the earth and it is good for business. But more than that, it raises awareness that water is precious and should be treated with respect.

Sustainable farming

Organically grown grapes for winemaking are the future, believes Pietie le Roux, senior farm manager of La Motte near Franschhoek, who has been with the farm for 25 years and has overseen the conversion from conventional to organic farming.

In that time he has seen many changes: "In 1984, this valley was not for red cultivars. There was not enough sun and vigour. We used to have 1 200 mm rain, now we have 800 mm. One heat wave a year was extraordinary, now we have eight to ten a year. The challenge is to cope and adapt to winter starting later – pruning is later, we used to prune 1 June; now in June it's not cold enough to stop the growth. There are big changes in viticultural practices."

Le Roux has adapted by changing the direction of planting rows, and using the cooler areas for white grape. Cover crops keep water evaporating from the soil; irrigation pipes are buried and there are temperature monitors in the canopies of the vines.

"Now I look at weather forecasts so I can plan for the rest of week; in the old days I knew from experience," he says.

Viticulture, like most agriculture, is a huge consumer of water – apart from the water needed for irrigation, every litre of wine requires between two to eight litres for its production. La Motte is a Biodiversity Champion and a large part of its BWI contribution is in its water management programme. Water used in the cellar is recycled here to drinking-water quality. That is a lot of water saved.

While the farm is fortunate to have mountain water for its use, Le Roux is well aware that water needs to be conserved. "Global warming is a problem. In 25 years the climate has changed rapidly, it's a big concern. We use all systems we can to save water, it rains less and less every year."

Each block of vines has what looks like a plastic lantern attached to a pole. This is part of a sophisticated system, using computers and infrared satellite, that monitors the temperature of each canopy every hour of every day. There is also a pipe a metre underground. This shows how much water the vineyards need, and when. It is irrigation on demand, with no waste. A drip irrigation system – 3,2 litres an hour per plant – ensures optimum use of water.

"The new Berg River Dam in Franschhoek is for Cape Town's domestic consumption – we don't get a drop from it, " Le Roux notes.

Soil analysis determines which cultivars should be grown on which slope – some need more water. "It costs R140 000 per hectare to re-establish a block of vines, so you have to make sure you plant correctly," he says.

Soil fertility is basic to organic viticulture – in fact, any agriculture – and the soil needs to have healthy micro-organism populations. Soil is a living organism but microbes are destroyed by chemical fertilisers and pesticides, and conventionally farmed soils are depleted, if not devoid, of these micro-organisms. Compost enriches soil and contributes to a healthy plant which is better able to resist disease, explains Le Roux.

Organic agriculture avoids or excludes the use of synthetic fertilisers, pesticides and plant growth regulators. It relies on crop rotation, crop residues, animal manures and cultivation to maintain soil productivity. Organic farmers may use copper (for powdery mildew) and sulphur (for downy mildew).

Le Roux plants lupin as a cover crop, which binds nitrogen to the soil and produces mulch when it dies back. Mulch conserves soil moisture, and increases soil fibre and organic matter. It is a good place for beneficial insects to breed. Lupin also dovetails perfectly with the grapes' growing season, dying off in November and acting as mulch until March/April.

As part of the BWI programme, 3 ha of spekboom (a carbon sink) has been planted. In addition, a 30-ha piece of mountain (on the 170-ha farm, 75 ha of which is under vines) has been cleared of aliens and the endemic "Blushing Bride" protea, a plant on the Red List of the world's threatened species (compiled by the International Union for Conservation of Nature), has been planted. "Since we started," Le Roux says, "we've found they don't grow where they used to grow. I've been a hiker in these mountains for many years. There are less and less disas. In previous years there were lots of Blushing Brides in the mountains, now you have to know where to find them."

Farming organically on a large scale is not easy, is initially costly, and at this stage has no financial benefits. And La Motte is a big farm. "But if you do it, do it properly, or not at all," says Le Roux. "Organics is growing 30% a year – if farmers are not organic in the next ten years, they will struggle to sell their product."

There are few organic farms in South Africa, and so organic practices are still being developed for our climate conditions, with little technical advice available. La Motte's experience will no doubt benefit others.

"It works," Le Roux assures. "You let nature do what it needs to. But before you do it, you as a farmer have to believe in it, you must want to do it, not just because it's a fashion. Otherwise you'll get fed up. You have to farm twice as hard, it's a huge effort."

But it is worth it.

"We farmers live close to nature. And as parents we have to save the earth for our children, it's incredibly important for the future," he says. His wish is that Franschoek will become a biodiversity valley. "I'm looking with big eyes at the outcome."

La Motte is owned by Hanneli Rupert-Koegelenberg and her husband Hein Koegelenberg is CEO of the farm. La Motte is SGS certified – an international certification that has stringent requirements.

The other farm Le Roux manages, Nabot in Walker Bay, started with virgin soil and has been an organic farm from Day 1, eight years ago. "It requires a big mind change, even from the workers on the farm. Those wines have different characters and smells."

But as he says, "the whole thing about organic is that you're giving back to nature. It's initially expensive, but after five or six years it evens out, and then gets cheaper."

Climate change and the future of farming

It may seem a daunting task to change the way agriculture is practised.

But, says Prof. Mohammed Karaan, dean of the Faculty of AgriSciences at Stellenbosch University, there has been an ethical shift in the way people think about agriculture.

"Climate change, erosion, chemical contamination – people have started focusing on those things. Many practices are not sustainable, and we need to look at low tillage and ecological ways of conservation," Karaan says. "There are much bigger changes happening in this field than most of us realise. We are seriously questioning the nature of farming. The leaders in the field are already doing what is tomorrow's science. Much of what academia does, however, is still teach yesterday's science. Of our research, 60 to 70% is conventional. But advances are being made in conservation ecology. Food science increasingly looks at environmentally and human-friendly products."

A carbon-neutral pioneer

Michael Back is the owner of Backsberg near Stellenbosch, the only carbon-neutral wine estate in South Africa, and the third in the world.

"It started, unknowingly, 12 to 14 years ago, when I employed a gardener to sort out the winery garden. And then we replanted what we'd pulled out. With access to big equipment nowadays, if there's a tree in the way, you get rid of it. We'd done a lot of damage, it was time to repair the damage."

What started as fixing up a garden to look pretty turned into a mission and a passion. "We've taken the route that with carbon neutral, everything is up for discussion; it's a total re-evaluation of what you do," he explains.

One of the first things Back did was an audit of the farm's timber – there are tons of it in trellising, roof beams, barrels – and then of the concrete, the tons of steel.

The audit helped them understand the carbon-emission consequences of Backsberg's farming and winemaking activities, reviewing all activities from overall energy consumption to CO_2 emitted during fermentation.

And then they started offsetting their carbon footprint, through things like skylights to save on electricity; smaller bakkies and tractors to save on carbon emissions, and a controller to control the pressure and volume of irrigation water to some of the vineyards. Their water banks are insulated with straw bales, so they need virtually no daytime electricity to cool the cellar buildings. They have a small nursery where they propagate trees; they also plant trees on behalf of their importers. They make their own compost; they make furniture from the used oak wine barrels.

Back shows me a plastic wine bottle, the next step in lighter bottles.

Already they are using lightweight glass bottles. Glass weight and wine quality have no relationship, he says, but the environmental cost of making lightweight glass is far less than that of producing standard glass. "It is also cheaper and helps us contain packaging costs." Now he is moving to plastic. He is confident that the wine public will buy into the concept within two years. "The problem is the short shelf life of wine in such a bottle – 18 months, so only some wines can be bottled in plastic."

Backsberg has a methane digester and offsets production with a greening programme in nearby Klapmuts, run by Food and Trees for Africa. "We plant a minimum of 1 000 trees a year, and we haven't run out of space yet . . . "

They are also one of BWI's Biodiversity Champions

"Everything we've done here we've found by seeking in history – clever people have gone before us. We have to take the systems of the past and layer in today's technology."

The most challenging aspect to making changes is to find the patience, Back says: "Farming and winemaking is a slow and lifelong business – I harvest once a year, I can only do one significant thing a year."

To him, "the biggest revelation around climate change was that we had to modify our behaviour. The biggest problem? Greed – we think we need too much, we've lost the balance between happiness and pleasure and real meaning in our lives." Back's aim is to do the same job, but own less. "I drive a Bantam bakkie," he tells me. "The first thing you do is to bury your ego."

There are a lot of options open to people, and there is a lot of talk.

"You can do it on a few levels, and people don't know where to start, they think 'I'm only one individual'." But each person can make a difference.

"Climate change is for everybody."

The future of wine

The future production of wine is not believed to be at risk in South Africa, as is the case in some other wine-producing regions such as southern California, writes Suzanne Carter.

Research shows that South Africa has the lowest increase in temperature (0,88 °C for the period studied) compared to all other global wine-producing regions. However, a few regions in the Northern Cape and along the Olifants River will potentially become too hot for viable production.

Wine-making is, however, likely to become more risky and more expensive, with production inputs increasing from higher water pricing, increased use of irrigation water, implementing drip irrigation schemes to all vines or uprooting of cultivars less suited to future climate conditions.

The most likely effects will be shifts in management practices to accommodate an increasingly limited water supply. According to Vink and his fellow authors, "(t)here is little doubt that climate change will influence berry ripening and the warming may lead to earlier dates of harvest and result in different wine styles. Producers will have to take cognisance that lack of water, increase in temperature, increase in evapotranspiration, etc., will have an impact on their viticultural practices."[292]

Carter concludes: "The wine industry seems to be in a fairly robust position for dealing with the changes that are projected for the mid-21st century. With careful management and early investment into water saving strategies as well as informed cultivar choices, there should be sufficient capacity to avoid major impacts on productivity in this industry."[293]

Sustainable farming practices incorporating resource-conserving methods and technologies (water, soil and genetic resource conservation) can lead to an increase in yield . . . as well as forming a cost-efficient means of adapting to climate change, says the report on climate change and the South African fruit and wine industry.[294]

Adaptation and mitigation measures need not always involve expensive, complicated interventions; simple, cost-efficient changes can make a substantial difference.

Climate change and changing consumer demands ask for constant innovation, aided by science and technology. But effecting change also requires people who will take the lead and try different approaches. Fortunately the grape and wine industries have no shortage of such leaders.

CHAPTER 11

Not black and white – shades of transformation

Ironically, farm workers today work and live in a more insecure environment than they did before the labour and tenancy laws of the mid-1990s.

Workers have less permanency because of pressures of globalisation, casualisation of labour and refugee labour, says Fatima Shabodien of the Women on Farms Project.

But Shabodien welcomes the changes that have happened since 1994. "We do have a legislative framework as the basis to claim rights. Laws around living and working conditions are a significant step. And there is more awareness of workers about their rights. But farm workers are still the most marginalised group in South Africa."

Accessing those rights, however, remains difficult, especially for rural farm workers. Transport is expensive and questioning the farmer could lose you your job.

"The political landscape has not translated into concrete action," she maintains, "and the lack of progress has embarrassed political parties, especially the ANC."

While legislation has changed, the social dynamics of unequal power relations between farmer and worker have not, and there are still large-scale violations of the law. According to Shabodien, the extent of that remains contested.

As we noted earlier, individual farmers or their export companies sell produce on a market that in most cases demands fair labour practices and good working conditions if it is to buy wine or grapes. However, while ethical trade initiatives have put pressure on producers to meet certain labour, environmental and safety standards (including social conditions on farms), this is not a generalised requirement and producers who continue business in the old way can still export. Not every client requires them to meet labour standards. Certification is also an expensive process.

There are now black-owned farms (though few and far between), black winemakers, and workers who own shares in farms they have worked on for generations. There is change, there is empowerment, there is upliftment. But not across the board, and living and working conditions on some farms remain problematic. As we have seen, farm communities still struggle with the legacy of the *dop* system; the health status of farm workers remains poor.

For Women on Farms, there are many success stories: "In Rawsonville, for example, we have a very active committee, who will approach farmers themselves with grievances. It's a strong group of women and a visible illustration of what's possible. That's empowerment. You can't train 80 000 people, but you can train a core group."

And in 2004 a union of mainly women farm workers was formed, Sikhula Sonke, which now has about 5 000 members. It is open to anyone who subscribes to its constitution. "We dreamt of the idea of a women-led social movement, the first prize being people who organise themselves," says Shabodien. Only about 10% of farm workers are unionised.

Land reform

Land reform has been dismally slow when it comes to the grape and wine industries: effective black involvement in the industry is limited, with less than 1% percent of land under wine grapes under black ownership, management or control in 2006 ("black" in this collective sense means South Africans that were classified into racial categories other than white under apartheid).[295] Wine farms and large commercial table grape farms are still mostly white owned.

Women on Farms would like to see farmers make part of their land available for transfer to workers. Land can be subdivided, says the organisation's Rose Horne: "The ideal scenario is to cut a portion off for housing, and allow for areas for food gardens. We don't want more poverty traps created." They are setting up four women-led agricultural co-ops. "We want 4 ha for them, but without exception we're without land. In the Rawsonville area farmers own six to seven farms."

Dirk Louw

Dirk Louw smiles as he tells of being part of a group who have lodged a land claim for the whole Northern Cape.

He is from Groblershoop, east of Upington, and a relative newcomer to table grape farming. For many years he worked as personnel manager for table grape farmer André Smith, running the farm Malmaison for him when he was away. "I reckon André saw my potential . . . I got close to him. He said he doesn't see me as an employee, and no longer wanted a 'boss-boy' relationship."

They looked around for opportunities, and Louw identified two projects he wanted to get involved in. "But André showed me how the sums wouldn't add up." Eventually, after a long process of negotiation, an empowerment project saw Dirk and nine others being given a farm. Although they wanted to go into partnership with Smith, they were told it could not happen; they had to resign from their jobs to be beneficiaries of Black Economic Empowerment (BEE), otherwise they could not give their best to the project.

The problem is that, in spite of promises that implements would be provided, nothing has been forthcoming. Without implements they cannot farm. But Louw is optimistic: "We will farm, there are funds available, we must just access them."

Louw has been trained in various business and agricultural skills. "There is a perception that when you have been given something, you are empowered. True empowerment cannot be bought: it is a process of personal development and you need to be involved in the process," he believes.[296]

Land reform is a highly charged issue in South Africa. Land costs are high, and so starting up is prohibitively expensive. "The moment you have to buy land, and then add to that production costs in year one, plus the learning curve, you're setting up people to fail," says Professor Mohammed Karaan.

Transformation of the agricultural sector requires extensive land reform. "We need a clever way of externalising cost," explains Karaan. "My radical view is that you have to nationalise land. Most commercial farms are not viable, most small farms are not viable, so why are we holding the system up?" In the commercial sector 10 to 20% of top farms are highly viable, with 20% of farmers producing 80% of produce. "Nationalise farmland, and give the top 20% their land back, free," he suggests. "Put the rest of the land into production under these farmers, and get each one to train two black farmers. Then you'll have 3 000 white farmers, and 6 000 black farmers."

That is not likely to happen, he concedes with a smile. The cost of land is a political issue. The commercial value of land today has exceeded its productive value. "You have to bring the cost of land down. Land is collateral, we can't destroy it."

Land reform in BEE is empowering white CEOs, not black people,

Karaan says. "We've got a mess; 60% of land is under claim, it will destroy the economy. It's got to be settled. Whether we nationalise or not, farmers will lose their land; they were built with government support, they are not viable."

BEE means many different things in the wine industry. The Wine Industry Transformation Charter[297] was adopted by the South African Wine Industry Council in July 2007, and in mid-2010 was still awaiting a response from the minister of agriculture. "Black Economic Empowerment legislation focuses on the creation of an entrepreneurial class amongst historically disadvantaged South Africans," the Charter states. "By implication, empowerment and transformation programmes in the wine industry must, therefore, be market based and business driven."

That viewpoint is challenged, however, in a paper written by researcher Andries du Toit and others in 2007: "... far from representing a decisive break with an inequitable past, BEE allows the South African wine industry to avoid potentially more uncomfortable options to redress current and past race-based imbalances such as land redistribution, import boycotts and better working conditions for grape pickers." According to these authors, a racial discourse, "pivoting on ahistorical and dislocated notions of 'blackness', has been used to displace the transformation agenda away from addressing the conditions faced by workers, and to an ameliorism that allows a small cohort of black entrepreneurs to become the preferred beneficiaries of 'transformation' in the wine industry. The new terrain is characterized by branding, advertising and image building on the one side: and by codes of conduct, a sectoral BEE charter, scorecards and auditing on the other."[298]

Landownership is not necessarily empowerment.

Introducing land reform as an element of BEE is "a disaster in its own right," believes agricultural economist Prof. Nick Vink. "The problem is that you are trying to alleviate poverty by putting people into debt; we've been doing it for 15 years and the land has ended up with the Land Bank." While the BEE scorecard is very innovative, it's too complicated, he says. "On the BEE scorecard a proportion of employees have to be black – that's not difficult, more than 50% are anyway, to start with. The second trick is procuring from someone who is – most are small and automatically qualify. There's no pressure on the system to change."

There are now some, very few, wine farms that are black owned. Human Settlements Minister and former businessman Tokyo Sexwale, chair of Mvelaphanda Holdings, for example, has part ownership in Constantia Uitsig[299], Bloemendal in Durbanville and D'Aria, also in Durbanville. He also owns

Oude Kelder, in Franschhoek, where he is reported to involve himself in the winemaking process.[300]

Another black-owned wine farm is Paardenkloof in the Overberg, which Mohammed Valli Moosa, former minister of environmental affairs, shares with his brother Mohseen. It was bought in 2003 and in August 2007 launched its wine under the Ecology label. And then there are the Rangakas, who own M'Hudi Wines.

The Rangakas – pioneers with a difference

They came to the Cape with no knowledge of farming, little knowledge of viticulture and no taste for wine. They bought a wine farm near Kraaifontein and named it M'Hudi.

The name comes from *mohudi* in Setswana, which means harvester. It is also the name of a book by Sol Plaatje "about a bold woman traversing South Africa to enter into an area she knows nothing about, but she relies on her internal resources and the resources around her, which are people," says CEO Malmsey Rangaka.

An apt name for the Rangaka family's new venture, which they refer to as the "M'Hudi Wines adventure".

The farm is on the R101, with a view of Table Mountain in the far distance. Its unassuming entrance makes me doubt that I am at the right place, this being unlike the old, established wine estates. But this is it – no Dutch gables and manicured gardens. A new entrance is being built, I am told, more fitting to the M'Hudi adventure.

The Rangaka parents cannot make our appointment, so daughter Lebogang steps in.

M'Hudi is the only black-owned family wine business. And while on the one hand, there is an advantage to be had by this, on the other, people dismiss their efforts. "Our story is different," says Lebogang. "We didn't come here to change anything; it could have been a trout farm. This was available, and we saw, oh my goodness, we have grapes. There was a standing arrangement with a co-op and we slowly started getting into it.

"For me, when I hear about empowerment stories, I ask: how meaningful are they really?" she says. "You allocate this part of the farm to workers, but they don't have the title deed, they don't own the land. Surely they need to be able to own some part of the means of production?"

More cynically, many also use share deals to their own advantage. "They use it to say we have, let's say, XY wine brand, some black name, but the owner of the brand still gets part of the profits. Why not give all the profits to the workers, why do you have to put your fingers in this one as well?

"I'm going to stick my neck out – I think a lot of opportunities are given to a small group in a clever way, so they can benefit from BEE.

"And now we're in the wine industry, and we're labelled as BEE wine. I don't dispute that we're black owned, but we are not funded, we're not the result of a handout or a deal. And we're saying, we worked for this; we haven't had a single cent from a government grant. We farm on the same terms as our neighbours. Our story is more compelling, we put in a lot of work and sacrificed a lot to be here.

"Being referred to as 'BEE' takes away from that. We've been told we are 'owned' by Villiera wine, and we have to set the record straight. It gets tiring, but we have to confront it tirelessly.

"This wasn't a crusade of ours, but it's become one, to remain a beacon of hope. We want to be something people can aspire to."

M'Hudi is truly a family affair, and that is not just advertising speak. The business is run by everyone; everyone makes decisions. In their previous careers, mother Malmsey was a clinical psychologist, father Diale a professor and administrator in higher education. Lebogang, who worked in human resources, is now the local marketer and is studying for an MBA at Stellenbosch University. Tsêliso, a journalist working in advertising, is brand manager and Senyane, a filmmaker, is now marketing manager. Diale is the operations manager.

Radical career changes for all.

"My mom came here first, and asked my brother to join her – he went from advertising to being a farm worker. But it did enable him to write about the wine industry. Now he's back in Johannesburg. We decided it was only right that he makes a living there, as he's soon to be married and will be starting a family."

Malmsey became CEO by being voted in. "We voted as a family," says Lebogang, "and my dad was the only one who voted for himself. She's the one – she's focused and the one person who can help us stay focused. We are lucky to have parents who have allowed us to make decisions as to how the family is run," she muses. "We've been able to challenge them, and we've ended up with a unit that's more than the sum of its parts."

The Rangakas of M'Hudi: Lebogang Rangaka, Diale Rangaka, Malmsey Rangaka, Rae-Leigh Adonis, Senyane Rangaka and Kwena, Lebogang's son. (Picture: Anna Lusty)

"Buying the farm wasn't a conscious decision," Lebogang explains, "it was fluke! It was a shock to all, including them (her parents). My dad, since the 1980s, has collected *Farmer's Weekly* magazines, his aspiration was to own a farm. He was tired of being an academic, he wanted to retire in the bush and watch his cattle graze.

"Instead he ended up with a vineyard. This was about the 22nd farm they looked at, and they looked all over the country. This farm was on the market, so they decided to look. The vineyard was a bit old, and there were guava trees."

They bought it, and moved here in 2003. Since then a tasting room has been added to the house, and the shed converted into a mini-maturation cellar.

It has been a steep learning curve for all.

If you own a wine farm, you should like wine, one would think. But that was not the case. "Where we come from, wine was frowned upon – people who drank wine were seen as alcoholics, as having fallen from grace. It was socially unacceptable. We didn't like wine and we weren't wine drinkers," says Lebogang.

"We had to learn. My dad mixed his wine with grape juice – half and half, and we just closed our eyes and swallowed." And now? "It's like olives: you can identify wines you like; what works for one palate doesn't work for another, and I have found some I like. And you can't taste one Pinotage and say 'I don't like it' and write all Pinotage off."

The first years were interesting, to say the least.

"We moved in at night," she recalls, "and in the morning woke up to find people waiting at the gate, it was Monday morning. We said hello, in Setswana, isiZulu – we tried many languages, to no avail. And then we said *goeie môre* (good morning). That got a response. We asked what they wanted, and what we should do next, and they said to open the gate. We didn't even know where the keys were, but they told us," she laughs.

These were the farm's workers, and they literally took over. "We didn't instruct them, we learned from them," Lebogang says. Their housing was in such bad condition that the Rangakas resettled them in nearby Bloekombos.

But the relationship was not long-lived: transformation in the Winelands has not happened fast, and they have come up against some disturbing attitudes. All the original farm workers have left M'Hudi.

"They are no longer with us. We found out – and it was a difficult pill to swallow – that they were not used to black farmers. They felt that taking instructions and money for work from 'Xhosas', black people, reduced them to the rank of slaves. Their friends were making fun of them." They left.

What a telling comment on the legacy of apartheid's years of separation and creating division among people. Lebogang agrees: "One time, when we told them we were Tswanas, not Xhosas, they asked: 'Is that closer to coloured?'"

Difficult as this was, it has been more difficult to deal with the neighbours.

"How do I put this? With the workers it was cut and dried, but the neighbours are strange. We have a neighbour who is very helpful, he'll be here in a flash to help. But there are issues – we keep on being told that we 'weaken security' in the area. It's difficult to pinpoint, but things aren't quite kosher. We applied for a rezoning to build a boutique hotel, and it was opposed by those around us, again for 'security' reasons. What does that actually mean?" Boutique hotels are popping up in many areas, an added income for wine farmers. Delaire and Zorgvliet West, both in the Banhoek area, come to mind, with no security concern from neighbours.

Today the Rangakas work with a smaller workforce; people are committed, they want to be here. At harvest time they employ 50 extra people. "There are enough people willing to work for us, many not from the Western Cape, so they come in with fresh ideas, and don't carry the past with them," she says,

The family has, fortunately, also had the rewarding experience of being mentored by their neighbours, the Griers. Jeff Grier is winemaker at Villiera and has over 20 years' experience making wine. "We had no winemaking experience. We've been very lucky, working with a reputable winery that's highly ranked and very ethical. The way they deal with us is really nice, they don't meddle. They took us step by step in the beginning, but have slowly backed off, and they don't impose on us. They give us a good product."

The result is, she says, that "they are marketing our story out there".

Their brand was launched in 2005, and they have a small range of wines. Their grapes are taken to Villiera and Koelenhof for pressing. "We buy in grapes for our Sauvignon Blanc; 15% of our wine is from our own grapes. Our vines are old, and quality is not that consistent."

The Rangakas do their own marketing, and Lebogang has been trained in marketing for the wine retail business by the British retailer Marks & Spencer. She believes that Marks & Spencer were willing to look below the surface of BEE as a mask: "They did research into who we were."

In May 2010, M'Hudi Wines was honoured with the prestigious Emerging Tourism Entrepreneur of the Year Award at the annual Indaba tourism show in Durban.

Su Birch, the CEO of Wines of South Africa (WOSA), says land reform is slow, but she believes that only 30% of land is suitable for high-volume mass-produced wines. To trade wine you have to build an image. And it is difficult to break into the industry as an outsider, she points out. "It's built on social networks, you need a lot of cultural knowledge of the wines of Europe and California, and of food and wine. Product knowledge is easier. If you have no experience, the learning curve is huge and difficult. It's a long-term commitment. What I get excited about is black winemakers and cellar masters who are qualified and competent – and that's happening. That's more sustainable than changing ownership of land."

Models of empowerment

There are many models of empowerment on grape and wine farms, from new ventures such as Dirk Louw's to share schemes and setting up farm workers' trusts.

One of the major table grape producers along the Orange River is Peu Bezuidenhout, whose story was told in Chapter 10. A few years ago Bezuidenhout sold a 25% stake in the farm to a group of permanent workers and set up Rekopane Estates, a land transformation project supported by the Department of Land Affairs and a loan from Standard Bank.

"I was the first in the area to do so," explains Bezuidenhout, "and it took three years to put things in place. To be 100% BEE compliant, we had to sell 26% shares; but that makes you liable for capital gains tax, so they changed the law. They now have a 25% share and a 1% voting share."

The 25% share is held by the Lorathebetse Trust (meaning "the sun has risen for us" in Tswana), made up of 65 permanent workers. Land Affairs put up R6,5 million for the workers to buy shares, and workers will pay off their loan.

"I did it for business reasons and to adhere to government policy – you must if you want to do business properly. But the other thing is that I have about 40 guys who have been with me from the beginning, and it was just fair for them to benefit from the land they helped build up through the years. It's changed things dramatically for them – they take more responsibility," he says.

Seasonal workers, if they prove themselves, can become permanent. About 60% are from Kuruman and Vryburg; 40% from local coloured communities. "The coloured community don't want to work in the vineyards preparing table grapes," says Bezuidenhout. "Which is why we recruited elsewhere. So now, 14 years later, we have skilled Tswana labour."

At Beyerskloof near Stellenbosch, Beyers Truter helped set up the Bouwland project in 2003.

"I started with all the families I'd worked with," he tells me. "We South Africans love the soil. In 1988 I smelt the soil and said, I want my own farm. So how much more people who have been working it for generations?"

There are 60 shareholders who have 75% ownership, and Beyerskloof has 25%. Things became political, Truter says, and he was accused of stealing money. "I was ready to sell my share. But the youngsters said, please Beyers, we grew up in front of you, we want this to work." And so he is still part of it: "We're not giving up the project." Problems encountered include a lack of marketing management and financial people. "There are many farm managers, and in 10 to 15 years there will be the capacity, but not now," Truter believes. "And while the state gives people grants, they have to borrow money at high interest rates for running capital."

There are many, many initiatives in many forms, which all contribute to transformation in the table grape and wine industries. Upliftment and empowerment are arguably different things, but each initiative makes a difference in someone's life. WOSA has recently published *Ithemba, 15 Years of Democracy, 350 Years of Winemaking,*[301] a glossy publication which charts the changing face of the wine industry. In the table grape industry, the Deciduous Fruit Producers Trust published *New Leaves,*[302] on transformation and training initiatives, in 2006.

There are companies such as Distell and KWV in which black consortia have shares: KWV signed an agreement in 2004 with Phetego Investments, which now owns a 25,1 % share in the company[303]; in 2005 Distell entered into a transaction with BEE consortium WIP Beverages, which acquired 15% of SA Distilleries and Wines Limited, the holding company for all Distell's operations.[304]

Branding is high on the list of "empowerment" initiatives: Epicurean Wines is the brand of former Gauteng premier Mbhazima Shilowa, businessman Moss Ngoasheng, Mutle Mogase of Vantage Capital, and American Ron T Gault, formerly of JP Morgan.[305] Ses'fikile ("we have arrived") is a brand owned by four black women, Nondumiso Pikashe, Jackie Mayo, Phelela Mgudlwa and Nomvuyo Xaliphi (they do not own the land; Bruce Jack of Flagstone Winery, based in Somerset West, does).[306] LaThiThá Wines is a 100% BEE-owned company founded by MD Sheila Hlanjwa who lives in Langa, a suburb of Cape Town. It was formed in 2005, and one of Hlanjwa's goals is to promote tourism in Langa by establishing a wine-tasting and conferencing venue.[307] Thabani, the Nguni word for "joyful", was the first wholly black-owned wine company in South Africa, with Jabulani Ntshangase, who pioneered the Wine Education Programme in 1995, and Trevor Strydom as directors. Based in the Cape winelands with a boutique blending cellar to be built in KwaZulu-Natal, Thabani operates throughout Africa.

Housing is often the first area where farmers can make a difference. Michael Back of Backsberg set up the Freedom Road housing project in 1997. "Most people want a roof over their heads and no debt. I don't believe in shareholding – how do you sell your share?"

Back provided the land and the money, the workers their sweat equity and the government a housing subsidy. "We didn't start the project until we had the money. We built some new houses and doubled the size of others in Klapmuts, 40 houses in all," he says.

"What does change require? Participation on all possible levels, whether it be housing, whatever," Back says. "Farming is high risk. I'd never invite someone to be a farmer, it doesn't necessarily help people. I don't believe in peasant farming, and commercial farming is not easy. Anyway, farm work is no longer a career of choice for many."

Changing ownership, changing attitudes

No one would question the fact that paternalism is deeply ingrained on the grape farms in South Africa.

While power relations have not changed everywhere, there are encouraging pockets of change. "The question is . . . whether relations between farmer and farm worker have changed to the extent that it has become something qualitatively and unmistakably different," notes the Wine Industry Transformation Charter. The Centre for Rural Legal Studies states in the Charter (2007) that most farm workers in South Africa do not have effective access to labour rights, tenure security and due process.[308] There is a long way to go.

However, as with most things, a commitment to change can make all the difference. "Farmers complain they can't get their sons to farm because it's 'politically insecure', but maybe it's not a bad idea to get new blood," says Fatima Shabodien of Women on Farms. "But of course there is also then a loss of knowledge." She speaks of a farm in Stellenbosch, Simonsig, where workers are encouraged to join trade unions and get medical care and transport allowances and are paid twice the minimum wage. "Workers are proud to work there."

From paternalism to partnership

When neuropsychologist Mark Solms bought the farm Delta (now Solms-Delta) in 2002 on his return from England, he was clear on one thing: "I didn't want to be a patriarch. My starting point was that I wanted to do it differently." Solms is South African, and knew the attitudes that existed here: "I'd never been a farmer, and all I knew was the archetype of 'the white South African farmer'. It was a burden to take on. I was an academic, not a farmer or a businessman."

Initially his idea was to just live here and not farm, but there were seven families on the farm, poor, uneducated and dependent. "I thought,

I can't fix South Africa, but I'll try to fix this little piece of farm. The farm was bankrupt, and so I met all the members of the seven families and asked each of them what they could do. They wouldn't even look at me, let alone tell me what they thought. It was like feudalism, like having serfs on the land. I realised that I had to create an economically viable farm to provide jobs. I couldn't just sit here and have a very big garden."

His ambition for the farm, economically, is to not lose money. "Wine is not the way to make money quickly; my long-term view is that what will make it truly sustainable is doing it excellently." You don't have to have proper housing, good salaries and health care, he says, "but it all translates in an indirect way into a more successful business."

Solms explains: "What we are producing is an art form, an aesthetic product, and it has qualitative considerations. Would you want to eat at a restaurant where the chef hates his job? If work is done in a way that creates beauty, you'll have a good product. Attitude affects outcome, care and love and attention are necessary to make a more successful farm."

There have been huge changes on the farm in just eight years, ownership being the biggest. "Ownership is crucial," he believes. "There is already enough that is wrong with relationships with farm workers; if the farmer owns the land, people are always at his mercy, always poor, unless workers own the land.

"When the first draft of the Wine Industry Charter came out, it said transformation couldn't come through landownership, as it was too expensive. And I thought, no, that's exactly what we do have to change. I came face to face with my human limitations. It was not a solution to just give up my farm; and you can't, legally, chop it up." He and a friend, Richard Astor, came up with a novel, simple solution: they mortgaged their adjoining farms Delta and Lübeck as collateral for a third farm, Deltameer, to be owned by workers in a trust.

"We took a risk, yes, but we must make sure it works. All three farms are farmed as one unit, one product. We own our own farms, the third is owned by a trust. The trust shares in the profits of the wine."

This empowered the 200 farm workers on the three farms as landowners, after generations of tilling vineyards on which they had no claim.

The three entities collectively form a 76-ha estate, home to around 25 families.

Transformation requires intention, and anyone can do it, believes Solms. "All I had was good intentions. I've had to learn on the job, transforming my bit of agricultural history. Financially, all it took was a loan from Investec Bank."

Transforming relationships is a bigger, and ongoing, challenge.

"Only by delving into the social history of the farm could I properly understand it. What needed to be done was to understand the nature of the problem in order to change it. I found things I wouldn't have anticipated: people had no hope, no sense of the future. They were at best fatalistic, and most were clinically depressed." Slavery was based on no hope; for farm workers hope has always been dangerous – hopes raised were too often hopes dashed.

Nico Jansen, now estate manager at Solms-Delta, lived on the farm when Solms arrived. When he first met the new owner, Jansen told him: "You can't just push people off the farms. This is how things stand in South Africa, you can't come here and make new rules."

Fortunately for him, Solms liked his outspokenness, and employed him. "Mark wanted to come back to the country, right the wrongs of the past, start a new life for the farm. Obviously I was sceptical, for me a good white was a dead white."

Jansen's chutzpah probably came from his early years. He was born on the farm Vrede en Lus, where he lived until he was four, and then went to live with his aunt in Paarl, who worked and boarded at a Jewish family. "I was the only coloured person allowed on Muizenberg beach (with my Jewish 'family'). After hours, coloureds were allowed, so I went again."

He lived in Paarl until high school. "Then all the trouble started," he says. At Noorder Paarl High School he was teased for having a domestic worker as a mother. He went to live with his granny who worked on a farm in Simondium, but decided to leave school in Standard 8, as travelling was expensive, and his grandmother could not afford it. "I was good at school. I thought, I've had an education and my 'Jewish' background will help. Anyway, I thought, I wouldn't get a job because I was coloured, so I could drop out of school, and allow my cousins to continue. It would help my grandmother."

He moved to Delta. "My wife worked here, on the farm, so I asked Michael Pickstone (the then owner) if we could live here, I'd pay rental. The farm was being sold and he needed the money.

"Never ever did I want to work on a farm, especially a grape farm," he smiles. "It was a challenge working with my own people, I was hated, I was going forward in life." At first there was resentment from co-workers, who thought he was enriching himself at their expense, but they soon realised he was working for a better lifestyle for all, he says.

Mark Solms says skills are sorely needed on a farm, and education is a priority. "Any estate making wine is a complicated business, we have to grow all kinds of skills." The farm's trust looked at how to best use its resources; the aim was to break the cycle of poverty. The decision was that children need education, so that they have options other than being farm workers. As long as they are in full-time study, the trust funds their education. A social worker is employed by the trust, and in that way the inevitable social problems on the farm can be dealt with in a professional way and on an objective basis.

Music of the vine

While you cannot measure transformation by one party, the *makietie* (celebration) that the annual *Oesfees* (harvest festival) at Solms-Delta always is, highlights the heart of change, which no scorecard or research paper can measure.

One area of life where people have always come together is music. Never mind the social segregation on farms, especially the more rural ones, when the sun went down and the *ramkiekie* (Khoi guitar) started playing, the party began.

Sometimes the instruments were more sophisticated, oftentimes the dances more structured, but always music was the language that spoke of longing, rebellion, unbridled expression and a chance to forget the hardships of life for a moment.

The Solms-Delta *Oesfees* grew out of a rural music project, based at Solms-Delta. "We saw it as a conservation task, to record what little remains, but we found music alive and well," says Mark Solms. Musician Alex van Heerden was employed to research the vernacular music of the rural Cape. The focus was to explore the origins of Cape music through an ethno-music audit of what had already been written about Cape music and to explore the influence on Cape music of indigenous Khoi and San traditions, European folk-songs and slave cultures from across India, Indonesia and Africa, as well as modern cross-cultural influences.

Van Heerden tragically passed away in a car accident in January 2009, aged 34. He had already discovered a wealth of musical talent among farm workers in the Winelands and made some close connections with people. In an interview in late 2008, he spoke about the power of dancing together: "Musicians would travel around, play on farms for farmers and workers, in halls.

Segregation was the official story, but not the real story. There's lots of evidence that smaller social events were organised by farmers, with a fiddler playing, where people would sing and make music together. Music, sex and alcohol are great social lubricators."

According to Solms, "Alex's job was to start at our farm, and move out. To our complete surprise Alex started a band on the farm, the Delta Optel Band." Now there are two other bands, the Delta Blues Stars, a minstrel band, and the Delta Langbroek Band, and a choir, the Soetstemme ("sweet voices"). The musicians are drawn from all around the area.

Apart from a good party, the *Oesfees* was a chance to help the farm workers recover their own history, says Solms. "This is music that unites the stories of the slave, European and Khoisan cultures that form the core of our unique Cape heritage. Just as Cape culture was forged by the confluence of these diverse ethnic groups, so was our music, which celebrates what really matters in life, despite all the hardships."

The *Oesfees* has now become an annual event, a celebration of local music, and it attracts large crowds. Children run around, grannies dance and food is provided. It is a feel-good harvest festival unlike any other, where there are no social barriers; whether you are a worker, a manager or just a visitor, you celebrate the bounty of the vine together. The Papier Langarm Orkes, whose members live in Franschhoek, appear regularly at the *Oesfees* .

The Papiers – a song and a dance to every farm

For a while we must part,
But remember me sweetheart,
Till the lights of London shine again . . .[309]

Johanna Alexander's sweet voice sings this song from the Second World War, her memory of the words strong. At 86 her voice is reedy, her delight written on her lined face. "I love to sing," says Johanna. "In the war years a lot of songs came out, and we sang in the factory (Rhodes Fruit Farms canning factory)."

And while I'm over there,
Think of me in every prayer
Till the lights of London shine again . . . .

Music, song and dance have filled Johanna's life; her brother Marthinus Papier brought a dance to every farm in the Franschhoek area with his violin and his talent, she says. Johanna well remembers the Wednesday nights on the farm where the family lived, when her brother would take out his violin and the people would dance the quadrille. "I couldn't wait for the people where I worked to finish eating so I could get home and join the dance. It was so nice, better than the *langarm* (which came later)," she says. A dance wasn't a success unless you'd danced the "*sopvleis*" (soup meat), the last of the series of square dances that made up an evening. Why "*sopvleis*"? She shrugs. Probably because there were no rules and you could move your body with abandon.

Marthinus was invited to a farm every Saturday night to play. He was the first man with a band in the valley, and he moved from farm to farm. "My mother loved dancing and while my youngest sister was still a baby, my parents would go with my brother – they'd walk even though it was far, sometimes returning only at 1am. They even went as far as Paarl, to play at Foresters Hall, and danced the whole night."

Those dances ended with the war, but Marthinus Papier didn't stop playing the music. He took up the saxophone and continued playing until he was too old to do so any more. He died in 2007, aged 88.

Part of his legacy was to pass his talent on to four of his sons, who today play under the name the Papier Langarm Orkes – Frank, Albert, Martin and Neville. Frank's son Regan and daughter Chanelle sing.

"We play *boeremusiek*" (light music associated with the culture of the Afrikaners), says Frank Papier, whose instrument is the accordion. "It's different from our culture's music, the *bruinmens se dans, die riel van die Noord-Kapenaars*" (the dance of the coloured people, the reel of the people of the Northern Cape). Frank started playing when he was 15.

Alex van Heerden heard about the Papier brothers and would come to the house and play along with them. "Music is the unofficial record of people's lives, a shared common experience," he said in an interview before he passed away.

"Music and dancing is an element of people's lives, an expression of life. And folk music is changing constantly, ephemeral in many ways."

Marthinus Papier was born in Vredenburg, but his parents moved to Drakenstein when he was four, recalls Johanna. She remembers walking to school in Languedoc, barefoot in the cold winter. "There wasn't money for shoes for everyone," she says. She got her first pair of shoes, brown ones with a flat heel, when she was a teenager. "The main road was still a gravel road, and I didn't want them to get dirty, so I carried them."

As a young man Marthinus worked at KWV and later at the sawmills. "He was very clever at music, and longed for a violin. My father had one and gave it to him when he turned 17. He still wore short pants!

"He knew how to play without tuition, he played out of himself," she says.

"Papa was a *ploegleier*, leading the donkey that pulled the plough, and he worked hard. The alarm rang at 6am, and we had to get up and make him coffee. Farmers didn't pay much – 3 shillings and 9 pennies a week."

A picture of the Eastern Star Christmas Band shows Marthinus in the middle, holding his saxophone. The Christmas Band would be dropped at one end of the valley and make their way back, stopping at each farm to play on Christmas Eve. That was in the late 1950s. The band would also play at Hollandsche Molen, a popular picnic spot, where people would come to dance. Johanna's husband Gert signed up for the war, seeing service in Egypt and Tobruk. When he came back he was given "only a bicycle and set of clothes," she remembers.

From the beginning of the settlement at the Cape, when people came together they would make music. The indigenous Khoikhoi and San used various instruments, and music was an essential part of ritual. In his history of the Nama Khoikhoi, published in 1897, Friedrich Ratzel writes: "The 'Bushman' is like the 'Hottentot' in his turn and capacity for music. Wherever he can snap up an old fiddle from a European, or make a rudimentary one for himself out of a gourd and two strings, he extracts a tolerable tone from the instrument, and reproduces any pretty airs that he may have heard at the mission or in his dances."

Slaves from different parts of the world – Indonesia, India, Madagascar, East Africa and Java – had an enormous impact on the settlement at the Cape, interacting with the indigenous people, the Dutch and other European settlers. Music and song have always been used to express feeling. Although slaves would not have been able to bring their instruments with them, some were taught to play the music of their Dutch owners. There are many accounts of slaves performing concerts and playing in bands. Thys van der Merwe, who has researched the history of Groot Constantia, says that the French traveller Francois le Vaillant and a companion called Larcher, on a visit to Constantia in 1780, awakened to the sound of beautiful music coming from outside. "They were surprised and flattered, assuming that the concert was in their honour. They were soon to be disappointed, however, when they discovered that Hendrik Cloete was customarily awakened each morning with a performance by 15 of his slaves who were good musicians."[310]

Van der Merwe says there is nothing else known of these slave musicians, their music and their instruments. The Slave Registers (which were officially kept only from 1816), mention only one slave on the farm as musician – he was Makelaar from Madagascar, aged about 60, whose occupation is listed as: Musician.

However, this was not the only slave orchestra in the area. The orchestra on the neighbouring farm Hoop op Constantia consisted of 16 slaves, and Martin Douwe Teenstra, who visited the farm in 1825, was "agreeably surprised by (their music), all slaves belonging to Mevrouw Colijn, who gave a rousing performance of martial music by a brass band, using the necessary wind and other instruments such as clarinettes, flutes, trumpets . . . and two great drums, and did it as well as the best English corps stationed in Cape Town."[311]

The nearby farm Bergvliet also had a slave orchestra, the same size as the other two, and the instruments similar to that of the orchestra at Hoop op Constantia.

The music of Europe, and the Calvinist Dutch, was not folk music; that developed as the slaves and the settler communities of the Boland influenced each other. Slaves played music for themselves, using the *ghoema*, a small drum made of a skin stretched tightly over one end of a wine vat.

The *ghoema* has its origins in the *gom-gom*, tom-tom or *ghoema*, all derivatives of "*ngoma*", the East African drum. "The Mozbiekers were well known for their drumming, use of tambourines and dancing," writes amateur historian Patric Mellét. "In 1820, the Comptroller of Customs notes that at the Cape, African slaves were distinguished by their 'passion for music'. Another documenter of life at the Cape, WW Bird, says 'the slave boys from Madagascar and Mozambique bring the stringed instruments, of their respective tribes and nations . . .' "[312]

The slaves also used music as a means to convey their frustration and their songs were often a form of protest, the true meanings hidden in the lyrics.

In late 2008, Alex van Heerden told of how he had found songs that were Boland specific. "I'm looking at music and dance, based on European quadrilles and waltzes. There must have been some interpretation involved, and I want to see how Cape style influenced them. There is no name for this style of music, but it was basically square dancing, based on quadrilles dating to the late nineteenth century. There would be choreographed stops and starts, and then a free-for-all, the '*sopvleis*', where there weren't any rules. The first time this music was recorded was in the 1930s, and it's mostly oral history that's available, from the old people in the valley."

Violin dance bands and the *boereorkes* were similar. "But basically the Cape Corps in the Second World War were exposed to the saxophone – it became the hip thing to have in your band." *Langarm* then evolved, based on square and ballroom dancing. Talented fiddle players played the "*Hotnots Riel*" and people danced.

But it was the *vastrap* that caught Van Heerden's attention. "It is the ethnic music of the Afrikaans-speaking people of South Africa," he wrote in his blog.[313] "It has the same roots as the Afrikaans language, arising from the meeting between Dutch, other European settlers, African and Eastern slaves with the indigenous Khoesan people of South Africa."

In his 1897 history of the Nama Khoikhoi, Friedrich Ratzel writes:

> Nama/Hottentot people have a culture that is rich in the musical and literary abilities of its people. Traditional music, folk tales, proverbs, and praise poetry form the basis for much of their culture . . . An example of a traditional dance is the well-known Nama-stap. Their music emulated the sounds made by animals and was played to accompany dances and storytelling. The early Nama used drums, flutes and stringed instruments; and the people who arrived later added marimbas, gourd rattles and animal horn trumpets. Missionaries established local religious choral groups.
>
> Among themselves they (the "Hottentots"), like the Bushmen, use the gom-gom or gora . . . They use also reed flutes, and drums made of an earthenware pot with sheep-skin stretched over it.

Vastrap also refers to the dance which is connected to the music, writes Van Heerden:

> *Vastrap* means 'fasten-tramp'. This could refer to dancing while trampling a newly-laid cow dung floor, newly harvested grapes, or simply trampling the dusty ground while dancing around an open fire. It is a rich and diverse style, there are as many variations of it as there are dialects of Afrikaans. In areas closer to large towns, the European influence on *vastrap* is more apparent, although the rhythm is still distinctly non-Western.
>
> Traditionally, couples danced the *vastrap* together to the sound of guitars, concertinas, accordions, banjos and violins, while more recently, bass guitars and drums have been added to most groups, while the "langarm" dance-bands

of the Western Cape have incorporated the saxophone as their lead instrument.

On the farms of the Groot Karoo, the *vastrap* dance is closer to the shamanic trance-dances of the San/Bushmen, he writes, with single dancers employing intricate foot movements to the pulse of the guitar-driven *vastrap* beat. In this region, there is a variation on the *vastrap* which is referred to as the "*riel*". The instruments, (mostly guitars and homemade violins) are often tuned to mimic the natural harmonics of traditional instruments such as the mouthbow, and thus sound slightly out of tune to the equal-temperament western ear.

Ratzel writes: "Besides the gourd-fiddle we find also the gora, and a drum, with a little water in it and a skin stretched over its mouth. The function of this music in the Bushman's life is to accompany the dance. The modulation of the voices is said to be intimately interwoven with the movements of the body. The Bushman dance is a gradual and methodical outbreak of licentiousness, reaching the point of convulsion."[314]

Vastrap's modern development was stunted by the fragmentation of Afrikaans culture, writes Van Heerden, brought about by colonialist ideals and apartheid. Afrikaner nationalists saw it as a threat to their fragile European identity, a threat to their position of power within the master/slave relationships so common in South Africa. After their defeat in the Anglo-Boer War, power and "European descent" became very important to the Afrikaner, and *vastrap*, with its association with abandonment, ecstasy, sexuality and African "lack of respectability", slowly became a marginalised music.

"Ordinary people, however, did not lose their love for it, and it stayed alive in 'langarm' dance bands all over the Cape, in 'boereorkeste' across rural Southern Africa, in 'klopse' carnival groups in the townships of Cape Town, in the countryside churches and farm-labourers' cottages of the Karoo."

When Van Heerden turned his attention to the rural areas of the Cape, "I found a musical tradition that was my own, but had been concealed from me, the rhythm of the '*Vastrap*'. It is a music that is impossible to play if you don't believe in magic."

Sarie Pietersen, 40, works at Solms-Delta in the vineyards. In 1986 her family – ma, pa and nine children – came to the farm Delta from the Koue Bokkeveld near Ceres. She joined the Solms-Delta band when it was started by Van Heerden.

"We had a keyboard at home, but my husband Isaac wanted to play the trumpet. As a household we do everything together. In our family, if one person is sick, the whole family goes along to the doctor; we go to church together. If invited somewhere, it must be the whole family, otherwise we pass the invitation on. So we decided to all take music up as a hobby," Pietersen tells me.

"Since September last (2008), we've been playing. Isaac plays the trumpet; Sheldon and I the trombone, and Brandon the drums. We practise Monday, Wednesday and Friday, from 6 to 8pm – it's only a pleasure to spend the time. We learn to play notes, church songs, *liedjies*. We have also appeared at Stellenbosch High School and in Simondium.

"It's a great feeling to learn how to play. Most of the young children want to be part of the band. In the times we live in, and when you hear what the children do, that's good."

She remembers Alex van Heerden fondly: "No matter who you were, Alex was friendly."

Solms-Delta have now established a Cape musical heritage centre as part of their Cape Music Project. It is based in a recently renovated building, known as the Music van de Caab centre, and will be used not only for archiving and displaying information accumulated during ongoing research, but also as an educational resource for the wider community.[315]

How is transformation to be measured? This will remain a much-debated question in the near future.

BEE scorecards, land ownership, share schemes or workers' trusts tell only part of the story. It is in the many personal stories that we get a feeling for what's really happening. Many times it's heartening; at other times it seems there's a long way to go. The story of the people of the grape is the story of transformation in process.

Last word

This small window we have looked through onto the world of the grape allowed us a glimpse of hidden histories. Hopefully we have gained some insight into the people of the vine.

As with wine, there are many sides to this story: wine can lift you from your ordinary state of being and inspire you; it can also lead to drunkenness and misery.

The 350 years of viticulture in South Africa have created both wealth and poverty.

Throughout this history run the myriad stories of the people who have worked in the vineyards, cellars and packing sheds. Their stories are revealing, a reminder of the diversity of their lived realities and the complexities of relationships between worker and farmer, employee and employer.

Uplifted by the grape or downtrodden by it, people have found ways to survive and sometimes flourish.

The history of the Cape has played out with viticulture as a backdrop.

In exploring the social history of the grape in South Africa we have uncovered some aspects that have been surprising, others that were predictable. Cheap labour has always been a concern of farmers; paternalism and the *dop* system played their parts in creating dependencies and social problems we are still grappling with today. But it has been a revelation to find that not only have wine farmers always struggled to survive, but that still today wine farming is marginal.

From a few decades back when wine was made largely by family-owned enterprises, the landscape has changed dramatically. Many foreigners have bought wine farms; consortia have invested in them and so too have the wealthy. The lure of wine farming is in the image, the lifestyle, and the making of fine wine. Wine farming is not a lucrative business, nor is that likely to change soon. The reasons may be different today: our wines are of good quality, we have the seventh largest wine industry in the world and exports have soared over the past ten years.

But the reality is that the wine industry is facing incredibly tough times.

Farmers today have to contend with soaring production costs and a poor return on their product. Add to that a changing climate.

A wine industry report at the end of 2009[316] quoted these figures: a wine farmer nets, on average, only 44c a bottle of wine from an average retail shelf price of R24 (750-ml bottle). This is in contrast to the R1,07 a bottle (4% of the retail price) that is required for a reasonable and justifiable entrepreneur's remuneration and return on capital.[317] And, while the average prices for bulk wine (red and white) have risen marginally from R3,54 a litre in 2004 to R3,89 a litre in 2009, the average total cost of wine production soared from R19 000 a hectare to R26 580 a hectare over the five years.[318] As with table grapes, there is strong competition from countries like Australia, Argentina, Chile and New Zealand. In addition, a strong rand is not good for exporters, and selling on a global market where supermarket chains often control prices is a tough business.

To exacerbate things, adverse weather conditions meant that the grape harvest in 2010 was down on average by almost 9% to 18% in areas like Stellenbosch.[319]

Very few farmers are making a profit; many wine farms are on the market.

Behind these figures are the thousands of livelihoods at stake; for every farmer who cannot survive, there are many permanent farm workers and even more casual workers who are affected. Wine, raisins and table grapes are today one of the biggest drivers of the economies of the Northern and Western Cape.

In these uncertain and troubled economic times, the challenges of transformation remain pertinent; there is much still to do.

The grape and wine industries will have to find new ways of remaining viable. Perhaps they will find new markets, or shrink; different crops may take the grape's place.

But there will always be wine. Wine holds a special place in people's hearts; wine has been used by many religions for thousands of years as a sacrament, to symbolise the immortal soul. The grape decays, as wine and brandy it endures.

We hope that this window onto the world of the grape has revealed the diversity of experiences and the spirit that make the people of the vine a resilient and a truly mixed bunch.

Select sources

INTERVIEWS

Jeanne Viall interviewed the following people:

Jakob Afrikaner
Johanna Alexander
Mercia Arendse
Michael Back
Jacobus Basson
Joa Bekker
Aubrey Beukes
Dina Beukes
Elize Beukes
Peu Bezuidenhout
Su Birch
Ntsiki Biyela
Louise Brodie
Phyllis Burger
Maxi Campion
Katrina Coetzee
Willie Coetzee
Louis Conradie
Mattie Cyster
Eleanor Damon
Jan Eksteen
Sylvia Erasmus
Joachim Ewert
Jan Filander
Quinton Fortuin
Jan Henning
Rose Horne
Elbré Jacobs
Martiens Janse
Nico Jansen
Mohammed Karaan
Nelie Kok
Pietie le Roux
Leslie London (e-mail interview)
Dirk Louw
Trevor Loxton
Lucien Luyt
Mary Malgas
Fred Meintjies
Annatjie Melck
Patric Tariq Mellét (e-mail interview)
Andrew Milne
Izak Nel
Leon Nel
Leana Olivier
Frank Papier
Jacob Peu
Dirk Pienaar
Sarie Pietersen
Pieter Raath
Tracey Randle
Lebogang Rangaka
Ebrahim Rhoda
Leonora Safoor
Hanno Scholtz
Fatima Shabodien
André Smith
Mark Solms
Nora Sperling
Spatz and Vera Sperling
Elmien Swartz
Beyers Truter
Thys van der Merwe
Richard van der Ross
Alex van Heerden
Danie van Schalkwyk
Paul van Wyk
Petrus van Wyk
Diko van Zyl
Denis Viljoen
Nick Vink
Willie Venneal
Hermanus Williams

BOOKS

Böeseken, AJ. *Slaves and Free Blacks at the Cape*, 1658-1700. Cape Town: Tafelberg, 1977.

Brink, A. *The Essence of the Grape: A South African Brandy Book*. Cape Town: Saayman & Weber, 1992.

Burman, J. *Wines of Constantia*. Cape Town: Human & Rousseau, 1979.

Cornelissen, Alwyn K. *Langs Grootrivier*. No publisher, no date. Copy accessed from Maxie Campion, Keimoes.

Cornelissen, AK. *Langs Grootrivier: grepe uit die kleurryke geskiedenis van die Noordweste*. No publisher, no date; possiby Upington, 1996.

Cyster, L, Cyster, M, Damon, E and Simpson, F. *Pniël en sy Mense*. Stellenbosch: Sun Media, 2008.

De Beer, Maria. *Keimoes en Omgewing*. Keimoes: Keimoes Municipality, 1992.

Dooling, W. *Slavery, Emancipation and Colonial Rule in South Africa*. Pietermaritzburg: University of KwaZulu-Natal Press, 2007.

Duckitt, HJ. *Hilda's Diary of a Cape Housekeeper*. London: Chapman & Hall, 1902.
Elphick, R. *Khoikhoi and the Founding of White South Africa*. Johannesburg: Ravan Press, 1985.
Giliomee, H and Mbenga, B (eds). *New History of South Africa*. Cape Town: Tafelberg, 2007.
Heap, P. *The Story of the Hottentots Holland*. Cape Town: AA Balkema, 1970.
James, W and Simons, M (eds). *The Angry Divide: Social and Economic History of the Western Cape*. Claremont: David Philip, 1989.
Kuttel, M. *Quadrilles and Konfyt*. Cape Town: Maskew Miller, 1954.
Lucas, G. *An Archaeology of Colonial Identity, Power and Material Culture in the Dwars Valley*. New York: Springer, 2006.
Macdonald, William. *Conquest of the Desert*. London: TW Laurie, 1913. Retrieved 22 August 2010 from http://www.archive.org/stream/conquestofdesertoomacdiala#page/x/mode/2up
Marais, E. *The Soul of the Ape*. Cape Town: Human & Rousseau, 1974.
May, Peter. *Pinotage: Behind the Legends of South Africa's Own Wine*. England: Inform and Enlighten, 2009.
Opperman, DJ (ed.). *Spirit of the Vine*. Cape Town: Human & Rousseau, 1968.
Penn, Nigel. *The Forgotten Frontier*. Cape Town: Double Storey Books, 2005.
Ratzel, F. *History of Mankind*, translated from the second German edition by AJ Butler, Volume II. New York: Macmillan, 1897.
Rosenthal, E. *We Want Fruit*. (New edition) Observatory: Quincunx, 2007.
Schoeman, K. *Early Slavery at the Cape of Good Hope* 1652-1717. Pretoria: Protea Book House, 2007.
Schutte, GJ (ed.). *Hendrik Cloete, Groot Constantia and the VOC* 1778-1799. Cape Town: Van Riebeeck Society, 2003.
Scully, P. *Liberating the Family? Gender and British Slave Emancipation in the Rural Western Cape*, 1823-1853. Cape Town: David Philip, 1997.
Shell, R. *Children of Bondage*. Johannesburg: Witwatersrand University Press, 1994.
Silberbauer, C. *Pniel and its First Missionary Superintendent*. Cape Town: Citadel Press, 1943.
Simons, HJ and RE. *Class & Colour in South Africa*, 1850-1950. Harmondsworth: Penguin. 1969.
Stander, Siegfried. *Tree of Life: The Story of Cape Fruit*. Cape Town: Saayman & Weber, 1983.
Steinbeck, John. *The Grapes of Wrath*. Sussex: Heinemann, 1969.
Terreblanche, Sampie. *A History of Inequality in South Africa* 1652-2002. Pietermaritzburg: University of KwaZulu-Natal Press, 2002.
Theal, GM. *Willem Adriaan van der Stel and Other Historical Sketches*. Cape Town: Thomas Maskew Miller, 1913.
Van der Ross, RE. *Buy My Flowers*. Observatory: Ampersand Press, 2007.
Van Zyl, D. *Klawer Wynkelder, 50 Goue Jare*. Stellenbosch: Rapid Access Publishers, 2007.
Van Zyl, L. *Boegoeberg se Mense,'n Flukse Draai van die Wiel*. Groblershoop: self-published, 1997.
Venter, AJ. *Coloured – A Profile of 2 Million South Africans*. Cape Town: Human & Rousseau, 1974.
Worden, N and Crais, C. (eds). *Breaking the Chains: Slavery and its Legacy in the Nineteenth-century Cape Colony*. Johannesburg: Wits University Press, 1994.
Worden, N. *The Chains That Bind Us: A History of Slavery at the Cape.* Cape Town: Juta, 1996.

WOSA. *Ithemba, 15 Years of Democracy, 350 Years of Winemaking*. Stellenbosch: Wines of South Africa, 2009.

OTHER

Adhikari, M. The Sons of Ham. Slavery and the Making of Coloured Identity, *South African Historical Journal*, 1992 November; 27(1), 95-112.

Agri SA. Presentation to the Portfolio Committee on Agriculture and Land Affairs on Farm evictions: Cape Town, 4 March 2008. Online: http://www.pmg.org.za/files/docs/080304agrisa.htm

Baldi, I, L Filleul, B Mohammed-Brahim, C Fabrigoule, J F Dartigues, S Schwall, J P Drevet, R Salamon, and P Brochard. Neuropsychologic effects of long-term exposure to pesticides: Results from the French Phytoner study. *Environmental Health Perspectives*, August 2001; 109(8): 839-844.

Bennion, LJ, and Li, TK. Alcohol metabolism in American Indians and whites: Lack of racial differences in metabolic rate and liver alcohol dehydrogenase. *New England Journal of Medicine*. 1976; 294:9–13.

Brodie, Louise. [Research and writing on the table grape industry] Unpublished writing and raw data made available to the author.

Brodie, Louise. *History of the establishment and development of the table grape industry in the lower Orange River Region of South Africa*. Unpublished manuscript.

Business Report, August 31, 2007.

Carter, Suzanne. The Projected Influence of Climate Change on the South African Wine Industry, Interim Report IR-06-043. The International Institute for Applied Systems Analysis (IIASA), 2006. Retrieved 22 August 2010 from http://www.iiasa.ac.at/Admin/PUB/Documents/IR-06-043.pdf

Clift, Harriet E. *The Assimilation of the Khoikhoi into the Rural Labour Force of Paarl, Drakenstein District*. Honours Dissertation, University of Cape Town, November 1995.

Cordyack, Brian. 20th-Century American Bestsellers: John Steinbeck, *The Grapes of Wrath*. Graduate School of Library and Information Science. Student assignment, University of Illinois, Urbana-Champaign, no date. Retrieved 22 August 2010 from http://www3.isrl.illinois.edu/~unsworth/courses/bestsellers/search.cgi?title=The+Grapes+of+Wrath

Du Toit, A, Kruger, S and Ponte, S. Deracializing Exploitation? 'Black Economic Empowerment' in the South African Wine Industry, *Journal of Agrarian Change*, January 2008; 8(1): 6-32.

Du Toit, JB. *Plaasarbeiders:'n Sosiologiese Studie van 'n Groep Kleurling-Plaasarbeiders in die Distrik Tulbagh*. (Farm Labourers: A Sociological Study of a Group of Farm Labourers in the Tulbagh District). MA Dissertation in Social Work, University of Stellenbosch, 1947.

Dugard, J, Mintoor, A, Ngwenya, M, Nkosi, P and Wilson, S. *Almost a Boss-Boy: Farm Schools, Farm Life and Social Opportunity in South Africa*. Centre for Applied Legal Studies, University of Witwatersrand, October 2005. Retrieved 22 August 2010 from http://www.sarpn.org.za/documents/d0001923/Farm-schools_Wits_Oct2005.pdf

Financial Mail, September 2, 2005.

Fourie, Johan. The South African Poor White Problem in the Early 20th Century: Lessons for Poverty today. Working Paper, University of Stellenbosch Department of Economics, 2006.

Foxcroft, Mary-Lyn. Growing the consumption of wine amongst emerging market consumers in South Africa. Cape Wine Master Diploma Student Assignment, January 2009.

Fruits of the Vine. National Library of South Africa online exhibition. 2007. http://www.nlsa.ac.za/vine/ [Page is no longer available.]

Harker, N, Kader, R, Myers, B, Fakier, P and Parry, C, Flisher, AJ, Peltzer, K, Ramlagan, S, Davids, A. Substance Abuse Trends in the Western Cape: A review of studies conducted since 2000. MRC/ UCT/HSRC collaboration. 2008. Retrieved 24 December 2010 from http://www.sahealthinfo.org/admodule/substance.pdf

Integrated Production of Wine (IPW) Scheme. Website. Retrieved 22 August 2010 from www.ipw.co.za

Jooste, GJ. *Die Geskiedenis van Wynbou en Wynhandel in die Kaapkolonie* 1753-1795. MA dissertation, University of Stellenbosch, 1973.

Legassick, Martin. The Will of Abraham and Elizabeth September: The struggle for land in Gordonia, 1898-1995. *The Journal of African History*, October 1996.

Letters Despatched from the Cape, 1652-1869. Precis of the Archives: Cape of Good Hope. The library of the University of California Los Angeles. Retrieved 22 August 2010 from http://www.archive.org/stream/precisofarchives13capeiala/precisofarchives13capeiala_djvu.txt

London, Leslie and J. te Water Naudé. Farm Workers in South Africa: The challenge of eradicating alcohol abuse and the legacy of the 'dop' system. *South African Medical Journal*, September 1998: 88.

London, Leslie. Human Rights, Environmental Justice and the Health of Farm Workers in South Africa. *International Journal of Occupational Environmental Health*, January/March, 2003.

MacGregor, James and Vorley, Bill. *Fair Miles? The concept of "food miles" through a sustainable development lens*. IIED Sustainable Development Opinion Paper, International Institute for Environment and Development, London 2006. Retrieved 22 August 2010 from http://www.iied.org/pubs/display.php?o=11064IIED

Master and Servant, Addenda to the Documents of the Working of the Order In Council of the 21st July 1846, Saul Solomon & Co, Cape Town, 1849.

Mellét, Patric Tariq. *Cape-Slavery-Heritage: Exploring the Roots of the People of the Cape - South Africa*. Blog. (no date.) Retrieved 22 August 2010 from http://cape-slavery-heritage.iblog.co.za

Moore, Jim. *Darwin's Sacred Cause*. BBC/Open UniversityOpen2.net. [Videos]. 2009. Retrieved 22 August 2010 from http://www.open2.net/historyandthearts/arts/darwin_biography.html

Museum van de Caab publications, Solms-Delta, 2004.

National Agricultural Marketing Council (NAMC). Report on the Investigation into the Effects of Eeregulation on the South African Wine Industry, December 2002. Online: http://www.namc.co.za/dnn/LinkClick.aspx?fileticket=uy_v8zRRcHQ%3D&tabid=72&mid=538

Nel, Salma. *Nel Familie* 1866-1999. Genealogy, in possession of Izak Nel.

Newton-King, S. Sodomy, Race and Respectability in Stellenbosch and Drakenstein, 1689–1762: The story of a family, loosely defined. Paper presented at a symposium on slavery at the University of Stellenbosch, 2008.

Nye, John VC. *Political Economy of Anglo French Trade*, 1689-1899*: Agricultural Trade Policies*,

Alcohol Taxes, and War. American Association of Wine Economists, AAWE Working Paper No 38, July 2009. Online: http://ideas.repec.org/p/ags/wbadwp/50295.html

Odendaal, J and Van Dyk, L. Conflict Sours the Grapes. *USB Leaders' Lab*, August 2008, pp 28-33. Retrieved 22 August 2010 from http://www.usb.ac.za/Media/thoughtleadership/leaderslab/Conflict_sours_grapes.pdf

Peele, Stanton. The Bottle in the Gene. Review of *Alcohol and the Addictive Brain*, by Kenneth Blum, with James E. Payne. *Reason*, 51-54. March 1992. Retrieved 22 August 2010 from http://www.peele.net/lib/blumrev.html

Peele, Stanton. The Implications and Limitations of Genetic Models of Alcoholism and other Addictions. *Journal of Studies on Alcohol* 47:63-73. 1986. Retrieved 22 August 2010 from http://www.peele.net/lib/genetics.html

Pesticide Action Network Europe (PAN Europe). European Wines Systematically Contaminated with Pesticide Residues. Press Release. 26 March 2008. Retrieved 22 August 2010 from www.pan-europe.info/Media/PR/080326.html

Pesticide Action Network Europe (PAN Europe). Message in a Bottle: Supporting information. No date. Retrieved 22 August 2010 from http://www.greens-efa.org/cms/default/dokbin/226/226177.supporting_information_message_in_a_bott@en.pdf

Petzold, C. Reading *Darwin's Sacred Cause*. Blog entry on *Petzold Book Blog*. 2009. Retrieved 22 August 2010 from http://www.charlespetzold.com/blog/2009/02/Reading-Darwins-Sacred-Cause.html

Pistorius, P and Todeschini, F. Idas Valley as an Example of the Cultural Landscape of the Cape Winelands (South Africa). International Council on Monuments and Sites (ICOMOS). ca. 2005. Retrieved 22 August 2010 from http://www.icomos.org/studies/viticoles/viticole8.pdf

Raath, Pieter. *Table Grape Science: Cultivation practices*. Viticulture 344 module notes, University of Stellenbosch, 2008.

Randle, T. *Grappling with Grapes: Wine Tourism of the Western Cape*. MA dissertation, University of Cape Town, 2004.

Rhoda, Ebrahim. The Islamic Da'Wah from the Auwal Masjid in the Bo-Kaap to Mosterd Bay 1792 -1838. *Quarterly Bulletin of the National Library of South Africa*, 61(2), April-June 2007.

Rhodes, Cecil John. Confession of Faith. 1877. Originally written on 2 June 1877, in Oxford. Retrieved 24 December 2010 from http://www.sianews.com/modules.php?name=News&file=print&sid=1882

Ross, Robert. Smallpox at the Cape of Good Hope in the Eighteenth Century. In *Proceedings of a Seminar on African Historical Demography*, 29-30 *April* 1977. 416-428. University of Edinburgh: Centre of African Studies. 1977.

SA Fruit and Wine Industry, Confronting Climate Change, a South African Fruit and Wine Initiative, February 2009. Retrieved 24 December 2010 from http://www.winetech.co.za/ docs2009/Component1-Summary-Feb09.pdf

SA Wine Industry Information and Systems (SAWIS). *SA Wine Industry Statistics*. No. 34, 2010.

Scheffler, H. *The History of the Historic Wine-Estate Muratie* 1699-1991. Translated by CJD Harvey. Vlaeberg, 1991.

South African Human Rights Commission (HRC). *National Inquiry into Human Rights Violations in Farming Communities*. 2003. Retrieved 22 August 2010 from http://www.

info.gov.za/otherdocs/2003/farming/nat.pdf
South African Human Rights Commission, 2008. *Progress made in terms of Land Tenure Security, Safety and Labour Relations in Farming Communities since 2003*. Retrieved 22 August 2010 from http://www.agbiz.co.za/Portals/0/SAHRC%20full%20doc.pdf
Sperling, Spatz. *The Memoirs of Spatz Sperling*. Unpublished manuscript dated 19 July 2005.
Theron, Jannie. Life on Rural Farms, Tape 104, Drakenstein Heemkring, 1987. Transcribed as a blog entry in *The History Webs blog: Ramblings through the archives*. Retrieved 22 August 2010 from http://historywebs.wordpress.com/2007/10/19/life-on-rural-farms-1930s/
Van der Merwe, Matthijs PS. *Groot Constantia* 1685-1885, *Its Owners and Occupants*. Cape Town: South African Cultural History Museum, 1997. Retrieved 22 August 2010 from http://www.grootconstantia.co.za/index.php?id=58
Van der Merwe, MPS. Slavery, Wine Making and the 'Dopstelsel'. A paper presented at the *Museums, tourism – en dop* symposium at Groot Constantia Jonkershuis Conference Centre, on Monday May 18 2009. Iziko Museums of Cape Town.
Van Heerden, Alex. Website. Retrieved 22 August 2010 from www.myspace.com/alexvanheerden. [Note that Van Heerden died in January 2009; the blogs are no longer available.]
Villa-Vicencio, Charles and Grassow, Peter. *Christianity and the Colonization of South Africa, 1652 to 1870*. Volume 1 of *The Social History of Christianity in South Africa, First Religious Encounters*, 1487-1795. Electronic publication. Cape Town: University of Cape Town Research Institute on Christianity in South Africa (RICSA). 2005. Online: http://web.uct.ac.za/depts/ricsa/projects/sochist/browse-volume-1.html
Vink, N, Deloire, A, Bonnardot, V, Ewert, J. Terroir, climate change, and the future of South Africa's wine industry. Paper for the pre-AARES conference workshop; Adelaide Convention Centre, Adelaide, South Australia, February 2010.
Watson, RL. Prize negroes and the development of Racial Attitudes in the Cape Colony, South Africa. Southeastern Regional Seminar in African Studies (SERSAS) page of the East Carolina University website. April 2000. Retrieved 23 August 2010 from http://www.ecu.edu/african/sersas/Watson400.htm
Weekend Argus, 26 May 2008.
Wine Industry Transformation Charter, Consultative Draft 1, August 2006. Retrieved 23 August 2010 from http://www.sawb.co.za/docs/ConsultativeDraft-August2006.pdf [This document was no longer available at the time of publication]
Wine Industry Transformation Charter, Adopted by the South African Wine Industry Council 30 July 2007. Retrieved 23 August 2010 from http://www.sawit.co.za/downloads/wine%20industry%20transformation%20charter%2030%20july%202007.pdf
Wines of South Africa: Variety is in our nature. Website. Retrieved 22 August 2010 from http://www.wosa.co.za

Endnotes

INTRODUCTION

1 SA Wine Industry Information and Systems (SAWIS), *SA Wine Industry Statistics* No. 34, 2010, p. 33.
2 Ibid., p. 14.
3 Ibid., p. 8.
4 Estimate provided by Prof. Joachim Ewert in an interview.

CHAPTER 1

5 John Steinbeck, *The Grapes of Wrath* (Sussex: Heinemann, 1969), Chapter 25.
6 Brian Cordyack, "20th-Century American Bestsellers: John Steinbeck, The Grapes of Wrath". Graduate School of Library and Information Science, University of Illinois, Urbana-Champaign. Online: (http://www3.isrl.illinois.edu/~unsworth/courses/bestsellers/search.cgi?title=The+Grapes+of+Wrath).
7 Gavin Lucas, *An Archaeology of Colonial Identity, Power and Material Culture in the Dwars Valley* (New York: Springer, 2006), p. 126.
8 Diko Van Zyl, "History of Wine" (www.wosa.co.za).
9 Wayne Dooling, *Slavery, Emancipation and Colonial Rule in South Africa* (Pietermaritzburg: University of KwaZulu-Natal Press, 2007), p. 63.
10 Patric Tariq Mellét, online: http://cape-slavery-heritage.iblog.co.za
11 Ibid.
12 Nigel Worden and Clifton Crais, *Breaking the Chains, Slavery and its Legacy in the 19th century Cape Colony* (Johannesburg: Wits University Press, 1994), p. 98.
13 Robert Shell , *Children of Bondage* (Johannesburg: Witwatersrand University Press, 1994).
14 Sampie Terreblanche, *A History of Inequality in South Africa 1652-2002* (Pietermaritzburg: University of KwaZulu/Natal Press, 2002), p. 161.
15 Dooling op. cit., p. 41.
16 Lucas op. cit., p. 129.
17 Pamela Scully, *Liberating the Family? Gender and British Slave Emancipation in the Rural Western Cape, 1823-1853* (Cape Town: David Philip, 1997), p. 65.
18 Dooling op. cit., p. 86.
19 Worden and Crais op. cit., p. 107.
20 Nigel Worden, "Between Slavery and Freedom", in Worden and Crais op. cit., p. 137.
21 Ibid., p. 118.
22 As quoted in RL Watson, "Prize Negroes and the Development of Racial Attitudes in the Cape Colony, South Africa" (http://www.ecu.edu/african/sersas/Watson400.htm)
23 Ibid.
24 Nigel Worden, in Worden and Crais op. cit., p. 134.

25 Ibid., p. 143.
26 *De Zuid Afrikaan*, as quoted in Dooling op. cit., p. 116.
27 Diko van Zyl.
28 Dooling op. cit., p. 116.
29 Ibid., p. 117.
30 Nigel Worden, *The Chains That Bind Us* (Cape Town: Juta, 1996), p. 42.
31 Scully op. cit., p. 88.
32 Lucas op. cit., p. 84.
33 *De Zuid Afrikaan* 1848, as quoted in Dooling op. cit., p. 121.
34 Ibid., p. 122.
35 Ibid., p.128.
36 Jack and Ray Simons, *Class and Colour in SA, 1850 to 1950*, Chapter 22 (http://www.anc.org.za/books/ccsa.html)
37 SA Human Rights Commission 2007 report: Progress made in terms of Land Tenure Security, Safety and Labour Relations in Farming Communities since 2003.

CHAPTER 2

38 DJ Opperman (ed.), *Spirit of the Vine* (Cape Town: Human and Rousseau, 1968), p. 235.
39 RE van der Ross, *Buy my Flowers* (Observatory: Ampersand Press, 2007), p. 10.
40 Ibid., p. 15.
41 Ibid., p. 73.
42 G Theal, *Willem Adriaan van der Stel and Other Historical Sketches* (Cape Town: Thomas Maskew Miller, 1913), p. 175.
43 Thys van der Merwe, Iziko Museum website. Online: http://www.iziko.org.za/grootcon/special/slavehist.html
44 Karel Schoeman, *Early Slavery at the Cape of Good Hope* 1652-1717 (Pretoria: Protea Book House, 2007), p. 27.
45 Ibid., p. 32.
46 The Library of the University of California Los Angeles, Precis of the Archives of Cape of Good Hope, Letters Despatched from the Cape, 1652-1869. Online. (http://www.archive.org/stream/precisofarchives13capeiala/precisofarchives13capeiala_djvu.txt)
47 Wayne Dooling, *Slavery, Emancipation and Colonial Rule in South Africa* (Pietermaritzburg: University of KwaZulu-Natal Press, 2007), p. 20.
48 Ibid., p. 21.
49 H Giliomee and B Mbenga (eds), *New History of South Africa* (Cape Town: Tafelberg, 2007), p. 51.
50 DJ Opperman (ed.) op. cit., p. 85.
51 National Library of South Africa online exhibition "Fruits of the Vine" (http://www.nlsa.ac.za/vine/)
52 G J Jooste, "Die Geskiedenis van Wynbou en Wynhandel in die Kaapkolonie 1753-1795" (MA thesis, University of Stellenbosch, 1973).
53 J Burman, *Wines of Constantia* (Cape Town: Human and Rousseau, 1979), p. 79.
54 DJ Opperman (ed.) op. cit., p. 89.
55 GJ Schutte (ed.), *Hendrik Cloete, Groot Constantia en die* VOC *1778-1799* (Cape Town: Van Riebeek Society, 2003), p. 291.

Note: On this farm, De Hoop op Constantia, as well as on the neigbouring farm, Groot Constantia, the world-famous Constantia wines were produced. A manuscript containing notes on winemaking, partly damaged, survived and is housed today in the Cape Archives. The part that survived mainly covers the period 1802 to 1821. From it much is to be learned about how Constantia wines were made on De Hoop op Constantia. In all probability, more or less the same methods were followed on Groot Constantia by the Cloetes and by the previous owners of both farms in the course of the eighteenth century.

56 GJ Jooste op. cit., p. 35.
57 Mary Kuttel, *Quadrilles and Konfyt* (Cape Town: Maskew Miller, 1954), p. 29.
58 GJ Schutte (ed.) op. cit., p. 291.
59 Karel Schoeman op. cit., p. 361.
60 HJ Duckitt, *Hilda's Diary of a Cape Houskeeper* (London: Chapman and Hall, 1902), p. 20.
61 Diko van Zyl, research notes for Wines of South Africa, "The Constantia wine tradition". Online (www.wosa.co.za)
62 GJ Schutte (ed.) op. cit., p. 259.
63 AJ Böeseken, *Slaves and Free Blacks at the Cape*, 1658-1700 (Cape Town: Tafelberg, 1977), p. 73.
64 GJ Schutte (ed.) op. cit., p. 15.
65 Ibid.
66 Ibid., p. 53.
67 Ibid.
68 Ibid.

CHAPTER 3

69 Peggy Heap, *The Story of the Hottentots Holland* (Cape Town: AA Balkema, 1970), p. 5.
70 Gavin Lucas, *An Archaeology of Colonial Identity, Power and Material Culture in the Dwars Valley* (New York: Springer, 2006).
71 Ibid., p. 73.
72 Museum Van de Caab publication, Solms-Delta 2004, p. 4.
73 Penny Pistorius and Fabio Todeschini, "Idas Valley as an example of the cultural landscape of the Cape Winelands (South Africa)". No date. Online: (http://www.icomos.org/studies/viticoles/viticole8.pdf)
74 Wayne Dooling, *Slavery, Emancipation and Colonial Rule in South Africa* (Pietermaritzburg: University of KwaZulu-Natal Press, 2007), p. 19.
75 Nigel Penn, *The Forgotten Frontier* (Cape Town: Double Storey Books, 2005), p. 28.
76 Helena Scheffler, "The History of the Historic Wine-Estate Muratie 1699-1991", translated by CJD Harvey (Vlaeberg, 1991).
77 Ansela's story and details come largely from Scheffler's research paper.
78 As quoted in Dooling op. cit., p. 18.
79 Nigel Penn op. cit., p. 40.
80 Gavin Lucas op. cit., p. 68.
81 For a fascinating insight into the northern expansion of the frontier, read Nigel Penn's *The Forgotten Frontier*.

82 Gavin Lucas op. cit., p. 69.
83 Harriet Clift, "The Assimilation of the Khoikhoi into the Rural Labour Force of Paarl, Drakenstein" (Honours Dissertation, University of Cape Towm, November 1995).
84 Robert Ross, "Smallpox at the Cape of Good Hope in the Eighteenth Century", African Historical Demography, Centre of African Studies, University of Edinburgh.
85 Wayne Dooling op. cit.
86 Ibid., p. 35.
87 Susie Newton-King, "Sodomy, race and respectability in Stellenbosch and Drakenstein, 1689 – 1762: the story of a family, loosely defined." Paper presented at a symposium on slavery at the University of Stellenbosch in 2008.
88 Wayne Dooling op. cit., p. 35.
89 Gavin Lucas op. cit., p. 80.
90 Ibid., p. 81.
91 Richard Elphick, *Khoikhoi and the Founding of White South Africa* (Johannesburg: Ravan Press, 1985), p. 155.
92 Karel Schoeman, *Early Slavery at the Cape of Good Hope 1652-1717* (Pretoria: Protea Book House, 2007), p. 377.
93 Patric Mellét, correspondence. His website contains a wealth of information: http://cape-slavery-heritage.iblog.co.za

CHAPTER 4

94 Gavin Lucas, *An Archaeology of Colonial Identity, Power and Material Culture in the Dwars Valley* (New York: Springer, 2006), p. 146.
95 Christian Silberbauer, *Pniel and Its First Missionary Superintendent* (Cape Town: Citadel Press, 1943), p. 3.
96 Ibid., p. 5.
97 Pamela Scully, *Liberating the Family? Gender and British Slave Emancipation in the Rural Western Cape , 1823-1853* (Cape Town: David Philip, 1997), p.137.
98 Ibid., p. 138.
99 Ibid., p. 139.
100 Wayne Dooling, *Slavery, Emancipation and Colonial Rule in South Africa* (Pietermaritzburg: University of KwaZulu-Natal Press, 2007), p. 117.
101 Master and Servant, Addenda to the Documents of the Working of the Order In Council of the 21st July 1846 (Cape Town: Saul Solomon & Co, 1849).
102 Ibid., p. 50.
103 Ibid., p. 51.
104 L Cyster, M Cyster, E Damon and F Simpson, *Pniël en Sy Mense.* (Stellenbosch: Sun Media, 2008).
105 Ibid., p. 41.
106 Gavin Lucas op. cit., p. 155.
107 Pamela Scully op. cit., p. 29.
108 Ibid., p. 28.
109 Ibid., p. 29.
110 Ibid., p. 28.

111 Ibid., p. 45.
112 Ibid., p. 32 .
113 Cyster et al. op. cit., p. 39.
114 Ibid., p. 41.
115 Christian Silberbauer op. cit., p.14.
116 Ibid., p. 48.
117 Ibid., p. 17.
118 Gavin Lucas op. cit., p. 148.
119 Cyster et al. op. cit., p. 50.
120 Ebrahim Rhoda, "The Islamic Da'Wah From the Auwal Masjid in the Bo-Kaap to Mosterd Bay 1792 -1838," *Quarterly Bulletin of the National Library of South Africa*, vol. 61, no. 2, April-June 2007.
121 Ibid.
122 Charles Villa-Vicencio and Peter Grassow, The Social History of Christianity in South Africa, First Religious Encounters, 1487-1795, Volume 1, Christianity and the Colonization of South Africa, 1652 to 1870. Online: http://web.uct.ac.za/depts/ricsa/projects/sochist/read-volume-1-chapter-1.html
123 Ibid.
124 Ibid.

CHAPTER 5

125 Quoted in Ebrahim Rhoda op. cit.
126 National Agricultural Marketing Council (NAMC), "Report on the Investigation into the Effects of Deregulation on the South African Wine Industry", December 2002, p. 32. Online: (http://www.namc.co.za/dnn/LinkClick.aspx?fileticket=uy_v8zRRcHQ%3D&tabid=72&mid=538)
127 JVC Nye, "Political Economy of Anglo French Trade, 1689-1899: Agricultural Trade Policies, Alcohol Taxes", American Association of Wine Economists, working paper no. 38, July 2009. "War with Louis XIV from 1689 led to the end of all trade between Britain and France for a quarter of a century. The creation of powerful protected interests both at home and abroad (notably in the form of British merchants, and investors in Portuguese wine) led to the imposition of prohibitively high tariffs on French imports - notably on wine and spirits - when trade with France resumed in 1714. Protection of domestic interests from import competition allowed the state to raise domestic excises which provided increased government revenues despite almost no increases in the taxes on land and income in Britain."
128 NAMC op. cit., p. 6.
129 André Brink, *The Essence of the Grape: A South African Brandy Book* (Cape Town: Saayman & Weber, 1992), p. 38.
130 Tracey Randle, "Grappling with Grapes: Wine Tourism of the Western Cape" (MA dissertation, University of Cape Town, 2004). p. 20.
131 SA Wine Industry Information and Systems (SAWIS), SA Wine Industry Statistics No. 34, 2010, p. 5. NAMC op. cit., p.5.
132 Ibid., p. 33.
133 Ibid., p 36.
134 Tracey Randle op. cit., p. 7. "In 1931, the K.W.V brandy expert, Mr. H J David, saw

the need for a wine industry magazine. With such a vision in mind, David went on to single-handedly create *Wine and Spirit - a South African Review*, later to be renamed *Wynboer*. At its 50th anniversary, G R F Meyer commented 'at the outset the magazine endeavoured to serve the wine farmer with information, technical advice and encouragement. *Wynboer* overcame many hurdles, mostly financial, saw many changes in the industry as well as amongst consumer needs. *Wynboer* has broadened its spectrum to reach the general public and in this has become an important educational tool in leading people to the enjoyment and proper consumption of products of the vine'."

135 Ibid., p. 10.

136 Mary-Lyn Foxcroft, "Growing the consumption of wine amongst emerging market consumers in South Africa" (Assignment submitted in partial fulfillment for the Cape Wine Master Diploma, January 2009).

137 NAMC op. cit., p.5.

138 Tracey Randle op. cit., p. 20.

139 NAMC op. cit., p. 5.

140 Ibid., p. 2.

141 Tracey Randle op. cit., p. 12.

142 Spatz Sperling, "The Memoirs of Spatz Sperling" (Unpublished, dated 19 July 2005).

143 Mary-Lyn Foxcroft op. cit., p. 43.

144 Ibid, p. 38.

145 From *South African Alcoholic Beverage Review* (Ramsay Son and Parker, 2007), as quoted by Mary-Lyn Foxcroft op. cit.

146 Diko van Zyl.

147 Quoted in André Brink op. cit., p. 33.

148 Ibid., p. 36.

149 Ibid., p. 33.

150 Ibid., p. 31.

151 Wayne Dooling, *Slavery, Emancipation and Colonial Rule in South Africa* (Pietermaritzburg: University of KwaZulu-Natal Press, 2007), p. 7.

152 Ibid., p 81 (quoted from M Rayner, "Wine and Slaves: The Failure of an Export Economy and the Ending of Slavery in the Cape Colony, South Africa, 1806-1834", PhD thesis, Duke University, 1986).

153 Ibid., p. 81.

154 Ibid., p. 83.

155 Ibid., p. 95.

156 Ibid., p. 99.

157 Ibid., p. 140.

158 Ibid. (as quoted from records in the insolvent case of George Stephanus Haubtfleisch, 9 March 1843).

159 Ibid., p. 141.

160 Ibid., p. 148.

161 Ibid., p. 190 (as quoted from Report of the Resident Missionary of Pacaltsdorp, 16 June 1863).

162 Ibid. (as quoted from Blue Books 1866).

163 Ibid., p. 192.

164 Ibid., p. 174.
165 Diko van Zyl, *Klawer Wynkelder, 50 Goue Jare* (Stellenbosch: Rapid Access Publishers, 2007), p. 64.
166 Many thanks to Diko van Zyl for this information.
167 "The early history of Pinotage". Online: (http://www.pinotage.co.za/filemanager/Pinotage___early_history.pdf)
168 Peter May, *Pinotage: Behind the Legends of South Africa's Own Wine* (England: Inform and Enlighten, 2009).
169 Online: http://www.pinotage.co.za/index.php?page=9

CHAPTER 6

170 JB du Toit, "Plaasarbeiders: 'n Sosiologiese Studie van 'n Groep Kleurling-Plaasarbeiders in die Distrik Tulbagh" (Farm Labourers: A Sociological Study of a Group of Farm Labourers in the Tulbagh District) (MA thesis, Dept of Social Work, University of Stellenbosch, 1947).
171 Wine Industry Transformation Charter, Consultative Draft 1, August 2006, p. 19.
172 Ibid.
173 Jannie Theron, "Life on Rural Farms", Tape 104, Drakenstein Heemkring, 1987. Online: (http://historywebs.wordpress.com/2007/10/19/life-on-rural-farms-1930s/)
174 Agri SA's Presentation to the Portfolio Committee on Agriculture and Land Affairs on Farm Evictions: Cape Town, 4 March 2008 (no page numbers, section 2). Online: (http://www.pmg.org.za/files/docs/080304agrisa.htm)
175 Agri Western Cape. (2007). Response to the request from the South African Human Rights Commission for submissions on the violations of human rights in farming communities. As reported in SA Human Rights Commission report: "Progress made in terms of Land Tenure Security, Safety and Labour Relations in Farming Communities since 2003", 2008.
176 Cecil John Rhodes, "Confession of Faith". Rhodes originally wrote this on 2 June 1877, in Oxford. Online: (http://www.sianews.com/modules.php?name=News&file=print&sid=1882)
177 William MacDonald, *Conquest of the Desert* (London: TW Laurie, 1913), p. 45. Online: http://www.archive.org/stream/conquestofdesertoomacdiala#page/x/mode/2up)
178 Ibid.
179 C Petzold, Reading Darwin's Sacred Cause, New York, 2009. Online (http://www.charlespetzold.com/blog/2009/02/Reading-Darwins-Sacred-Cause.html)
180 Ibid.
181 Jim Moore, Darwin's Sacred Cause. Online: (http://www.open2.net/historyandthearts/arts/darwin_biography.html)
182 JB du Toit op. cit., p. 50.
183 Ibid.
184 Quoted in Leslie London, "Human Rights, Environmental Justice and the Health of Farm Workers in South Africa", *International Journal Occupational Environmental Health*, January/March, 2003.
185 Ibid., p. 65.
186 J Dugard, A Mintoor, M Ngwenya, P Nkosi and S Wilson, "Almost a boss-boy: Farm schools, farm life and social opportunity in South Africa." (Centre for Applied Legal

Studies, University of Witwatersrand, October 2005). Online: (http://www.sarpn.org.za/documents/d0001923/Farm-schools_Wits_Oct2005.pdf)
187 Ibid., p. 37.
188 Ibid., p. 36.
189 Ibid.
190 Ibid., p. 37.
191 Ibid.
192 Ibid., p. 34.
193 Ibid., p. 36.
194 Ibid.
195 Ibid., p. 39.
196 Ibid., p. 35.
197 Ibid.
198 Ibid., p. 36.

CHAPTER 7

199 Jan Bouws, "Wine, Words and Music", in DJ Opperman (ed.), *Spirit of the Vine* (Cape Town: Human & Rousseau, 1968), p. 242. This comes from an "old custom to praise the tot", writes Bouws.
200 Mary Kuttel, *Quadrilles and Konfyt* (Cape Town: Maskew Miller, 1954), p. 6.
201 South African Human Rights Commission, "Report on National Inquiry into Human Rights Violations in Farming Communities", 2003.
202 Leslie London, "Human Rights, Environmental Justice and the Health of Farm Workers in South Africa", *International Journal of Occupational Environmental Health*, January/March, 2003, p. 62.
203 CJ Orffer, "To the Southern Point of Africa", in DJ Opperman (ed.), *Spirit of the Vine* (Cape Town: Human & Rousseau, 1968), p. 82.
204 André Brink, *The Essence of the Grape, A South African Brandy Book* (Cape Town: Saayman & Weber, 1992, p. 31.
205 GJ Jooste,"Die Geskiedenis Van Wynbou en Wynhandel in die Kaapkolonie 1753-1795"(MA thesis, University of Stellenbosch, 1973), p. 37.
206 Ibid., p. 50.
207 Ibid. p. 56.
208 Dr C Graham Botha, Chief Archivist of the Union of South Africa, quoted by Diko van Zyl, WOSA website.
209 Ibid.
210 In Thys van der Merwe, "Slavery, wine making and the 'dopstelsel'", a paper presented at the "Museums, tourism – en dop" symposium at Groot Constantia Jonkershuis Conference Centre, Iziko Museums of Cape Town, on Monday 18 May 2009.
211 Ibid.
212 Pamela Scully, *Liberating the Family? Gender and British Slave Emancipation in the Rural Western Cape , 1823-1853* (Cape Town: David Philip, 1997), p. 91.
213 Wayne Dooling, *Slavery, Emancipation and Colonial Rule in South Africa* (Pietermaritzburg: University of KwaZulu-Natal Press, 2007), p. 163.
214 AJ Venter, *Coloured – A Profile of 2 Million South Africans* (Cape Town: Human & Rousseau, 1974), p. 47.

215 Hermann Giliomee, "Aspects of the rise of Afrikaner capital and Afrikaner nationalism in the Western Cape, 1870-1915", in W James and M Simons (eds), *The Angry Divide* (Claremont: David Philip, 1989), p. 66.
216 Wayne Dooling op. cit., p. 213.
217 Ibid., p. 215.
218 http://www.nlsa.ac.za/vine/viewimage.asp?image=1203a.jpg
219 JB Du Toit, "Plaasarbeiders: 'n Sosiologiese Studie van 'n Groep Kleurling-Plaasarbeiders in die Distrik Tulbagh" (Farm Labourers: A Sociological Study of a Group of Farm Labourers in the Tulbagh District). (MA thesis in Social Work, University of Stellenbosch, 1947.)
220 Ibid., p. 50.
221 AJ Venter op. cit., p. 53.
222 Spatz Sperling's memoirs, unpublished, p. 19.
223 Ibid., p. 22.
224 Thys van der Merwe.
225 AJ Venter op. cit., pp. 48-49.
226 Ibid.
227 Ibid., p.50.
228 Ibid p. 51
229 Martin Legassick, "The will of Abraham and Elizabeth September: the struggle for land in Gordonia, 1898-1995", *The Journal of African History*, October 1996.
230 AJ Venter op. cit., p. 17.
231 Eugène Marais, *The Soul of the Ape* (Cape Town: Human & Rousseau, 1974), p. 106.
232 Adapted from "Alcohol metabolism, an update: July 2007". Online: (http://pubs.niaaa.nih.gov/publications/aa72/aa72.htm)
233 Stanton Peele, "The Implications and Limitations of Genetic Models of Alcoholism and Other Addictions", *Journal of Studies on Alcohol*, 47:63-73, 1986. Morristown, New Jersey. Online: (http://www.peele.net/lib/genetics.html)
234 LJ Bennion and T-K Li, "Alcohol metabolism in American Indians and whites: Lack of racial differences in metabolic rate and liver alcohol dehydrogenase", *New England Journal of Medicine* 294:9–13, 1976.
235 AP Blignaut, "Thy Bane is in Thy Shallow Skull", in DJ Opperman (ed.) op. cit., p. 340.
236 Tracey Randle, "Grappling with Grapes: Wine Tourism of the Western Cape". MA thesis, University of Cape Town, 2004.
237 http://www.peele.net/index.html
238 Martin Legassick op. cit.
239 Ibid.
240 Leslie London and J Te Water Naudé, "Farm workers in South Africa – the challenge of eradicating alcohol abuse and the legacy of the 'Dop' system." *South African Medical Journal*, 88, September 1998.
241 Nadine Harker, Rehana Kader, Bronwyn Myers, Nuraan Fakier and Charles Parry (MRC), Alan J Flisher (UCT), Karl Peltzer, Shandir Ramlagan, Alicia Davids (HSRC), "Substance abuse trends in the Western Cape, A review of studies conducted since 2000", p. 10. Online: (http://www.sahealthinfo.org/admodule/substance.pdf)

CHAPTER 8

242 Leslie London, "Human Rights, Environmental Justice and the Health of Farm Workers in South Africa", *International Journal of Occupational Environmental Health*, January/March 2003, p. 61.
243 Ibid., p. 63.
244 Ibid.
245 *Business Report*, 31 August, 2007.
246 Leslie London op. cit., p. 65.
247 Baldi et al., "Neuropsychologic effects of long-term exposure to pesticides: results from the French Phytoner study", *Environmental Health Perspectives*, 109 (8): 839-844 (2001), in Pesticide Action Network Europe.
248 Online: (www.pan-europe.info/Media/PR/080326.html)
249 Quoted in Leslie London op. cit., p. 59.
250 Wine Industry Transformation Charter, Consultative Draft 1, August 2006, p. 27. Online: (http://www.sawb.co.za/docs/ConsultativeDraft-August2006.pdf)
251 Jacobus Odendaal, "Conflict Sours the Grapes", reported in University of Stellenbosch Business School, *Leaders' Lab*, August 2008, based on his MBA thesis: "Konflik in die werksplek: Gevallestudie met verwysing na vyf tafeldruifuitvoerplase in die Benede-Bergrivier", March 2008. See Odendaal and Van Dyk (2008).
252 Eric Rosenthal, *We Want Fruit* (Observatory: Quincunx, 2007), p. 56.
253 Siegried Stander, *Tree of Life: The Story of Cape Fruit* (Cape Town: Saayman & Weber, 1983), p. 7.
254 Eric Rosenthal op. cit., p. 59.
255 Ibid., p. 55.
256 The SA Fruit and Wine Industry, "Confronting Climate Change, a South African Fruit and Wine Initiative", February 2009, p. 3. Online: (http://www.winetech.co.za/docs2009/Component1-Summary-Feb09.pdf, p. 3.)
257 James MacGregor and Bill Vorley, "Fair Miles? The concept of 'food miles" through a sustainable development lens," IIED Sustainable Development Opinion Paper, London: International Institute for Environment and Development 2006. Online: (http://www.iied.org/pubs/display.php?o=11064IIED)

CHAPTER 9

258 Martin Legassick, "The will of Abraham and Elizabeth September: the struggle for land in Gordonia, 1898-1995", *The Journal of African History*, October 1996.
259 William McDonald, *Conquest of the Desert* (London: TW Laurie, 1913).
260 Maria de Beer, *Keimoes en Omgewing* (Keimoes: Keimoes Municipality, 1992), p. 13.
261 Quoted in Martin Legassick op. cit.
262 William McDonald op. cit.
263 Martin Legassick op. cit.
264 "The fate of the farm Ouap provides an intriguing case-study in land alienation from Basters to whites," writes Legassick. "It is a case-study which would have been impossible to investigate without the tenacity with which the September family has continued to query the original 'sale', and without the evidence of oral tradition."
265 Martin Legassick op. cit.

266 Percy Nightingale, Cape Parliamentary Papers, 25 July 1887, quoted in Martin Legassick op. cit.
267 Nigel Penn, *The Forgotten Frontier* (Cape Town: Double Storey Books, 2005), p. 156.
268 Ibid., p. 166.
269 Maria de Beer, p. 20
270 Ibid.
271 Online: (http://www.fairtrade.org.uk/what_is_fairtrade/default.aspx)
272 Maria de Beer op. cit., p. 16.
273 Ibid., p. 19.
274 Martin Legassick op. cit.
275 Johan Fourie, "The South African poor white problem in the early 20th century: Lessons for poverty today", Working Paper, University of Stellenbosch Department of Economics, 2006.
276 Ibid.
277 Nigel Penn op. cit., p. 162.
278 Alwyn K Cornelissen, *Langs Grootrivier* (no publisher; no date). Copy accessed from Maxie Campion, Keimoes.
279 Maria de Beer op. cit., p. 16.

CHAPTER 10

280 Pieter Raath, "Table Grape Science: Cultivation Practices." (Viticulture 344 module notes, University of Stellenbosch, 2008).
281 Ibid.
282 N Vink, A Deloire, V Bonnardot and J Ewert, "Terroir, Climate Change, and the Future of South Africa's Wine Industry". Paper for the pre-AARES conference workshop, Adelaide Convention Centre, Adelaide, South Australia, February 2010.
283 Midgley et al.(2005), quoted in N Vink et al. op. cit., p. 4.
284 The SA Fruit and Wine Industry, "Confronting Climate Change, a South African Fruit and Wine Initiative", February 2009.
285 N Vink et al. op. cit., p. 9.
286 Suzanne Carter, Interim Report IR-06-043: The Projected Influence of Climate Change on the South African Wine Industry. Online: (http://www.iiasa.ac.at/Admin/PUB/Documents/IR-06-043.pdf)
287 Ibid.
288 IPW website, www.ipw.co.za
289 N Vink et al. op. cit., p. 9.
290 Ibid.
291 Online: (http://www.hwt.co.za/wine_cellar_treatment.htm)
292 N Vink et al. op. cit., p.13.
293 Suzanne Carter op. cit., p. 28.
294 The SA Fruit and Wine Industry op. cit.

CHAPTER 11

295 Wine Industry Transformation Charter, Consultative Draft 1, August 2006, p. 3.
296 Louise Brodie, *New Leaves* (Paarl: The Deciduous Fruit Producers Trust, 2006), p. 20.

297 Wine Industry Transformation Charter, adopted by the South African Wine Industry Council 30 July 2007.

298 Andries du Toit, Sandra Kruger and Stefano Ponte, "Deracializing Exploitation? 'Black Economic Empowerment' in the South African Wine Industry", *Journal of Agrarian Change*, Volume 8, Issue 1, pp. 6–32. (Published online: 12 December 2007).

299 *Financial Mail*, 2 September 2005.

300 *Weekend Argus*, 26 May 2008.

301 WOSA, *Ithemba, 15 Years of Democracy, 350 Years of Winemaking* (Stellenbosch: Wines of South Africa, 2009).

302 Louise Brodie op. cit.

303 WOSA op. cit., p. 10.

304 Ibid.

305 Ibid., p. 11.

306 Ibid., p. 33.

307 Ibid., p. 35.

308 Wine Industry Transformation Charter, 2006, p. 20.

309 Song by Tommy Connor, Eddie Pola.

310 Information given in personal correspondence, sourced from Matthijs P S van der Merwe, *Groot Constantia 1685-1885: Its Owners and Occupants* (Cape Town: South African Cultural History Museum, 1997). It is also available online at: http://www.grootconstantia.co.za/65/chapter_5__hendrik_cloete_senior__1778-1799_

311 Ibid.

312 Patric Tariq Mellét (no date). Online: (http://cape-slavery-heritage.iblog.co.za)

313 www.myspace.com/alexvanheerden (blogs no longer available, accessed in January 2009).

314 F Ratzel, *History of Mankind*, translated from the second German edition by AJ Butler, Volume II (New York: Macmillan, 1897), p. 274.

315 Online: http://www.solms-delta.co.za/wp-content/uploads/2009/11/music-van-de-caab.pdf

LAST WORD

316 "Macro-economic Impact of the Wine Industry on the South African Economy (also with reference to the Impacts on the Western Cape)." Conningarth Economists, December 2009, for South African Wine Industry Information and Systems (SAWIS). Online: http://www.sawis.co.za/info/download/Macro_study_2009.pdf

317 Ibid.

318 Ibid.

319 SAWIS, "Harvest Report 2010: Tricky in the vineyard, great in the cellar." Online: http://www.sawis.co.za/info/download/2010_Harvest_Report.pdf

320 Pamela Scully, *Liberating the Family? Gender and British Slave Emancipation in the Rural Western Cape, 1823-1853* (Cape Town: David Philip, 1997), p. 137.

321 Ibid., pp. 13-15.

322 Gavin Lucas, *An Archaeology of Colonial Identity, Power and Material Culture in the Dwars Valley* (New York: Springer, 2006), p. 142.

323 Mohamed Adhikari, "The Sons of Ham: Slavery and the Making of Coloured Identity", *South African Historical Journal*, Vol. 27, No. 1, November 1992, 95-112.

324 Ibid., p. 95.
325 Ibid., p. 97.
326 Ibid., p. 98.
327 Ibid., p. 111.
328 Nigel Penn, *The Forgotten Frontier* (Cape Town: Double Storey Books, 2005), p. 165.
329 Ibid.
330 Adhikari op. cit., p. 109.
331 Quoted in Gavin Lucas op. cit.
332 Adhikari op. cit., p. 99.

Index

About the authors

JEANNE VIALL was born in Rehoboth, Namibia, on 18 January 1960. She received a BA at the University of Natal, Pietermaritzburg and started her career as a journalist in 1985 at the *Pretoria News*, moving to the *Cape Argus* a few years later. She worked as a sub-editor for many years before joining the newsroom. Her specialist beats included health and features. In 1998 she won a MASA (Medical Association of SA) award for her reporting on medical issues in a changing healthcare system. In 2008 she went freelance, and now works from her home in Stellenbosch. Her articles have appeared in several magazines. She has compiled, edited and contributed to a journal called *Conversations – A Forum for the Changing Health Paradigm* (to be published early 2011). With her husband, Dr Bernard Brom, she writes for and edits a website (www.creatinghealth.co.za) which explores health from an integrative perspective. Her interest in health is broader than the health of people; it includes the health of food systems and the health of the planet.

DR WILMOT JAMES was born in Paarl on July 5 1953. He is a noted academic-turned-politician, who currently is a Member of Parliament for the Democratic Alliance (DA). He serves as Shadow Minister of Basic Education and is the Federal Chairperson of the DA. Dr James is an Honorary Professor of Sociology (University of Pretoria) and in the Division of Human Genetics (University of Cape Town). He also chairs the Board of the Africa Genome Education Institute. Dr James has a PhD in sociology from the University of Wisconsin at Madison (1982) and a BA Hons cum laude from the University of the Western Cape (1977). He has held visiting positions at Yale University, Indiana University, American Bar Foundation (Chicago), the California Institute of Technology and Edinburgh University. He has served as Chairperson of the Cape Philharmonic Orchestra and the Immigration Advisory Board of South Africa. He is also a former Trustee of the New York based Ford Foundation. This is the 18th book Dr James has either written or edited, the latest being *Nature's Gifts: Why we are the way we are* (Wits University Press, 2010).

PROFESSOR JAKES GERWEL was born on 18 January 1946, and grew up on a sheep farm in Somerset East in the Eastern Cape. Prof Gerwel holds a BA and BA Honours in Afrikaans-Nederlands from the University of the Western Cape, a Licentiate in Germanic Philology from the Free University of Brussels as well as a Doctorate in Literature and Philosophy from Brussels. He is the chancellor of Rhodes University, chairs the Nelson Mandela Foundation, the Mandela Rhodes Foundation and the Allan Gray Orbis Foundation. He is also vice-chair of the Peace Parks Foundation. Prof Gerwel was vice-chancellor and rector of the University of the Western Cape from 1987 to 1994, during which time he instituted far-reaching curriculum changes and a host of research and outreach projects. He served as a Director General in the office of President Nelson Mandela and Cabinet Secretary of the Government of National Unity from 1994 to June 1999. He is Distinguished Professor in the Humanities at the University of the Western Cape and Honorary Professor in the Humanities at the University of Pretoria. He is also a non-executive director of Naspers and non-executive chair of Brimstone, Life Healthcare, Media24 and Aurecon. Dr Gerwel was awarded the Order of the Southern Cross (Gold) by then President Nelson Mandela. He holds several honorary doctorates from South African and international universities. His prevous publications include the groundbreaking study *Literatuur en apartheid* (Literature and apartheid).